SHAKESPEARE

SHAKESPEARE

A LIFE IN SEVEN CHAPTERS

EDWARD S. BRUBAKER

ISBN: 978-0-615-24057-2

CONTENTS

A WORD FROM
THE EDITORS

SHAKESPEARE: *A Life in Seven Chapters* was written over a period of years, and our task as editors was therefore somewhat different from the usual. Although the manuscript was complete in its content and organization, it required several readings to assure consistency of form and mechanics. We decided, however, not to modernize the form of the footnotes since they reflect in themselves the author's temperament and attitude toward his subject. The writing style and organization, in particular the flow of the discourse from topic to topic, are Professor Brubaker's.

At some point Professor Brubaker refers to his book as a "sketch of Shakespeare's life." It is indeed much more than that but, in a sense, it is not really that. The theoretical basis of the book lies in Professor Brubaker's belief that an author's writings are informed by the experience of the events and circumstances that occurred during his or her life from childhood to old age. Professor Brubaker shows how Shakespeare's work is a reflection of his life and times and how his life and times can be seen as a reflection of his work. He is convinced that it is possible to find in the writings themselves the manifestations and influences of those events and circumstances. Thus, in the course of reading the book we are not just educated about, for example, Shakespeare's father's and perhaps his own Catholic sympathies, but we also see where and how in the dramas evidence for such sympathies appears. Professor Brubaker's plot summaries and critical analyses are interesting and necessary adjuncts to his project, but the fascination is to follow the paths of arguments he lays out when he deals with the Robert Greene pamphlet or attempts to determine the roles Shakespeare might have played as an actor.

The impetus and financial support for publication came from former students and colleagues: William D. Bloodgood, Richard Hay, Bruce A. Maza, Benjamin F. Mittleman, Lisa Phyllis Seidman, David Alan Sitler, Leslie Anne Stainton, Laurence Brockman Tighe, Betty S. Wickstrom, Gordon M. Wickstrom, Pamela Williams, and R. Treat Williams. We wish also to note the generosity of the The C.E. and S. Foundation of Louisville, Kentucky, and the support of Ann Steiner, Provost of Franklin & Marshall College, for making available the resources of the College. In addition, a word of gratitude is owed to Professor Emeritus Gordon Wickstrom, a former colleague of Professor Brubaker. It was he who brought to the attention of the College the existence of the manuscript, thus providing the inspiration and persuasion for its publication.

It is the intention of the donors that the publication of the book serve as a tribute to and acknowledgement of Professor Brubaker's long and distinguished career as Alumni Professor of English Literature and Belles-Lettres at Franklin & Marshall College, where with great success he taught drama and brilliantly directed plays, especially Shakespeare's.

Professor Brubaker has asked us to acknowledge his wife Mary for her support and encouragement during the writing of the book and his daughter Jenny Black for her help in preparing the manuscript for electronic transmission. In addition, he has asked that we convey his thanks to friends Michael Wyatt and Larry Tighe for their helpful advice.

Robert J. Barnett
Judith A. Chien

PROLOGUE

What news on the Rialto?

(Merchant of Venice 1.3.38)

S O many biographies of William Shakespeare have been published that one may well ask, what is new about this one? I can't say I have any new discoveries to report. If I have anything new to say, it comes from taking a fresh look at the well-known facts and at the old theories and stories. Most biographies of Shakespeare are not based so much on original research as on speculations about materials discovered by others. Perhaps my approach may produce some results that will not survive critical scrutiny, but I think the game is likely to yield something worthwhile.

It can be said, however, that this book is organized in a new way. The plan developed from reading Gail Sheehy's book, *Passages* (1974). Her book presented the thesis that every seven years or so, we find ourselves in quite different circumstances. The idea is not unrelated to Shakespeare's classic statement on the theme of the "Seven Ages of Man." The world around us changes, and we change with it. This brought to mind Grant Wood's wry picture of young George Washington chopping down the cherry tree. The little boy with the hatchet was given the face of the old president as portrayed by Gilbert Stuart. This kind of double image often comes into play when we think about famous people. We imagine the child as having had the bearing and dignity of the person we recognize from portraits made in a later stage of life.

The dominant images we have of Shakespeare are the bust of the obese gentleman placed in his monument in Stratford Church and the engraving of the fellow with the enormous forehead used as the frontispiece of the folio collection of his plays. Both had been created after his death, possibly from likenesses taken earlier, but certainly with the accomplished poet in mind rather than the young

actor who wrote *The Comedy of Errors.* Concentrating on older figures is bound
to happen when little is recorded about anyone before they become famous.
The traditional stories about Shakespeare's early years are no more reliable than
Parson Weems' moral fable of Washington and the cherry tree.

Although little is known about the earlier stages of Shakespeare's life, I thought
it would be interesting to organize a biography by taking what could be called his
seven ages and imagining them one at a time through a series of questions. What
was going on in his life at age seven? At fourteen? At twenty-one? And so on.
How had he, his family, his work, and the world around him changed? Through
what crises had he passed?

Considering how Shakespeare spent his lifetime, it would be sensible, if not
inevitable, to assume that from a young age, the center of his life must have
included performing and writing for the theatre, and that such would have to be
an important part of his story. During the passages of his life, the theatrical world
he knew, and later worked in, changed as new circumstances and techniques
of playmaking, performing, and producing developed. To explore the kind of
theatre activity Shakespeare might have known throughout his life, I decided to
select a play for each one of Shakespeare's passages of life, none that he himself
wrote, but plays that were popular and influential during the different stages of
his theatrical career. The titles of the selected plays are used as the titles for the
chapters of this biography. This plan provides an efficient way of introducing
discussions of fads and changes in the Elizabethan theatre. These matters have
been well researched by theatre historians, but biographers of Shakespeare have
not given as much attention to them as they deserve. If such matters are not
reviewed, readers are likely to imagine that Shakespeare worked alone at a desk
as it is supposed modern writers do, rather than with others in the collaborative
stimulus and atmosphere of a theatre company. He was no doubt a genius, but
not one whose life will fit the modern pattern of a struggling artist, starving in a
garret, waiting for something to turn up.

Obviously there are other circumstances aside from Shakespeare's theatrical
background whose understanding requires a sense of history. Even the basic
records that show that Shakespeare was born in Stratford, that his father was
a glover involved in the wool trade, that he went to a grammar school, was
married, had children, lived in London, became rich and famous—these records
only have meaning if we have enough information to imagine what it could
have been like to have lived through those experiences in his time. That calls for

speculations necessarily involving some fiction, but nonetheless built on facts. That is, if a story is to be fashioned at all, the help of specialized studies provides an opportunity of getting it right.

Some crucial questions to be explored include, for example, how large would a village like Stratford have been on an Elizabethan scale? What sort of a person was John Shakespeare? How did the Reformation, the undeclared war with Spain, court politics, affect his life? What went on in an Elizabethan grammar school? Do the irregularities in Shakespeare's marriage mean he was involved in a shotgun wedding? How might Shakespeare have become familiar with the stage and then a member of the foremost acting company of his time? What did those activities involve? Why did Robert Greene attack him? What reputation did he have in his own time? All biographies review these topics with the intention of bringing the facts into some sort of coherent relationship. The difference between one book and another depends on the way the writers interpret the facts, that is, what they make of them.

We may never know enough about Shakespeare's life to satisfy our curiosity, but many additional records and documents have been discovered than can be worked into a story. A more lengthy biography, one that surveys the life and times of Shakespeare in all its fullness, would be beyond my reach. And there are many items I have stumbled across, but which I judged to be of minor importance. Just as one has to interpret facts and documents, so one has to select for discussion what can be useful in developing and presenting a plausible picture of Shakespeare's career in the theatre.

Biographies of Shakespeare usually include discussions of the literary merits of his plays, reviewing and commenting on what critics have said and the way the plays have been produced in the last three centuries. These are fascinating subjects and cannot be entirely omitted from a biography, but they lead, I think, to discussions that wander far from the central topic of biography. This book could no more be subtitled the "Life and Art" than the "Life and Times" of Shakespeare.

From the beginning my project was influenced by the good fortune I had in being part of the company and staff of the Shakespeare Festival in Ashland, Oregon, from 1955 to 1969. It was as it is today, a real repertory company. "Stay four days, see four plays!" was the advertising slogan. The repertory changed from year to year, which made it possible for me to work on productions of all of Shakespeare's plays as they were scheduled and rescheduled every ten years or so. At that time critical analyses of the seldom produced plays were not easy to find. And in many instances we were committed to producing plays no one knew much about and were launched willy-nilly into unknown territory. We may not have been first-rate, but we were surprised to discover that even without cutting or revision, these old scripts were still theatrically valid, entertaining, and affecting.

The important discovery of this experience was that Shakespeare is a much more intelligent and creative person than the one I was told about or imagined as I read his works in undergraduate and graduate studies. Realizing what a genius we have on our hands is certainly not a surprising insight reserved for theatre folk; lots of people have come to it by other roads, even those who would rather not attend a live production. There are few who would want to argue about the genius of Shakespeare, although if that is granted, a biographer must still face an important question: what were the circumstances of his life that allowed his theatrical genius to flourish?

These are certainly not evident in the story of Shakespeare's life as it is usually presented. It is often repeated and generally assumed that he had few advantages and was far from being a privileged person. That hardly makes sense. If that view were correct, we would have to wonder how the poor boy from Stratford could have written the plays attributed to him. There must be something wrong in the way the documents are read. The problem with that view is not that it is misleading: it is wrong.

It is surprising to notice the way the story line of "poor-boy-makes-good" has wormed its way into so many discussions of Shakespeare's life, distorting the interpretation of facts. It crops up in the suggestion that the driving force in his life was to repair the fortunes of a bankrupt father. But when we examine what is known about the range and size of John Shakespeare's business dealings, there is not enough available evidence to support the conclusion that the family was poor. The only advantage to that view is that it makes it possible to think of Shakespeare as a hero who overcame the deprivations of a humble childhood. The "poor-boy" myth returns in mutterings about Shakespeare's lack of university training, as if that experience were necessary to make a playwright, especially if we consider what went on at the Elizabethan universities. Some good playwrights like Marlowe and Fletcher were university men and some good playwrights like Kidd and Jonson were not.

Another source of imaginary sorrows arises from the irregularity of his marriage. This leads to the supposition that with a wife and children to support he was forced into a disreputable life in the theatre. He must have begun taking whatever bit parts he could get until he was "discovered." That would make another blot on the family escutcheon he would want to erase. And it all seems plausible if modern marriage customs are projected onto Elizabethan times, and if we want to cling to Victorian attitudes toward the stage. Closely related to that attitude toward the theatre are statements that Shakespeare cared nothing for his playwriting achievements. He only wrote for money and hardly bothered to see his plays into print.

Finally, there is a rather subtle form of the "poor-boy" legend that crops up in assertions that he was so intent on amassing a fortune to compensate for his poor beginnings and to support himself in the style of a gentleman that he became a grasping miser.

The story of Dick Wittington rising from orphan to Lord Mayor of London is a fable, like the stories Ben Franklin told of his rise to fortune, and the story of George Washington and the cherry tree. Perseverance, thrift, and honesty are virtues promoted by the rags to riches fable. It makes a good story, especially when we can't know for sure what happened. But in the case of Shakespeare's life, I think enough is known not to have to fall back on the theme of "poor-boy-makes-good" to tell a fair story.

CHAPTER I

THE CRADLE OF SECURITY
1564–1571

More. I prithee tell me, what plays have ye?
Player. Divers my Lord: *The Cradle of Security, Hit Nail o'th Head*
Impatient Poverty, The Play of Four P's, Dives and Lazarus,
Lusty Juventus, and *The Marriage of Wit and Wisdom*
(*The Book of Sir Thomas More*)

THE Avon flows gently south and west from the center of England to join the Severn as it turns toward the Bristol Channel. Above the valley of its headwaters stands Coventry, once the home of Lady Godiva, later the center of the cloth industry in the midlands and the largest inland city in Tudor England. Coventry dramatized its free status with an impressive circle of walls and displayed its wealth and merchandise in lavish annual productions of a cycle of mystery plays. Not far off to the west is Kenilworth made famous by Sir Walter Scot, where Elizabeth's favorite, the Earl of Leicester, rebuilt the castle, expanding palatial halls, pleasure gardens, and hunting parks to entertain his Queen.

The first town the Avon passes on its seaward journey is Warwick, forever associated with the legends of Guy of Warwick. As the river circled round the mass of rock from which the castle dominates the region, its channeled waters filled the moat and turned the mills of the town. About eight miles farther downstream lies Stratford-upon-Avon, the birthplace of William Shakespeare. Here the river widens, providing a ford for the old Roman road as it headed northwest from London. After the fifteenth century, Stratford Bridge was built to span the Avon, carrying traffic north to Henley-in-Arden and Birmingham and west to the then larger town of Worcester on the Severn in whose cathedral lies the tomb of King John. At Stratford, the mid-point of its rambles, the Avon becomes a navigable waterway, passing between farms and grazing lands and the abbey village of Evesham, once the goal of pilgrims visiting the shrine of St. Egwin.[1] Finally the Avon joins the Severn sixteen miles south of Worcester.

There at the confluence is the town of Tewksbury that gave its name to the battle in the bloody meadow where in 1471 the House of York won its last, deceptive victory in the War of the Roses. Farther downstream stands Gloucester, a favorite residence of the Plantagenet kings. Despite its rich association in history and legend, the Avon remains in our thoughts a quiet country stream in curious contrast to the astounding and many-minded Shakespeare who was born and buried on its banks. The pleasant image of the "Sweet Swan of Avon" that Ben Jonson gave us carries us back to the murmuring stream, to a peaceful landscape unspoiled by the turbulence of time and to a picture of natural easy goodness, unsophisticated by theatrical anxiety and artifice. However rich Warwickshire is with legendary and historical associations, it explains little about the genius whose life and work fascinates us. As with so many of his dramas, Shakespeare's life intrigues us with its contradictions. It begins at Stratford.

William, the son of John and Mary Arden Shakespeare was baptized on April 26, 1564 in Holy Trinity, the parish church of Stratford. He was their third child. Two daughters, Joan and Margaret had died in infancy, so William was for a brief time their only child. Other children followed, Gilbert, another daughter named Joan, Anne who died in infancy, Richard, and finally Edmund who was born when William was sixteen.

If children are apt to be like their parents, the life of Shakespeare's father and mother bears examination. John Shakespeare was an important man in his time and place.[2] He was by trade a glover, a manufacturer and seller of fine leather goods, purses, hatbands, and above all gloves. They were decorated, laced, embroidered, perfumed, and pranked with pearls if the buyer could afford them. Gloves were especially valued as gifts to give during a courtship and were often distributed at weddings to attendants of both bride and groom. For example, in *Much Ado About Nothing* [3.4] Hero receives gloves of an "excellent perfume" on the morning of her marriage to Claudio. In *Love's Labour's Lost* [5.2] the lords send wooing gifts to the ladies; one is given pearls, another a miniature encircled with diamonds, and the third a pair of "sweet" gloves. There is no suggestion in the script that the gloves were of less value than the jewels. Another indication of the regard given to gloves is shown by their appearance in official portraits. In the betrothal portrait of Queen Mary in the Prado, she is seated, a red rose in one hand and gloves in the other. In Southampton's portrait memorializing his imprisonment in the Tower, he displays an elegant pair of gloves garnished with black silk bows. Edward Alleyn holds a pair of gloves in his portrait as founder of Dulwich College. It seems as important to have and display gloves as to wear them. In short, John Shakespeare was engaged in a luxury trade—not quite like a silversmith or goldsmith, but he was by no means in a poor man's craft. There is a tale of the time Alexander Aspinall, the Stratford schoolmaster, in 1594 bought a pair of gloves from John Shakespeare to give to his betrothed. William came up with this impromptu posey, "The gift is small/ The will is all/ A shey ander Aspinall." The story may not be factually true, but it got passed along as it squared with customs and the persons involved. Aspinall married Anne, the widow of Ralph Shaw; she carried on her first husband's business in the wool trade. He had left her twenty-one tods of wool and six tods of yarn. A tod weighs about twenty-eight pounds. Her wool and yarn was worth more than the £20 annual salary Aspinall received as schoolmaster.

John Shakespeare was likely to have extra money to loan or invest. After serving an apprenticeship, usually a seven-year term, a glover in a market town would work as a paid journeyman for a master of the craft, or if he had borrowed or inherited enough, he could immediately establish his own workshop. After paying the accustomed fees, he was granted the freedom of the town, which allowed him to pursue his craft without competition from others not similarly trained and licensed. Although John Shakespeare was a glover by trade and so identified in public documents, he was free to invest in lands and commodities and to deal in loans. He made substantial investments in houses and fields and became an important buyer and seller of wool.

According to Peter J. Bowden, "the attraction of the wool trade for so many different classes of persons suggests that there were few better investments available in Tudor and Stuart England."[3] If Schoolmaster Aspinall was introduced to the wool trade by marrying the widow Shaw, John Shakespeare, as a glover, was automatically involved. To quote Professor Bowden again, glovers and other leather workers came to deal in wool through their interest in sheepskins, which they bought as a normal part of their business. When purchased from the farmers these skins were covered by a growth of fell wool, and this had first to be removed before the pelts could be [used] … As the wool was of no use to the leather industry it was then sold… From selling superfluous wool to dealing in fleece wool was but a short step.

Recent research has completely confirmed the statement in Nicholas Rowe's 18th-century biography of Shakespeare that his father was "a considerable dealer in wool."

The records found so far are impressive, particularly if we remember that for every recovered record, others may yet be found and others have been lost. In the matter of dealing in wool, what we know of John Shakespeare's activities is on record because some of them may have been illegal. After 1552 a law largely restricted the buying of wool to manufacturers or merchants of the staple. That is, middlemen were not to get between the sources of wool and those who used it in manufacture or exported it to foreign countries. To enforce the law, the government relied on informers to report violations and offered a reward if the information proved to be correct.

One informer who pointed the finger at John Shakespeare was James Langrake of Wittlesbury in Northamptonshire. He gave information in 1572 that John Shakespeare and John Lockeley, both of Stratford, bought two hundred tods of wool at fourteen shillings per tod from Walter Newsam and others. Newsam was possibly from Chadshunt, Warwickshire. Also in 1572, Langrake gave information that John Shakespeare bought from Edward and Richard Grant in Snitterfield, one hundred tods of wool at fourteen shillings per tod.[4] No evidence of the outcome of these cases has been found.

It may seem odd that James Langrake of Wittlesbury in Northamptonshire would know about John Shakespeare's buying wool in the Stratford area, which is about forty miles distant from Wittlesbury. There seems to have been a lot of wool in the area. Not all farmers had large herds, but many kept at least some sheep. We know for instance that the Hathaway family, into which William Shakespeare married, grazed sheep in their pasturelands.[5] There would be many sellers in the Midlands and some of the buyers may have been on the lookout for a chance to push their competitors out of the market by subjecting them to crippling fines.

James Langrake may have been as interested in the rewards of giving information as in harassing a competitor, for he also made charges against John Shakespeare for violating the statutes against loaning money at usurious rates. He claimed that in October 1568, at Westminster, John Shakespeare loaned John Musshem of Walton, Warwickshire, £80 to be repaid a month later with £20 interest, an amount well over the ten percent legal limit. John bargained to pay a forty shilling fine, rather than letting the case go to trial. Was John used to carrying £80 about him or did he have an agent in London? In a similar case, Anthony Harrison of Evesham, Worcestershire, claimed that in October 1568 at Westminster, John Shakespeare had given the same John Musshem £100 to be repaid at the end of November with £20 interest.

It is possible that Musshem and Shakespeare were something like partners, because both were sued in 1573 for a debt by Henry Higford of Solihull, a town northwest of Stratford, almost in Worcestershire, who claimed they each owed him £30. In 1556 Thomas Such of Armscot, Worcestershire, sued John Shakespeare for £8. In 1572 John Shakespeare sued John Luther of Banbury, Oxfordshire, for a debt of £50, contracted a year earlier in London.[6]

A somewhat different case came up in 1580. John Shakespeare and John Audley, "a hat-maker of Nottingham were bound over in the Court of the Queen's Bench to give security against a breach of the peace."[7] They did not answer and were fined. John Shakespeare had to pay £20 for himself and the same amount as surety for Audley. Another person named in the case was Thomas Cooley of Stoke, Staffordshire. We don't know who claimed to be threatened by Shakespeare, Audley, and Cooley, but it seems likely that John Shakespeare could hold his own in a row.

There are other cases where John Shakespeare's name appears in court records, but I have mentioned enough to give a picture of the kind of man he was. It seems that we are in no position to draw conclusions about John Shakespeare's fortunes from what can only be a partial list of transactions, except to conclude that he spent, borrowed, and loaned large sums of money. However, the cases I mentioned suggest that his operations covered a lot of territory. He got around London and Westminster and had business dealings in the midland shires of Nottingham, Northampton, Oxford, Stafford, and Worcester.[8] Considering all this, it is difficult to accept a picture of John Shakespeare as an illiterate, stay-at-home craftsman. Furthermore, John Shakespeare's career as an official in the market town of Stratford is rather testimony that he was a highly competent person.

He grew up in Snitterfield, a farming hamlet three miles north of Stratford. There is no record of where he served an apprenticeship, or when he located in the market town. His name first appears in the town records in 1552 when he was fined at the leet court of the manor of Stratford for making a muck hill in Henley Street. From this record of a one shilling fine, it can be inferred that he had completed an apprenticeship and was a householder on his own; otherwise his master would have been the one to be fined. In 1556 he purchased two houses with garden plots in Stratford, one on Henley Street and another on Greenhill Street. The Henley Street property became his home and shop. It had to have been a valuable and expensive property because it had a large frontage on a busy street convenient to the Stratford market and on the main road north. Although he seems to have bought more properties than were needed for his family or his business dealings, it is not easy to know exactly how much property he owned or bought or sold at various times during his life. It is probable that some were investments to provide additional income. In September of 1556 John Shakespeare was appointed a taster to inspect ale and bread, the first of many offices he held in Stratford, which put him in a position to levy fines.

The following year, 1557, he married Mary Arden, the youngest of eight daughters of Robert Arden, a prosperous yeoman farmer of Wilmcote, a hamlet about three miles northwest of Stratford and west of Snitterfield. No doubt John Shakespeare married well, as men were expected to do. Mary Arden inherited some land and money from her father who had died the previous year. His will also provided for his widow, another unmarried daughter, and for a distribution to his other daughters. Robert Arden may have been a wealthy man, but with all those daughters and a widow to provide for, the family purse was hard pressed. He had to do well by his youngest daughter if she were to be married at all. For in those days marriage was a matter of business and would not take place until a couple was able to set up a separate household and provide for children. Since John Shakespeare had to have property or prospects in some proportion to what his wife brought to the marriage, his marriage might even have doubled his wealth.[9] Mary Arden was one of the executors of her father's will, fair evidence that she brought business sense to the marriage as well as inherited property. When we consider that John Shakespeare worked as a glover and in the wool trade, it is easy to imagine that the Shakespeares had many employees, and that

Mary Shakespeare would have played an important role in the management of those business operations.[10]

It is not likely that John and Mary arranged their marriage themselves. That is not the way things were done. Marriages were negotiated by the parents or others representing the families and with an eye to their financial interests. Since her marriage took place within a year of her father's death, it is likely that Mary's inheritance had been determined by marriage negotiations carried out before or while his will was being drawn up. The families had known each other for a long time. Richard Shakespeare, John's father, rented farm land and buildings from Robert Arden. Some take this to mean that the Shakespeares of Snitterfield may not have been as well off as the Ardens of Wilmcote. It is true that the Arden name was prominent in the forest or Arden region of the Midlands and can be traced to the time of William the Conqueror. But even in families whose ancestry can be traced, some branches are privileged and some are not. The name Shakespeare has been traced to the twelfth century—which is almost as good as the time of the Conquest—and has a very ancient and heroic sound. John Shakespeare claimed that his grandfather was rewarded by King Henry VII for valiant service.[11] Strictly speaking, the branches of the Shakespeare and Arden families were both substantial farmers, although neither would be listed as gentry. It seems likely that John Shakespeare's father would have helped his son to establish himself as a glover in Stratford.

After his marriage Master John Shakespeare began to play an increasingly important part in public life, as substantial householders were expected to do, as much to look after their own interests as to serve the public. He served briefly as one of four constables in Stratford. William was to make good fun of constables in *Much Ado About Nothing* and *Measure for Measure*, portraying them as illiterate, officious, and stupid, but in real life constables were not appointed for comic effect. When in *Measure for Measure* the Deputy sees the limitations of Constable Elbow, he asks for "the names of some six or seven, the most sufficient in your parish" [2.1.272-273] who would be better suited for the post. He means by the word "sufficient" solvent as well as capable. In 1561 John Shakespeare was appointed one of two chamberlains who kept track of the finances and property of the Stratford Corporation. It was an exacting responsibility which he apparently did very well, for he was asked to do it for several years. In 1565, the year after William was born, John Shakespeare was made an Alderman, one of a body of fourteen who governed Stratford. This came not simply as a sign of John

Shakespeare's competence, but can be taken as evidence that he was among the most financially substantial householders in the town.

To be an Alderman in such a town may seem to us to be a big fish in a small pond. Stratford had about two thousand inhabitants—three thousand if we include the people in the small settlements nearby which were included in the parish. But we must see this figure on an Elizabethan scale. In 1600 the largest English city, London had about two hundred thousand. The next largest had not much more than ten thousand, and there were only a few of them, all sea ports, namely Norwich, Bristol, York, and Newcastle. The English population was made up almost entirely of farmers widely dispersed in hamlets and villages surrounded by fields, pastures, and forests. Market towns like Stratford served an area not wider than a ten-mile radius, the distance of a day's walk and return with time allowed for whatever business or visiting the market afforded. Given this wide dispersal of the working population and the difficulties of travel, towns did not get much larger than Stratford.[12]

The history of Stratford as a self-governing corporation with the privilege of holding a weekly market and an annual fair goes back to the twelfth century when it was a manor belonging to the Bishop of Worcester. During the Reformation the manor, like many other church properties, passed to the crown and then to the Earl of Warwick. The customs and traditions of its governance were confirmed by a royal charter of incorporation in 1553. This gave the leading citizens, that is, the wealthiest citizens, what may be called the duties of self-government, but they were required to govern, not to let things slide. There was a council of twenty-eight Burgesses made up of the principal householders from whom fourteen Aldermen were selected to manage the town. If service as a Burgess or Alderman was refused, a fine had to be paid. Members of those bodies did not stand for election; they were appointed by their colleagues and continued in service until old age or their neglect of duty made it necessary for them to be replaced. Annually the Aldermen selected or drafted one of their members to serve as Bailiff and another to serve as Chief Alderman. (The office of Bailiff in a manor town would be equivalent to that of a Mayor.) These two officers were responsible to the Lord of the Manor or his steward. Additionally, by virtue of their place they were officers of the crown and Justices of the Peace.

The kingdom was governed by a complex variety of courts, commissions, and officers as well as by the surviving feudal, manorial, and ecclesiastical jurisdictions. But the central government, or rather the administrative bureaucracy that ran it, was very small. Parliamentary statutes and proclamations by the Queen's Privy Council tended to put responsibility directly on local authorities. Thus the Aldermen and Mayor, or Bailiff as in the case of a manor town like Stratford, were held accountable for maintaining order and upholding the laws and statutes of the realm. They were responsible for compliance with the poor and vagrancy laws, for the highways and bridges, for regulating prices and wages, furnishing soldiers and equipment for military service, and the collection of assessments and subsidies. In Stratford, the School, the Guild Hall and Chapel, the almshouses, and the salaries of the schoolmaster and the vicar were all responsibilities of the Bailiff and Aldermen.

Elizabethan life was regulated to an extraordinary degree. Much of private life was controlled by rules and fines. Church attendance was required and there were rules about dress, the hours of work and play and sleep. There were fines for disrespectful or obstreperous talk. People seemed not to be much concerned for personal liberty.

John Shakespeare wore the furred gown of an alderman from 1565 to 1586. He took a turn as High Bailiff in 1569 and as Chief Alderman in 1572. Although the tenure of these offices was only for a year, and the offices were usually passed to different aldermen each year, the positions were not treated casually or with democratic indifference to ceremony. Sergeants in buff colored uniforms and bearing maces escorted the magistrates to their official duties, to meetings and court sittings, to Sunday worship and other gatherings where they would find places of honor reserved for them.

All this meant that as William Shakespeare was growing up, he enjoyed the delights and difficulties of being the son of an imposing and influential father. His earliest memories of John Shakespeare might have been of the country justice:

> In fair round belly with good capon lined,
> With eyes severe and beard of formal cut,
> Full of wise saws and modern instances.
>
> *(As You Like It* 2.7.154–156)[13]

There is another contrasting picture of John Shakespeare that survives in an anecdote written down in the mid-seventeenth century by Thomas Plume:

> Sir John Mennis saw once his old father in his shop—a merry cheeked

old man—that said—Will was a good, honest fellow, but he durst have cracked a jest with him at any time.[14]

Although this sketch of the old man has only the authority of gossip, it rings true. There is something that seems right about thinking of Shakespeare's father as both the busy, public man of his middle years and in his later years as the jest cracker, a bit silly with age, getting a laugh on his then famous son.

John Shakespeare lived through a time of see-saw changes in the policies and practices of religion as the children of Henry VIII succeeded each other. He was a young man when the ministers of the boy king, Edward VI, brought the English church more fully into line with the programs of the Protestant reformers on the continent. Then in 1553, about the time John Shakespeare opened his shop in Stratford, the King died and his half-sister, Mary, the daughter of Katharine of Aragon, became Queen and tried to return the country to the Roman fold. Five years later Mary died and Elizabeth reclaimed authority as governor of the church in England and reestablished the forms of worship set down in a revised Book of Common Prayer. These changes were accompanied by dramatic reversals of fortune for the nobles and ecclesiastics trapped by the shifts of power from one side to the other. Surely many ordinary folk missed the traditional devotional practices they knew from childhood and accepted the new forms of worship with some reluctance.[15] How strictly the innovations were observed depended somewhat on the zeal of officials in a town or diocese. What seems curious is that the country survived these changes without more troubles. Perhaps this is true because the situation was politically dangerous and not simply a matter of doctrine or ritual. It involved the question of the legitimacy of the regime of Queen Elizabeth.

When the Pope refused to annul the marriage of Henry VIII to Katharine of Aragon, Henry's subsequent marriage to Anne Boleyn created an adulterous union, at least in the view of Rome. The Princess Elizabeth was a bastard, because she was born to Henry's second wife while he was still married to his first. Given this view of the matter, the throne rightfully belonged to someone else—Mary of Scotland, a great granddaughter of Henry VII, or to Philip II of Spain, the surviving husband of the late Queen Mary. To argue such a thing was high treason. Similarly, to accept the Pope's authority over Elizabeth's in church affairs was equally treasonous. In these circumstances Elizabeth and her Council felt duty bound to control public discussion of any matter touching on politics or religion. Licensing was a well established method of controlling what books got into print, and Bishops, whether Anglican or Catholic, were accustomed to disciplining any of their clergy who strayed off limits. In addition to the press and the pulpit, the stage was readily available for attacking as well as defending the political and religious settlement that Elizabeth hoped to establish. The stage, however, had not proved easy to control.

Actors do not always follow a script, but they always play off the current concerns and excitements of an audience. Another aspect of the problem was that there was a growing number of acting companies touring the country. Since suppressing theatrical activity entirely would have been impossible, some machinery for controlling the stage had to be devised. The Queen decided to order the local authorities to handle the problem. By proclamation in the first year of her reign Elizabeth forbade "all manner of Interludes to be played openly or privately" unless they were licensed by the mayor or chief officers of a city or town, by lieutenants in the shires, or by two justices of the peace in the area where performances might take place. And these officers were charged "as they will answer: that they permit none to be played wherein either matters of religion or of the governance of the estate of the commonweal shall be handled or treated." The proclamation also gave authority to the officers to arrest and imprison offenders for fourteen days or more until they had assurances the offense would not be repeated.[16]

Note that this censorship was designed to prevent discussion of political and religious questions, unlike modern censorship, which is often primarily concerned that bawdy players not fiddle with sexual themes and innuendoes. In practice a system developed whereby the approval and licensing of plays became the responsibility of the Master of the Revels, an officer under the Lord Chamberlain. While this determined what plays might be performed, the Mayor, or Bailiff in a manor town like Stratford, still had to give his permission before a performance could take place.

The small touring companies of about eight men and a boy that flourished in the early days of Elizabeth's reign were already under considerable control. Strict laws against vagrancy made it difficult for any group to travel from town to town without some authorization. Playing companies were required to have the nominal protection of a particular nobleman who gave them the right to wear his livery and badge and granted them a patent certifying that they were his servants and that he had licensed them to travel and perform. Of great importance, the patent included a request, almost a command from the noble lord to the townsmen to treat his players well and to allow them to perform in suitable places.

After checking their credentials, the magistrate, like King Claudius in *Hamlet* would probably ask about the argument of the play, "Is there no offense in it?" To which expected question the leading player had ready a speech delivered in tones of assurance that all their plays were duly licensed by the Master of the Revels. At this point, if the Mayor or Bailiff had a taste for theatre, it became customary to allow a trial performance in the Guild Hall or other convenient place to which were invited the Aldermen and leading citizens together with their wives and children and as many others as could be squeezed into the Hall. The Mayor was host for the performance, like the Queen at Court. If all went well, the actors were rewarded by the Chamberlain and allowed to perform in public where they could collect the customary fees for admission. Apparently permission to perform might be refused, but not necessarily because the play was suspected of being seditious. The Mayor might be opposed to any activity that disturbed the orderly routine of town life, or he simply might not like plays. In such a case, a flat refusal ran some risk of offending the powerful patron of the company, so the practice developed of contributing to the expenses of the players with the understanding that they would not perform but move on to the next town. The wishes of the town officials could not be lightly flaunted, as is illustrated by two cases involving the Earl of Worcester's Men, a touring troupe.

In the summer of 1583 they arrived in Norwich when there was a fear of an outbreak of the plague. So they were given the rather large sum of twenty-six shillings, eight pence with the understanding that they would not perform. That night they went back on the agreement and played at their inn. Next morning the Mayor and Aldermen decided to inform the Earl of Worcester of the contemptuous conduct of his men which could lead the Earl to recall their patent. The town officials also decreed that Worcester's Men should never receive reward in Norwich again and that they be sent to prison unless they immediately left the city. The players went down on their knees, admitted their fault and begged that the letter to the Earl not be sent.

But they had not learned their lesson. A year later Worcester's Men came to Leicester and the Mayor gave them an angel, about ten shillings, toward their dinner and asked them not to play for the simple reason that "the time was not convenient." About two hours later they approached the Mayor again and asked to be allowed to play in their inn. Again the Mayor refused. Whereupon they said they would play in despite of him and with "diverse other evil and contemptuous words" they went through the town beating drums and sounding trumpets to announce a performance. They were brought before the Mayor and had to say they were sorry and beg pardon, "desiring his Worship not to write to their Master against them." Fortunately the Mayor of Leicester had a good heart, so upon their submission and repentance he allowed them to play that night in their inn, but not in his hall. They had to announce to the audience that "they were licensed to play by Master Mayor and with his good will and that they were sorry for words past."[17]

This kind of confrontation must have been unusual in Leicester, for the records suggest it was a most hospitable place for actors to visit. In fact, during the reign of Elizabeth more groups toured to Leicester than to any other English town. The second most frequently visited town was Coventry and Bath was third. These towns lie almost in a line following the southwesterly course of the Avon. Other towns on this line that frequently entertained players were Bristol, Gloucester, and Stratford.[18]

It is a most interesting fact that payments to traveling players are first mentioned in the Chamber Accounts of Stratford in 1569 when the Bailiff was John Shakespeare. Rewards were given that year to the company of the Queen's Interluders and to the Earl of Worcester's Men to whom was given a negligible reward of one shilling. They must have been a small, unimpressive group, or not very good that day. Since that was fifteen years before they had their troubles with the Mayors of Norwich and Leicester, they would hardly have had the same personnel even if they had the same patron. The Queen's Interluders were however rewarded with nine shillings. Five-year-old William Shakespeare could hardly forget their parade in the red livery of the royal household, a livery that one day would be granted to him.

The Queen's Interluders did not appear again in Stratford, but Worcester's Men made four more visits. In the early 1580's one of their actors was the young Edward Alleyn who later, as leader of the Lord Admiral's Men, astounded audiences in the title roles of Marlowe's plays *Doctor Faustus, Tamburlaine,* and, *The Jew of Malta*. In the 1570's the Earl of Leicester's Men came to Stratford three times. One of their players was James Burbage, who built the first playhouse in London and, it could be said, started the city on its way to becoming the center of theatrical activity in England. His son, Richard, the finest player of the next generation, was to become Shakespeare's fellow actor and the creator of his most demanding and exciting roles. Sometime after 1583, the Queen created a new company called the Queen's Men headed by Richard Tarleton, the most popular clown of the age. This company appeared in Stratford four times. It is often assumed that a company on tour is a company that can't make it in the big city. That would be true in some cases, but not in the case of the Queen's Men. In a recent study, Scott McMillin and Sally-Beth Maclean demonstrate that the Queen's Men toured the country extensively, perhaps more so than any other company. Touring was their main business and their most rewarding. It seems the Queen wanted her livery to be recognized even in out-of-way places.[19]

The satirist Thomas Nashe tells this story of the popular clown, Tarleton of the Queen's Men, and a "wise Justice" in a country town:

> Having a play presented before him and his Township by Tarleton and the rest of his fellows, her Majesty's Servants, ... the people began exceedingly to laugh when Tarlton first peeped out his head. Whereat the Justice ... seeing with his becks and nods he could not make them cease, he went with his staff, and beat them round about unmercifully on the bare pates, in that they, being but farmers and poor country hinds, would presume to laugh at the Queen's Men, and make no more of her cloth in his presence.[20]

There were four other companies who came to Stratford one or two times.[21] From 1569 to 1589, all the years Shakespeare was growing up, hardly a year went by without a professional troupe performing in Stratford. Some of them may not have been very good, but the best English actors found their way to Shakespeare's bailiwick.

No one wrote down the titles of the plays that were performed, and sometimes the name of the company was not recorded. There is, however, an eyewitness description of a performance in Gloucester that gives a fairly accurate picture of the kind of dramatic fare the professional troupes had to offer. It is found in a book by Ralph Willis, *Mount Tabor, or Private Exercises of a Penitent Sinner*. The performance took place about the same time John Shakespeare first introduced traveling players to Stratford and to his son. They may have seen the same production. Here is Willis' description:

> In the city of Gloucester the manner is (as I think it is in other like corporations) that when players of interludes come to town, they first attend the Mayor to inform him what nobleman's servants they are, and so to get license for their public playing. And if the Mayor like the actors, or would show respect to their lord and master, he appoints them to play their first play before himself and the Aldermen and Common Council of the city. And that is called the Mayor's play. Where every one that will comes in without money, the Mayor giving the players a reward as he thinks fit to show respect unto them. At such a play my father took me with him and made me stand between his legs, as he sat upon one of the benches where we saw and heard very well.

> The play was called *The Cradle of Security*, wherein was personated a king or some great prince with his courtiers of several kinds, amongst which three ladies were in special grace with him. And they keeping him in delights and pleasures drew him from his graver counselors, hearing of sermons, and listening to good counsel and admonitions, that in the end they got him to lie down in a cradle upon the stage, where these three ladies joining in a sweet song rocked him asleep that he snorted again. And in the mean time, closely conveyed under the clothes where withal he was covered, a vizard like a swine's snout upon his face with three wire chains fastened thereunto, the other three ends whereof being held severally by those ladies, who fall to singing again, and then discovered his face, that the spectators might see how they had transformed him, going on with their singing. Whilst all this was acting, there came forth of another door at the farthest end of the stage, two old men. The one in blue with a sergeant-at-arms his mace on his shoulder, the other in red with a sword in his hand and leaning with the other hand upon the other's shoulder. And so they went along in a soft pace round about by the skirt of the stage, till at last they came to the cradle, when all the court was in greatest jollity. And then the foremost old man with his mace struck a fearful blow upon the cradle. Whereat all the courtiers, with the three ladies and the vizard all vanished. And the desolate prince did personate in the moral, the wicked of the world; the three ladies, Pride, Covetousness, and

Luxury; the two old men, the end of the world and the last judgment. This sight took such impression in me that when I came towards man's estate, it was as fresh in my memory as if I had seen it newly acted.[22]

Although Willis felt it important to tell exactly what the characters represented, the morality is impressive for more complicated reasons. The Prince could just as well be labeled Mankind or Everyman; the ladies, Flattery, Selfishness, and Do-Your-Own-Thing; the old men, Reality and Retribution. The play gets its energy from its straightforward presentation in the manner of a cartoon of a recurring human situation—what it is like to be lulled by a false sense of security. And there are related concerns that play off that situation, uniting the world of the play and the world of the audience. What if we are under similarly false and giddy illusions? Are we being turned into swine? What will happen when we wake up? Notice too how the audience is in on the trick being played on the Prince, a sure-fire device to hold their attention and ensure their participation.

If Shakespeare did not see *The Cradle of Security* as a boy, at least he had absorbed the themes and techniques of similar moral interludes. Echoes of them can be found in many of his works. The story of a Prince seduced by flattery, enraged by sound counsel, and brought to grief and death gives shape to Shakespeare's *Richard II* and *King Lear*, and a comic variation of the pattern can be seen in the relationship of Falstaff and Prince Hal in the Henry IV plays.

There are also verbal echoes as well as story snippets. When Iago is being most false to Othello he speaks lines that could be used as a final cry by the Prince in *The Cradle of Security*:

> Oh, 'tis the spite of hell, the fiend's arch-mock,
> To lip a wanton in a secure couch
> And to suppose her chaste!
>
> (*Othello* 4.1.71–73)

The meditation by Henry VI describing the contrasting life of a shepherd and a king, evokes a picture of a false court in the morality play tradition:

> the Shepherd's homely curds,
> His cold thin drink out of his leather bottle,
> His wonted sleep under the fresh tree's shade,
> All which secure and sweetly he enjoys,
> Is far beyond a Prince's delicates—
> His viands sparking in a golden cup,
> His body couched in a curious bed,
> When Care, Mistrust, and Treason waits on him.
>
> (*III Henry VI* 2.5.47–54)

Perhaps the most memorable moment in *The Cradle of Security* came when "all the court was in greatest jollity" and the old man with the mace struck a fearful blow. For, as Hamlet says, "that fell sergeant Death is most strict in his arrest." The sharp contrast of the full tide of life meeting the menacing and unexpected figure of death is an effect Shakespeare exploited with many variations, for example in the entrance of Mercade in *Love's Labour's Lost,* which darkens the scene with news of the death of the King just as the performance of the play-within-the-play reaches its peak of comic frenzy. We might add the moment the body of Juliet is found by her nurse as the household bustles to prepare her wedding. Richard III announces the death of Clarence as the court is about to celebrate a love day. And more subtly, the skull uncovered by the grave digger in *Hamlet* is the skull of the King's jester, whose flashes of merriment were wont to set the table on a roar.

One more variation is this meditation by Richard II, where Death is seen as a court jester:

> For within the hollow crown
> That rounds the mortal temples of a King,
> Keeps Death his court, and there the antic sits
> Scoffing his state, and grinning at his pomp,
> Allowing him a breath, a little scene
> To monarchize, be feared, and kill with looks,
> Infusing him with self and vain conceit,
> As if this flesh, which walls about our life,
> Were brass impregnable. And humour'd thus,
> Comes at the last, and with a little pin
> Bores through his castle walls, and farewell, King.
>
> (*Richard II* 3.2.160–170)

Consider the relationship of King and entertainer from another angle. At a performance of a play in the Guild Hall, two figures are the focus of the attention of the audience, each reflecting in his own way the community gathered about them: the Bailiff secure on the bench of honor and host of the occasion, and the actor in the playing space creating the picture of humanity distracted by vices and heedless of the approaching shadows. The spectacle says little of current events, of politics or religion, but through the music, the false face, costumes and symbolic props, the audience can see their own life with a quickened sense of its drama. It is wonderful to sponsor such a performance and wonderful to create such illusions.

But not all time was for pastime. John Shakespeare's term as High Bailiff of Stratford running from October 1568 to October 1569 happened to coincide with the time of the Northern Rebellion, the first serious challenge to the authority of Queen Elizabeth.

In May of 1568 Mary Stuart, the deposed Queen of Scots, escaped her prison in Lock Leven Castle and crossed the Solway Firth to English territory. Although she was only twenty-six years old when she came to England, Mary's life had already become sad and sordid. She was crowned Queen of Scotland as a child and while her mother ruled as regent, Mary was betrothed to the Dauphin and sent to France. At sixteen she was Queen of France, widowed a year later, and returned to Scotland. As long as Elizabeth remained unmarried and childless, Mary was next in line to the English throne. But that was not good enough for Mary. She claimed the title of Queen of England. No one knew at the time how seriously she might assert her claims should the opportunity arise, but being a Catholic, Mary's claim might find ready support among the disaffected nobility with Catholic sympathies. In the meantime the rival queens dissembled a friendship as Mary looked for a new husband whose position could bolster her title. Elizabeth took a hand and proposed her own trusty favorite, the Earl of Leicester, a match for Mary that would be in line with English interests. The Duke of Norfolk was another possibility.

During these desultory negotiations, Lord Darnley, a shallow and dissolute youth of some royal blood and Catholic sympathies, happened to be visiting

Scotland and caught the eye of Mary. Without time to consider her own thoughts, let alone the objections of her council or of her powerful neighbor to the south, Mary married Darnley. A year later in 1566 her son James was born, but everything went wrong after that. By then Mary had become a bitter enemy of her husband. In a jealous rage Darnley had Mary's secretary, David Rizzio, taken by force from her presence and murdered outside her chamber while he held her pinned to the wall. Mary knew she had married in haste but she was not one to repent at leisure. Not having the option of divorce, Mary connived at the murder of her husband, and then married Lord Bothwell who was believed to have arranged the murder. That was too much for the Kirk of Scotland. After a brief show of force, Bothwell fled to Denmark, Mary was taken to prison and deposed in favor of her year-old son, James. A year later she escaped to England. Her plan was to gather an army and restore herself to the throne of Scotland. Her hope was that Elizabeth would come to the aid of a sister monarch or at least give a safe conduct to France where her relatives, the powerful Guise family, would take her cause in hand. Elizabeth did neither. Instead she had the Earl of Shrewsbury take Mary into custody at Carlisle Castle.

Despite these ugly facts surrounding her deposition, Mary's plight and her determination to fight provoked both sympathy and some very unrealistic expectations. What began as talk about returning her to power, hatched into a plan to restore Roman Catholicism to Scotland and subsequently evolved into a mad scheme to overthrow Elizabeth as well. Put in its simplest terms the scheme could be outlined like this: the Northern lords of Catholic sympathies in alliance with the Duke of Norfolk would raise their followers, capture strongholds, meet up with troops and supplies sent over from the Spanish Netherlands. They would free Mary and after they gained the upper hand, Mary would marry Norfolk, and England would have a new king and queen. In November 1569 the hotheads in the North, yearning for the good old days, took to the field before plans could be coordinated. Perhaps they knew they didn't have time, for Elizabeth's ministers knew well beforehand what was afoot. The Duke of Norfolk was arrested and sent to the Tower. The Lieutenants in the shires were ordered to have troops trained and equipped for service.

The first year the rebels had an easy time augmenting their forces as they moved south. At Durham they took over the cathedral, threw out the communion table and prayer books, set up altars, and celebrated mass. They went on their way rejoicing with banners displaying the five wounds of Christ. At Hartlepool where soldiers and supplies from the Spanish Netherlands were to be landed, they were fired on by English warships that had taken control of the harbor. Another rebel force bypassed the strong garrison at York and headed south toward Tutbury, where Mary had been moved. But she had already been moved a second time—all the way south to Coventry.

Gradually a large body of English troops was assembled in Lincolnshire, Leicestershire, and Warwickshire under the Earl of Warwick and Lord Clinton to block the southern movements of the rebels. Lord Hunsdon took another army to reinforce the Earl of Sussex at York. The rebellion collapsed in front of him. There followed a devastating campaign of reprisals, looting, and executions as the cold winter of 1570 added to the suffering in the northern counties. It took many years before the consequences of this violence played out. The Duke of Norfolk and the Earl of Northumberland were brought to trial and executed. On the other side, the Pope issued a bull branding Elizabeth a bastard heretic and releasing English subjects from allegiance to her. The Pope also supported the claims of Philip II of Spain to the English throne. The bull had little effect beyond making it necessary for English Catholics to practice their religion in secret. Elizabeth refused to take further action against Mary herself or to return the fugitive queen to the hands of the Scots. Nonetheless Mary continued to plot against her protector.[23]

The town of Stratford had a share in the excitement of the year of the rebellion, although the forced marches and fighting took place far to the north. Rumors stirred about as soon as Mary crossed the border in May. In the fall, Bailiff Shakespeare as a Justice of the Peace was ordered to have men in readiness. Weapons from the town armory were repaired and training began. Finally the trained bands were off to service with the Lord of the Manor, the Earl of Warwick. Some of the bands from the more southern counties passed through on their way north. It is not likely that young Will Shakespeare, about to enter grammar school, would remember in detail the excitement of that year. It is possible, however, that the recruiting scenes he invented as comic additions to his plays on the reign of King Henry IV owe something to memories of soldiers mustered and marched through Stratford at the time of the Northern Rebellion.

Perhaps more important than any personal memories or the descriptions he might have read in the chronicle history books, Shakespeare inevitably thought of history and politics as concerned with the issues raised by the Northern Rebellion which continued to be the focus of attention through his lifetime.

There came the eventual trial and execution of Mary, the attempted invasion by the Armada of Philip II, and the Gunpowder Plot after Mary's son James became King of England. Further, there were the campaigns in France, the Netherlands, and Ireland, raids on Spanish harbors and shipping. While censorship would make it difficult to comment directly on the political and religious issues raised by contemporary events, Shakespeare's history plays are shaped by those issues. His early histories dealing with the Wars of the Roses are bound together by the double issues of a disputed title to the crown and the horrors produced by civil war as partisans of the rival claimants battle it out. His *King John* displays a variety of ways in which claims might be made: primogeniture, possession, conquest, marriage, the published will of a previous monarch, papal decree, all of which just about cover the claims put forward in various combinations by Elizabeth, Mary, and Philip. In Shakespeare's later histories such as *Richard II* and *Henry IV, Parts I* and *II*, the basic story is of usurpation followed by a revolt that ends in disaster because the rebels take to the field before their plans can be perfected. In *Henry V* the king's dubious title to the throne of France is settled by conquest and marriage.

The histories deal with events that transpired some two hundred years before the plays were written, but both Shakespeare and his audiences would read them in the light of current events and the political issues brought sharply into focus by the Northern Rebellion.

CHAPTER 2

JACK JUGGLER
1571–1578

Dem. What's here? a scroll, and written round about.
   Let's see: [*reads.*]
      "*Integer vitae, scelerisque purus,*
      Non eget Mauri jaculis, nec arcu."
Chi. O, 'tis a verse in Horace, I know it well,
      I read it in the grammar long ago.

(*Titus Andronicus* 4.2.18–23)

BEFORE the Reformation, the life of Stratford's more solid citizens centered on the Guild of the Holy Cross, or to give its name in full, the Guild of the Holy Cross, the Blessed Virgin, and Saint John the Baptist. The Guild was a social, charitable, and religious organization. Members, both men and women, paid an annual fee, elected their own officers, and enjoyed the privileges of the fraternity. They wore a distinctive hood when they went in procession with banners and crosses on saints' days, at funerals of fellow members, and at their annual feast.

Although not everyone could afford the expenses of belonging, membership in the Guild was not limited to residents of Stratford or its surrounding villages. The advantage of prayers and masses for the dead attracted many to join and endow the Guild with rich legacies. Among its most distinguished members were George, Duke of Clarence, then Earl of Warwick, his wife and two of his children—the same unfortunate George whose murder in the tower is dramatized in Shakespeare's *Richard III*. At the height of its prosperity the Guild came to possess much real estate and a treasury of jewels, plate, banners, vestments, and other furnishings.

The Guild was in many ways a constant presence in Stratford. Through its officers, by-laws, and meetings, a measure of self-government and local initiative became customary in the town. The Guild maintained its own hall, almshouses, chapel, and school, and provided four priests to say masses through the day, and one to teach in the Latin grammar school. It took over maintenance of the bridge over the Avon. Of the four annual fairs held in Stratford from the earliest times, the best known lasted four days beginning on September 13th, the day before the Feast of the Holy Cross and the focus of devotion by the Guild.

In 1547, as the Reformation began to work its way into English life, the Guild was dissolved. Its property, the revenue of which was largely dedicated to maintaining the chantry priests, was confiscated, although provision was made to keep the school open. The charter granted to Stratford in 1553 by King Edward VI created a corporation which replaced the governmental structures of the Guild. The corporation took over the Guild Hall and was given responsibility to maintain the almshouses, the bridge, and the school, which was renamed "The King's New School at Stratford-upon-Avon."

The chapel continued to be used by the scholars for morning prayers but its sumptuous decor, which rivaled the parish church, was gradually reduced to Protestant plainness. In 1563, when John Shakespeare served as Chamberlain to the Corporation, his accounts show that the wall paintings were covered with whitewash. They included a "Last Judgment" on the great arch separating the chancel from the nave, a "Legend of the Cross" on the ceiling, and a "Dance of Death" on the side walls. By the time William entered the school, the rood screen had been taken down, the stained glass had been replaced by clear glazing, and the elaborate vestments had been sold.

There is some question whether Shakespeare attended the Stratford Grammar School. Since the records of students from that time do not survive, we have no way of knowing whether he did or not. There is, however, no question that he had a Latin grammar school education. It is of little consequence which school he attended, for the course of study was very much the same throughout the kingdom. Given the circumstances of his father's position as one of the aldermen charged with maintaining the school, and the fact that if he had gone elsewhere his parents would have had to pay for his lodging, the sensible assumption is that he did indeed attend the King's New School at Stratford-upon-Avon.

Like many others in Elizabethan England, the Stratford school was a free school. That is, students did not have to pay tuition fees, but not everyone could attend. Classes lasted all day, and there were only brief holidays at Christmas and Easter, so children of poor parents, who might be placed in service or needed to work at home, could not afford the time their education would require. Then too, the curriculum was very demanding with tedious drills in Latin, and not all children would be apt scholars. Schoolmasters were notorious for not sparing the rod. It is likely that many a whining schoolboy gave up the struggle. There is a story that illustrates the alacrity of Elizabethan schoolmasters to whip their scholars for infractions of one sort or another. A schoolmaster, enraged when a dullard could not recall the catechism's answer to the question "What is God?," thrashed the offender soundly and then flung him back in his seat yelling, "Now maybe you'll remember what God is. God is Love!"[24] Those who survived the mental and physical demands of the Grammar Schools were an elite group.

In many other ways Elizabethan schools were different from modern ones. The most striking difference would be in the curriculum, which was designed to develop facility in speaking, reading, and writing the Latin language, the key to higher education at a university. The modern sciences, history, mathematics, the fine arts, and humanities were not in the curriculum. Students could pick up some notion of history, geography, and literature from their Latin exercises and readings, but the emphasis was on three topics: the Christian religion, Latin, and classical rhetoric.

As to the Christian religion, it must be noted that although town officials, trade guilds, and private endowments became sponsors of many schools after the Reformation, the schools were as much religious institutions as ever. Schoolmasters had to be licensed by the bishop of the diocese in which they taught and were subject to periodic examination. Given the political implications of the disputes generated by the Reformation, it is hardly surprising that a prospective teacher's views on such matters would be looked into. All schoolmasters were university graduates, where any taint of questionable views noticed by officials of the university would be nipped in the bud.[25] In the case of the Stratford Grammar School, the Lord of the Manor could reject a schoolmaster appointed by the Aldermen, and the master's conduct would be subject to examination by the Bishop of Worcester. During the time Shakespeare was in school, the Lord of the Manor was Ambrose Dudley, Earl of Warwick, a soldier who led an expedition into France on behalf of the Protestants and who played a key role in crushing the Northern Rebellion. The Bishop of Worcester was John Whitgift, later Archbishop of Canterbury, a man zealous for learning and for the prerogatives of bishops.

The schoolmaster's university training and the supervision of the bishop of the diocese would not be the only reasons grammar schools kept their character as religious institutions. The day began with psalms and prayers. The study of the catechism, creed, commandments, and biblical passages, at first in English and Latin and later on in Greek, was a regular part of schoolwork. Students were commonly assigned to listen carefully to the long Sunday sermon and to reconstruct the main points in class on Monday morning.

Beyond the formal readings and religious exercises, there was a general assumption that the purpose of education was ultimately to serve the cause of religion. The point is succinctly expressed in a letter from the Council of the North to the Burgesses of York:

> It is the duty of all Christian magistrates to have a care of the good education of all youths and children within their charge, that they may be instructed and seasoned at the first with the true knowledge of God and His religion, whereby they are liable to become good members of the Church and commonweal and dutiful subjects of her majesty and the state.[26]

In his plays Shakespeare often demonstrates an apt familiarity with the chief points of Christian doctrine and of biblical story, scarcely surprising when we consider the curriculum of the grammar schools. We need not suppose he acquired it by being particularly attentive at services and sermons, by searching the scriptures, or by reading theological disputations. The main points of Christian doctrine were rehearsed and reviewed regularly during his years of schooling.

Another point to consider is that a common exercise in the schools would have the master read a passage of scripture in Latin and require the students to translate it to English, and the other way around, from English to Latin. A lot of scripture was memorized in the process, and a student had to reach beyond recognizing words toward understanding of whole sentences.

The second important difference between modern schools and the Stratford grammar school was that instruction was in the Latin language; grammar meant Latin grammar. Of course, everyone knew their regional dialect of English, but since a countrywide standard for pronunciation and spelling had not yet developed, the students spent little time on the formal study of English. This helps to explain why Elizabethan writers spelled English words as they heard and spoke in their home counties. As for Latin however, the schoolmasters were careful to drill the standard forms, at least as they understood them.

The concentration on Latin was of such importance because most learning was only accessible through that language. It was the language of instruction at the universities and thus a rigid requirement for careers in the church, government service, and the learned professions. It was the language of European diplomacy and trade. From the beginning, grammar schools were designed to develop a full command of Latin, and teachers were prepared to take the time necessary to accomplish the task. As soon as students were able to read and write English, they began memorizing the authorized textbook, William Lily's *Grammatica Latina*. Passages from classical authors were recited by the master and the students were set to parsing the passages, word for word, and scratching their heads to come up with English phrasing that might be equivalent in tone and style. Eventually students were set to making their own Latin sentences, verses, and speeches. In a short time they were expected to speak only Latin, at least within the hearing of the master, and were punished for infractions. From the ages of five to fifteen, or six to sixteen, this tasteless and tedious training went on. The slow of study were sorely tried and tormented; the quick to learn could look forward to being introduced to Greek.

Such training may seem inappropriate for students who would not be going on to study theology or medicine at the university or to read law at one of the Inns of Court. English was after all the language of daily life, and no doubt those who had Latin in school forgot much of what they had learned. But if we ask what use a person of wit and imagination like Shakespeare could make of such training, the answer is not hard to find. Consider, for example, the way translating gives facility in coming up with borrowed words to enrich the native language. Schoolmasters developed the trick of mixing Latin and English synonyms. In *Love's Labour's Lost*, Shakespeare ridicules a village schoolmaster who can hardly get through a sentence without using a Latin word and then exploring its range of meaning by throwing in a thesaurus of English synonyms. One of his speeches describing a wounded deer goes like this:

> The deer was (as you know) *sanguis*, in blood, ripe as the pomewater, who now hangeth like a jewel in the ear of *caelo*, the sky, the welkin, the heaven, and anon falleth like a crab on the face of *terra*, the soil, the land, the earth.
>
> (*Love's Labour's Lost* 4.2.3–7)

Shakespeare himself very often writes back and forth from one vocabulary to the other. A Latin word suggests an English equivalent and vice versa. In *Hamlet* he padded many lines by stringing synonyms together—as in the phrase, "melt, thaw, and resolve itself"—very often pairing a native English word with a Latin import. Here are some examples, also from *Hamlet*:

> Thy knotted and combined locks to part—1.5.18.

> And I, of ladies most deject and wretched—3.1.155.

> And I do doubt the hatch and the disclose—3.1.166.

> To sing a requiem and such rest to her—5.1.237.

> For though I am not splenitive and rash—5.1.261.

In the advice to the players there is a grand cluster of such phrases:

> Nor do not saw the air too much with your hand, thus, but use all gently, for in the very torrent, tempest, and, as I may say, whirlwind of your passion, you must acquire and beget a temperance that may give it smoothness. (3.2.4–8)

Yoking nearly synonymous words together is a form of redundancy, but in this case, the combination of borrowed and native words, of the exotic and the ordinary, gives such a rich display of verbal energy as to arrest our ears. Some phrases produced by this method are simply unforgettable, as in these lines from *Macbeth*:

> No, this my hand will rather
> The multitudinous seas incarnadine,
> Making the green one red.

> (2.2.58–60)

It is obvious that Shakespeare had an active mind and a talent for languages, but it seems unlikely that such gifts would have been brought into play or his larger-than-life vocabulary developed without the training offered by the grammar school.

However much the rigorous and systematic study of Latin may have contributed to Shakespeare's great sensitivity to words and his eagerness to play with them, that was not the only advantage the study of Latin gave him. Of equal, if not greater importance, would be the world of Latin literature, of thoughtful, imaginative, and artistic Latin writing. Reading the Roman orators, poets, playwrights, and historians would open a door to another culture which would be closed to those otherwise locked in their native tongue. The rich treasury of English literature which plays so large a part in modern liberal education was not then in existence. Aside from Chaucer and Malory, there was practically no English literature in print except for tales of knightly adventures which grew out of the traditions of storytelling—the sort of thing that turned the head of Don Quixote—and there were broadside ballads of marvels, strange crimes, and disasters. The great ones yet to come, such as Spenser, Sidney, and Marlowe, were Shakespeare's contemporaries and still in grammar school themselves. Given these circumstances, we can hardly overstate the value of the introduction to Latin literature that Shakespeare's schooling provided.

We can tell by allusions, paraphrases, and direct quotation that Shakespeare knew choice passages from the classical authors, Ovid, Virgil, Plautus, Terence, Juvenal, Cicero, Horace, Caesar, Seneca, Livy, and Suetonius, as well as the Latin Bible and such neo-Latin writers as Erasmus and Mantuanus. He encountered these writers not so much from reading whole books as from passages in the grammar and copybooks and from dictation by the master. He may not have read a great deal, but so persistent was the practice of repetition, memorization, analysis, recitation, and imitation that what was learned was not soon forgotten.

There was, however, one classical author he knew thoroughly, imitated profoundly, and could be said to have taken as his model. That was the poet Ovid. Like Shakespeare himself, Ovid is a writer of great variety. In his masterpiece, *The Metamorphoses*, an ingenious combination of ancient myth, fable, and history, Ovid interweaves in an intricate and continuous pattern a vast series of miraculous transformations, charming fantasies, horrible atrocities, sexual infatuations, pastoral landscapes, and bloody battles. His technique involves putting story within story, developing some at length, briefly alluding to others, delaying one narrative while another is brought forward, pausing here for an affecting monologue and there for a brief satiric comment, but always switching mode and pace. Shakespeare called him "the most capricious poet, honest Ovid." In addition to being the master of delightful surprises, Ovid consistently demonstrates a sophisticated mastery of the art of reshaping traditional material for new purposes.

It is not surprising that Shakespeare took Ovid as a model, as did many Renaissance writers. Ovid's breezy artifice, his mix of the marvelous, both erotic and heroic, seemed to be more classical than the qualities of dignity and restraint we have come to associate with the art of Greece and Rome. When Shakespeare writes of the gods and mortals of ancient myth and fable, he follows Ovid rather more often than Virgil.

While there is probably nothing of Shakespeare's which is not indebted in some way to Ovid, several of his works are indirect imitations. The most obvious is *A Midsummer Night's Dream*, which borrows the theme of magic transformation and the story of Pyramus and Thisbe. *Titus Andronicus*, his early tragedy, derives from Ovid's horror story of Tereus and Philomel. There are also borrowings in the narrative poems *Venus and Adonis* and *The Rape of Lucrece*. The theme of the inevitable change wrought by time is a recurring topic in many of Shakespeare's finest sonnets. There is both direct borrowing and imaginative imitation of Ovid in *The Tempest*. In his discussion of the influence of Ovid, Gilbert Highet wrote:

> Shakespeare's greatest debt to Ovid is visible all through his plays. It was
> the world of fable which the *Metamorphoses* opened to him, and which he
> used as freely as he used the world of visible humanity around him.[27]

Years later when Shakespeare became famous, his contemporaries, who enjoyed and suffered the same grammar schooling he did, were reminded of the Roman poet when they read Shakespeare. In 1596 when Francis Meres published his *Palladis Tamia, or Wits Treasury*, an anthology of notes on a variety of topics, he included among some comparisons of English poets with Greek, Latin, and Italian ones the following observation:

> As the soul of Euphorbus was thought to live in Pythagoras, so the sweet, witty soul of Ovid lives in mellifluous and honey-tongued Shakespeare, witness his *Venus and Adonis*, his *Lucrece*, his sugared Sonnets among his private friends, &c.[28]

The suggestion of one soul living in another implies a creativity that goes beyond the kind of imitation a bright boy might pull off in school. Jonathan Bate, who has examined Shakespeare's debt to Ovid in great detail, makes the point that Shakespeare used Ovid as a "precedent" rather than as a "source" for his own work. *Venus and Adonis* and *The Rape of Lucrece* are "dazzling proofs of Shakespeare's art, self-conscious Renaissance exercises in the imitation and amplification of Ovid."[29]

There are some beside Meres who were willing to say Shakespeare was better. In *The Second Part of the Return from Parnassus*, a play performed during the 1601 Christmas revels at St. John's College, Cambridge, there is a scene where two graduates out of pocket in London apply to the Lord Chamberlain's Men for an acting job. Before they arrive for the audition, Richard Burbage, the leading actor in the company, suggests that they might be useful in writing plays. Will Kemp, the chief clown and jig maker of the company, responds with this tongue-in-the-cheek opinion:

> Few of the university men's pen plays well, they smell too much of that writer Ovid, and that writer Metamorphoses, and talk too much of Proserpina and Jupiter. Why here's our fellow Shakespeare puts them all down, aye and Ben Jonson too.[30]

The fact that neither Jonson nor Shakespeare was a university man, says a great deal about the quality of education they were able to get in their grammar schools—Jonson in Westminster, Shakespeare in Stratford.

Another aspect of education in Elizabethan grammar schools sets it apart from a modern undergraduate school. In addition to instruction in the Christian religion and the Latin language, students were trained in the principles of rhetoric. It hardly needs to be said that our current attitude toward rhetoric is not very friendly. We invariably use the word in a pejorative sense. We label fancy talk, political spin, and emotional pleading as rhetoric, implying that language is being used to conceal and mislead, not in a candid and sincere way.

Rhetoric, in the sense it was understood by Aristotle and rhetoricians since his time, was defined as the art of persuasion. It was the art of finding arguments, calculating the nature of the intended audience, arranging those arguments in an effective order, choosing the style of language appropriate to the subject and occasion, and a *persona* and tone of voice that was most appropriate. Once rhetorical skill was developed, one would be able to speak, listen, and read with greater precision, be able to notice the structure of an argument and the strategy of its presentation. Rhetoric could be well described as the disciplined and artful use of language. It was assumed to be a requirement for success in public life and thus held an important place in the curriculum.

In the time before printing and communication were speeded up by electronic technology, when paper was expensive and ink was difficult to handle, affairs were necessarily conducted more by speech than by writing. Instruction in the schools was done by lecture and recitation, sermons and legal pleas were expected to be long-winded, enthralling, embellished with memorable phrases and classical allusions. Speakers had to face their audience rather than a microphone, and speak from memory, not from a pile of papers.

Benjamin Franklin tells us in his autobiography how he trained himself to write. Admiring the essays of Addison and Steele, he set about imitating their work by a series of exercises. He would make an outline of the topics and arguments in one of their essays and place his notes aside for a week or two. Then, following the outline, he would write an essay of his own on the same subject. Comparing his effort with the original, he came to understand and acquire their strategy for writing. He was not so much trying to develop original thought as trying to develop skill in expressing commonplace ideas in a fresh and engaging manner.

That was the traditional method of rhetorical training. Students were not asked to develop their thoughts on a topic. They were asked to remember and recast the thoughts of others. Copiousness, fluency, and artfulness were prized, not originality. Some exercises might be given a dramatic twist. After reading Ovid's story of Theseus' desertion of Ariadne, students might be asked to imagine themselves as the girl and then compose a speech to express the girl's feelings when she sees Theseus sail away. Confronted with this assignment, many modern students, unless they are in a playwriting class, could not get much further than screaming. The next assignment might be to compose a speech for Theseus. What might he say by way of excuse for his perjury and desertion?

In his book, *Shakespeare's Use of Learning*, Virgil Whitaker gives a translation of a model composition from a textbook that Shakespeare's schoolmaster probably used—a speech for Niobe after her children had been struck down by Apollo:

> Wretched am I; what one calamity shall I weep above the rest, bereft now of the children for whom I was once pre-eminent? What wealth has for my wretched self been reduced to what poverty? In my misery I am no longer the mother of one child, who once walked famous for so many. How much better were it to have been barren rather than fertile in tears and grief. For those who weep their loss of children are far more unhappy than those who have never given birth. Their experience of the love of children causes the bitterest grief in destitution.[31]

It is interesting, perhaps even appalling, to have it pointed out that this speech concentrates on Niobe's reaction to the present while another example cited by Whitaker gives her thoughts on the past and yet another on the future.

Shakespeare's characters never seem to be at a loss for words. They are like Niobe in the example, rather too verbose. But we can see, as Whitaker points out, where Hamlet's phrase, "Like Niobe, all tears," came from. Consider as well how members of the audience who had the same grammar school training might appreciate similar rhetorical showpieces that turn up in so many plays in the Elizabethan theatre.

Aside from training in finding what to say, which they called "invention," students were trained to recognize and practice the high, middle, and low styles, figures of speech, arresting turns of phrase, balanced sentences, devices of versification, and various schemes of repetition. These were all classified in handbooks of rhetoric and given hard names, usually derived from Greek, such as, epanalepsis, chiasmus, zeugma, as well as ones we still recognize, oxymoron, peroration, anapest, climax, and so on and on. How many of these terms were drummed into the heads of students probably depended on the value their master placed on their recognizing and using that sort of analysis. But as most pieces of imaginative writing from Elizabethan times are patterned and elaborate, it seems that a good many writers admired such artifice. Few took plain, simple, and unaffected writing as an ideal.

When Polonius in *Hamlet* presents his theory as to the cause of Hamlet's madness, he stumbles into this rambling tangle of phrases:

> That he is mad 'tis true; 'tis true 'tis pity;
> And pity 'tis 'tis true. A foolish figure—
> But farewell it, for I will use no art.

(2.2.97–99)

Polonius realizes that in turning the phrase about, exchanging the placement of the key words *true* and *pity*, he is using a figure of speech that will almost always seem foolish, not simply redundant, and if he is going to get to the point, he had better stop being artful. Shakespeare did not stumble here; he was aware of the use and abuses of rhetorical figures and used this one to satirize Polonius. If the point of this has to be explained to us, there is good reason to suppose the educated ones in Shakespeare's audience would catch and relish it, for they had the same training.

Epanados and *chiasmus* are the technical names for these rhetorical figures.[32] Shakespeare used them to somewhat the same effect in a speech by Falstaff, "If then the tree may be known by the fruit, as the fruit by the tree," [*I Henry IV* 2.4.428–429]—expanding a point from the Sermon on the Mount. Such figures can have powerful dramatic impact. Coming from the mouth of witches, "Fair is foul and foul is fair" [*Macbeth* 1.1.11] has a threatening ambiguity.

Elocution is another side to rhetorical training that was not neglected. It was not enough to have a well-organized speech with the ornaments of language; the speech had to be delivered in an effective manner. Or to put it another way, the speaker had to play to an audience. The grammar schools in the time of the Tudors usually included the acting of plays, especially the plays of Plautus and

Terence in Latin and sometimes in English adaptations to reinforce a feel for the spoken language and to practice declamation.

Before the expansion of professional acting in Queen Elizabeth's time, one of the most important playwrights in English was Nicholas Udall. He was Master of Eton College from 1534 to 1541, when he was dismissed after being charged with "buggery." One would think that would put an end to his teaching career, but we find him gathering considerable reputation as a scholar and, despite his Protestant leanings, serving as the deviser of entertainments for the court of Queen Mary. In 1555, the year before his death, he was installed as master of the newly reorganized Westminster school.

Although Eton was called a college, it was essentially a grammar school like the one at Stratford. In fact, Udall's salary was the same at Eton as the Master's at Stratford. Udall wrote many of his plays for students to perform, which they did at the courts of King Edward VI and Queen Mary. He is credited as the author of five plays that found their way into print in the 16th century. The most famous one, *Ralph Roister Doister*, used material adapted from Plautus. It is still read by students of early English drama although rarely performed. Another based on a Plautine model is *Jack Juggler*.

A former student of Udall's and himself a later master at Eton, William Malim, describing the customs which were observed at Eton at the beginning of Elizabeth's reign, wrote that during the Christmas season the schoolmaster chose a play:

> which the boys may act, not without the elegance of Roman plays,
> before a popular audience sometime during the Christmas season.
> Occasionally he may also present dramas composed in the English
> tongue which have cleverness and wit.[33]

Not only was the custom of performing plays in school continued at Eton after Udall's time, but also the custom was widespread. Perhaps the most famous school producer was Richard Mulcaster, the first master and guiding spirit of the Merchant Taylors' School in London from 1561-1586 and later at St. Paul's School. His boys presented plays at court from 1574 to 1583. They were rivals to the professional men's companies playing in London and at times were serious competitors. One of his students, Sir James Whitelock, wrote:

> I was brought up at school under Master Mulcaster, in the famous school
> of the Merchant Taylors in London ... Yearly he presented some plays at
> court, in which his scholars were [the] only actors, and I one among them,
> and by that means taught them good behavior and audacity.[34]

"Good behavior" in this instance means something more than good manners; I think it includes what we would call expressive gestures. "Audacity," suggests the kind of confidence that makes one willing to take risks. In Francis Beaumont's play, *The Knight of the Burning Pestle*, a citizen's wife reacts to a boy actor's performance:

> Sirrah, didst thou ever see a prettier child? How it behaves it self, I warrant
> ye, and speaks, and looks, and perts up the head! I pray you brother, with
> your favor, were you never none of Master *Monkesters* scholars?[35]

The play was produced at a time when Mulcaster's boys from St. Paul's were performing weekly at the private theatre in the Blackfriars.

In 1581, Mulcaster published a book with the running title, "Positions Concerning the Training Up of Children."[36] It is perhaps surprising that one third of the book is devoted to physical training and the necessity of exercise. He recommended running naked as being more healthful. And he argued in Chapter 35 that physical training was just as much the master's duty as teaching grammar, "For I do assign both the framing of the mind, and the training of the body to one man's charge ... both [are] not to be uncoupled in learning." He saw no reason why capable girls should not be sent to schools as well as boys. These may have been innovative positions, but on another topic his views are more traditional: "For the rod may no more be spared in schools, than the sword may in the Prince's hand."

Despite his reputation for taking his student actors to court, Mulcaster's book says nothing about play-acting, although vocal and breathing exercises, singing, and dancing are recommended as part of physical training—all of which may account for much of the skill his student actors displayed.

Mulcaster could not only achieve polished performances from his scholars, but several of them later made their mark as playwrights, Thomas Lodge, Thomas Kyd, and possibly John Webster, although it is uncertain when he was at the Merchant Taylors' School. Nathan Field, a student when Mulcaster was at St. Paul's School, became a playwright and the leading actor of a later generation.

It is certain that Mulcaster was carrying on the tradition of school drama he picked up at Eton, for he was a student there during the mastership of Nicholas Udall. Our interest in Master Mulcaster's teaching arises because that tradition touches on the life of William Shakespeare. From 1575 to 1579, the period that would have been Shakespeare's last four years at school, the Master at Stratford was Thomas Jenkins, who was a former pupil of Richard Mulcaster at the Merchant Taylors' School. Jenkins was a graduate of St. John's College, Oxford, earning his Bachelor's and Master's degrees, and then elected Fellow until 1572. After a brief stay in Warwick, he took charge of the Stratford Grammar School.

It is very likely that Udall's play, *Jack Juggler* was performed by the boys at the Stratford School. The play is described on the title page as "A new Interlude for Children to play," and there is evidence that it was printed at least three times in the 1560's, so it must have been well known and often produced. Whether or not it was produced by Master Jenkins at Stratford, it is worth examining because it probably is a good example of the sort of dramatic fare offered by the schools during the Christmas season.

Jack Juggler could be called a one-act farce, not much more than 1,000 lines or about an hour's playing time. There are only five roles, plus a prologue and an epilogue, which might have been spoken by the schoolmaster. Many of the speeches are directed to the audience, and they are long speeches demanding considerable skill to play them effectively. They require an ability to elicit reactions and play off whatever the actor gets by way of response from the audience, as well as the ability to vary pitch, pace, and tone. The surprising thing is that this "Interlude for Children to play," could be so demanding. There is nothing easy or childlike about it.

The staging of the play is rather simple, though "staging" is not quite the right word to use in this context, because no stage or platform is required. There must be a door to knock on, but the play was designed to be performed in a hall, flat on the floor. In many places the actors mingle among the audience, kidding and questioning. Thus a platform separating actors and spectators would only interfere with the kind of interplay implied by the script. However, it would be a mistake to think of this as an unusual arrangement to make it easier for children to perform. It was the standard way of staging an interlude or play at the time, particularly an indoor performance during the Christmas season. Professional troupes used a platform when playing outdoors to a standing crowd, but when they played indoors, they were on the floor. If platforms were provided, they would be for seating some members of the audience.[37]

The title role of Jack Juggler is listed in the *dramatis personae* as "the Vice," the name given to a traditional character in early English drama, a sort of trickster who takes the audience into his confidence and sets up a practical joke to be played on another character. In comedy the joke is little more than a parlor game, but in tragic drama, the Vice is a kind of devil who sets up others for a fall, Iago in Shakespeare's *Othello* being an example. The name Juggler may not suggest much more than a clown who comes to make us merry, but the word was also used for a magician who creates illusions. Macbeth calls the witches who tricked him, "juggling fiends."

Jack Juggler is on "stage" almost all the time. However, the largest and the most demanding role is not Jack Juggler, but Jenkin Careaway, a lackey, a happy-go-lucky lazy liar, a petty thief and gambler, but charming despite all that. Jack has a grudge against Jenkin and sets him up to believe he is not himself. Jack dresses like Jenkin, tells him to get away from his master's house because he, Jack, is Jenkin. That is the gimmick that gets things started. It is adapted from a memorable sequence in Plautus' *Amphitruo* in which Mercury disguises himself as a servant of Amphitruo and bamboozles the real servant into thinking he is not himself. In Udall's adaptation, as the slapstick action accelerates, Jenkin is beaten by Jack, persuaded that he is not himself, and beaten by his master and mistress when he tries to clear up his incredible confusion. What is so demanding in the role of Jenkin is that he goes through a wide spectrum of moods and reactions. He is happy, self-satisfied, brags then pleads, blusters, then cringes, gets mad, and goes mad.

There is a significant difference between Udall's adaptation and Plautus' *Amphitruo*. In the original, Mercury tricks Sosia into believing he is not himself. The trick is only one of several farcical situations, but in *Jack Juggler*, that one trick is stretched out, farced or "stuffed" to make a play as long as the Plautine original. The play exemplifies what the rhetoricians admired as copiousness.

Although the playwright did not make the play easy for schoolboys to perform, it probably would have had a special appeal for them if they had spent some time reading Plautus' *Amphitruo* in the original Latin. They would have struggled for weeks, perhaps months, through the play word by word, figure by figure, idiom by idiom, and line by line, asked over and over again to catch and render the meaning in the English of their day, perhaps acting some of the scenes in class. After all that, inevitably many of the boys were bored out of their minds and sick of the whole thing. However, when they began rehearsing, although the play takes great liberties in adapting Plautus, *Jack Juggler* would give them a glimpse of how racy and funny the situations become in front of an audience. More importantly, perhaps the adaptation from Plautus would give a sense of what a creative person could accomplish with the audacity to cut loose from as well as to borrow from a classical pattern.

It is pleasing to imagine that William Shakespeare performed one of the roles in *Jack Juggler* before the leading townsmen and the bench of Aldermen who were the supervisors of the Stratford School. But if he did not, at least he knew Plautus and knew how to make the Plautine situations serve his turn. In *The Taming of the Shrew* [5.2] and in *The Comedy of Errors* [3.1], he incorporated the same farcical situation from Plautus' *Amphitruo*. And he did a superb updated version of Plautus' *Menaechmi* as the main story in *The Comedy of Errors*. The imitation is so obvious that anyone who knew Plautus' original—and everyone with a grammar school education probably did—could see that Shakespeare was inviting a comparison, having the audacity to ask the question, "Isn't this better?" And it is better, and better in exactly the way Elizabethans thought ancient models could be improved, by making them bigger, more intricate, complex, and sophisticated. *The Menaechmi* is built on confusion that arises when twins, separated at birth, happen to show up in the same town and each is mistaken for the other. Shakespeare doubles the fun by having the twins each have a twin servant. The masters are not only mistaken for each other, but they mistake their servants and the servants mistake their masters. Perhaps the way Shakespeare displays mastery beyond the work he is imitating is by drawing more and more people into the story. They become confused, angered, and finally terrified by the weird sight of doubles, so the whole world of the play gets turned upside down. Shipping is held up in the harbor, fighting breaks out in the streets, and just as the boiling point is reached, the whole noisy mess is cleared up as the separated twins face each other at last.

Of course, Plautus was not the only Roman playwright whose works were read in the grammar schools. Terence was studied for the elegance and polish of his writing and for the many moralizing maxims that decorate his dialogue.

Everyone who compares Plautus and Terrence finds Plautus better at popular comedy, including the famous Julius Caesar, who is reputed to have said that Terence lacked comic force. His plays were read in schools, but there isn't much evidence that Terence's plays were reworked for the popular stage. The third Latin playwright commonly read in the schools was Seneca. His tragic dramas are largely adaptations of Euripides, although they have nothing of Euripides' theatrical brilliance. In fact, Seneca's plays are a string of lengthy speeches, extravagant and tortured outbursts by characters in extreme situations. The speeches are models of declamation and no doubt useful when studied from a rhetorical point of view. However tedious Seneca may seem to modern readers, the Elizabethan dramatists were strongly influenced by him.

Shakespeare's *Titus Andronicus, Hamlet,* and *Macbeth* owe much to Senecan tragedy. Antony Hammond, citing the researches of Harold Brooks, points out that Shakespeare imitates passages from a variety of Seneca's plays in his *Richard III.*[38] The player's speech in *Hamlet* on the slaughter of Priam and the reaction of Hecuba [2.2.450-518], may have been suggested by Hecuba's opening speech in Seneca's *Trojan Women,*[39] made by combining materials from two plays of Euripides: *Hecuba* and *The Trojan Women.* Although the exciting climax of Euripides' *Hecuba* is not part of Seneca's adaptation, Shakespeare knew about it either by reading or hearing about Euripides' version of the story. It is alluded to the opening scene of *Titus Andronicus.* One of the Gothic princes brought captive to Rome comforts his mother, the Gothic Queen by saying:

> The self-same Gods that arm'd the Queen of Troy
> With opportunity of sharp revenge
> Upon the Thracian tyrant in his tent
> May favor Tamora, the Queen of Goths
> (When Goths were Goths and Tamora was queen),
> To quit the bloody wrongs upon her foes.
>
> (1.1.136–141)

The allusion is to the climactic scene in Euripides' *Hecuba* where the King of Thrace who had murdered Hecuba's son, Polydorus, is lured into Hecuba's clutches. She gets the opportunity of sharp revenge by offering to tell the King where the gold of Troy is hidden if he will come to her tent with his two sons.

Once he is there she binds him, kills his two sons before his eyes and then blinds him. The scene is Euripides at his most horrendous.

Although this incident is not in Seneca's play, Shakespeare had other ways of knowing about it. Ovid tells the story in Book XIII of *The Metamorphoses*, which was also borrowed from Euripides. And there were many Latin versions of Euripides' *Hecuba* specially made for school use. Erasmus prepared one with his Latin on opposite pages from the original so the book could be used as a pony for students working their way through the Greek text. There is more evidence, beside the allusion to Hecuba's revenge, that Shakespeare was familiar with some version of the story Euripides used. Emrys Jones has developed an argument that Shakespeare's *Titus Andronicus* follows the design of Euripides' *Hecuba*. Shakespeare's play falls into two parts. In the first part Titus is driven mad by a series of calamities visited on his family by his enemies. In the second part, Titus consummates a terrible revenge on them. Euripides' *Hecuba* has the same two-part structure. In the first part Hecuba, already a prisoner after the murder of her husband and the fall of Troy, sees her daughter taken away as a sacrifice to appease the spirit of Achilles. She then finds the body of her murdered son washed up on shore. These calamities drive her mad. In the second part, Hecuba inflicts a terrible revenge on the Thracian King who murdered her son.[40]

In the modern theatre Euripides' *Trojan Women* is regularly produced. As an anti-war play it no doubt deserves a hearing, but it is rather a play of suffering than of action, and is not nearly as exciting as *Hecuba*, which by contrast is seldom even read today. Not so in Shakespeare's time, when through translations into Latin and English, it was the Greek play most often printed. If Shakespeare didn't read it in school, he may well have studied it on his own. Indeed, the story featuring Hecuba as an avenger must have been widely known or there would not have been much point in alluding to it by a few lines in a play for the public stage.[41]

This review of the some of the features of Shakespeare's grammar schooling suggests that such an education would have provided many opportunities to develop skill in the art of writing, public speaking, and acting, and to become familiar with the work of the classical playwrights, Plautus, Terence, Seneca, and Euripides.

Aside from occasional performances by visiting professional acting companies and the traditional school entertainments at Christmastime, there is not much known about other forms of theatrical activities in Stratford. However, folk games, sword and Morris dancing, May Day and Midsummer revels, Robin Hood and Maid Marian high jinx, no doubt continued in Stratford as in other English towns all through Shakespeare's boyhood. Official records seldom deal with matters of long-standing tradition, unless they happen to get noted in the Elizabethan equivalent of the police blotter. The puritanical side of the Protestant movement opposed the traditional folk games and eventually suppressed May pole dancing. As late as 1622, however, one John Allen along with five others was cited "for dancing the morris in prayer time on the feast of Philip and Jacob"— that is on May Day. Another cited was John Hobbins of Shottery, "for being the Maid Marian."[42] But he was pardoned because he was a minor.

We know that more formally organized theatrical entertainment was customary at Whitsuntide on or about Pentecost, the seventh Sunday or fiftieth day after Easter. Stratford records show that in 1583 the Stratford Corporation paid their fellow townsmen Davy Jones and his company thirteen shillings four pence "for his pastime at Whitsuntide,"[43] a reward to those who provided the pastime either as a gratuity or to help with the expenses. If Shakespeare had no part in Davy Jones' company for that "pastime," he certainly would have heard of it because of several kinship connections. Davy Jones was the son-in-law of Adrian Quiney, and he later married one Frances Hathaway, probably a relative of Anne Hathaway, Shakespeare's wife. Adrian Quiney was an Alderman with John Shakespeare. When John was Bailiff, Adrian was his assistant or Chief Alderman, and when John was the Chief, Adrian was the Bailiff in times when the Bailiffs served as Justices of the Peace for Stratford. Much later, Adrian's grandson, Thomas Quiney, married Shakespeare's daughter, Judith. The town was small, and those who ran it knew each other.[44]

In *The Two Gentlemen of Verona*, Shakespeare alludes to the Davy Jones kind of amateur theatrical. Julia, after disguising herself as a boy, invents a story to explain how much like Julia she looks:

> for at Pentecost
> When all our pageants of delight were played,
> Our youth got me to play the woman's part,
> And I was trimmed in Madam Julia's gown

> Which served me as fit, by all men's judgments,
> As if the garment had been made for me....
> And at that time I made her weep a good,
> For I did play a lamentable part.
> Madam, 'twas Ariadne passioning
> For Theseus' perjury and unjust flight.
>
> (4.4.158–168)

The country of Shakespeare's comedies is very often the England of his boyhood. Here he assumes that the youth of Verona followed the same customs as the youth of Stratford. The tradition of plays at Whitsuntide must have been widespread and well known to Shakespeare's audience or Julia's brief mention of the custom would need a fuller explanation. In *The Winter's Tale* similar customs are assumed to be followed in Bohemia. There the Shepherd's daughter, who is really the lost princess, presides at a country sheep-shearing feast dressed like the goddess Flora. Presenting flowers to her guests, she is momentarily embarrassed to find herself in a role:

> Methinks I play as I have seen them do
> In Whitsun pastorals. Sure this robe of mine
> Does change my disposition.
>
> (4.4.133–135)

Calling the Whitsun plays "Pastorals" fits the mode of the scene in *The Winter's Tale*, but it suggests as well that perhaps many of the Whitsun pastimes were also pastorals. The reenactment of the legend of Theseus and Ariadne reflects the immediate experience of actor and audience, and both are moved to tears. If the country entertainments were sometimes capable of such effects, the achievement of amateur folk theatre in the English countryside was certainly not primitive.

CHAPTER 3

THE DESTRUCTION
OF JERUSALEM
1578–1585

Do like the mutines of Jerusalem,
Be friends awhile, and both conjointly bend
Your sharpest deeds of malice on this town.

(*King John* 2.1.378–380)

THE most popular forms of theatre in England in the 15th and 16th centuries were the various versions of "The Play Called Corpus Christi," usually produced in annual festivals by the craft and religious guilds of the larger cities. Coventry, some eighteen miles from Stratford, was famous for its version, and seeing it would have been an impressive and influential theatrical experience of Shakespeare's youth.

The play developed around the Feast of Corpus Christi, a celebration of the institution of the Holy Eucharist placed on the church calendar the Thursday after Pentecost, fifty days after Easter. Thus the feast always came in the spring of the year when the hardships of winter were over, when traveling was easier and it was good to be out of doors. Although it seems that in the beginning Corpus Christi day was simply marked by a procession carrying the Host or Body of Christ through a circuit of a town, by the end of the 15th century it had become, at least in the larger towns that could afford the display, the occasion for a very large and elaborate dramatic festival which lasted from dawn to dusk, and in some cases for several days. A London production in 1409 is recorded as going on for eight days. The Coventry play was the centerpiece of an annual Corpus Christi Fair that sometimes lasted eight days.

The Corpus Christi Play was actually a cycle of shorter plays or pageants, each of them a "page" illustrating a section of a larger work. The pageants dramatized materials taken from the Bible and other sacred writings to expound on no less a theme than God's plan of salvation for mankind. This theme determined the materials that would be used. There are many biblical narratives that have obvious theatrical potential—the story of David and Bathsheba or of Joseph in Egypt, for example—but in the Corpus Christi Play, the mission and sacrifice of Christ was the predominant theme of the cycle. The task and expense of producing the individual pageants were assigned to the various craft guilds by the town council. Although the pageants were produced and acted by townsmen, they were written by the clergy, men learned in the theology and doctrines of the church. There is nothing naive about their work.

The typical program of the cycles as produced in England dramatized stories and legends in four groups. The first group began with the creation of the world, followed by the fall of Lucifer and the fall of Man. That group was followed by stories from the Old Testament which were interpreted as prefiguring the ministry and passion of Christ, such as Noah's flood, the sacrifice of Isaac, Moses leading his people out of slavery in Egypt, and the prophecies of the coming of Christ. Then came the second large group of pageants, which dealt with events surrounding the nativity of Christ. The third large group jumped to material dealing with the betrayal and passion of Christ. Another group showed the resurrection, the harrowing of hell, Christ's appearances to his disciples, and the ascension, finally going out of history and time to the Last Judgment. These stories were of course alluded to in sermons, paintings, stained glass, and sculpture, indeed in all the decorative arts. Thus, everyone knew at least bits and pieces of the story which was given a full and resonating coherence by the cycle.[45]

Something of the scale of the production can be surmised from the number of plays or pageants in the manuscripts that have survived. The York "register" includes forty-eight plays, and although the average length is less than three hundred lines, the whole cycle, managed on a very tight schedule, would have taken more than fifteen hours to perform. It is not likely that everyone in the audience would be able to pay close attention all day long, but the whole scheme might one day become clearer as the annual revivals accumulated in memory.

As part of the Festival of Britain in 1951, for the first time in nearly four

hundred years, some surprisingly impressive pageants from the York Corpus
Christi Play were produced. Since then other productions of the old scripts have
been undertaken in many places. Producers and actors recognized the theatrical
richness of the pageants, and scholars undertook a major reevaluation of the
place of the Corpus Christi Play in the history of English drama. Canon Purvis,
who prepared the text for the York revival, described the reaction of the first
modern audience:

> The actual performance was, indeed, a real revelation of something fresh,
> direct, and powerful, and of greatness hitherto unrecognized. A treasure of
> English literature had been rediscovered, and the rediscovery was to all who
> experienced it, in their various ways and degrees, deeply moving both
> aesthetically and spiritually.[46]

It must be pointed out that the Corpus Christi Play was anything but a
simple exercise in devotion; the play is more than an invitation to contemplation.
It tells a story, and stories, whether we believe them or not, whether we recognize
their symbolic dimension or not, are intentionally entertaining. For example,
while there is certainly a solemn, even majestic tone in many places in the
Corpus Christi Play, a jarring note of raucous comedy often intrudes in a way
that is shocking to people who believe that sacred story must always be treated
in spiritual tones and attitudes. Unlike the ancient drama of Athens and Rome,
where the forms of drama were almost strictly either comic or tragic, the Corpus
Christi Play was a mixture of both. Indeed it is a strange combination of circus
and sermon, and the way to get it wrong is to read the Corpus Christi plays in a
reverential frame of mind.

How comic material is made to work within the sacred story is worth
considering. Biblical stories are written in a concentrated way, leaving much for
the reader to fill in. As the dramatists developed the Corpus Christi plays, they
invariably added satiric and comic details from contemporary life, to provide
a refreshing contrast to the more serious and affecting treatment given to the
materials anchored in history and legend. Thus Noah's wife, about whom the
account in Genesis has nothing to say, became the type of recalcitrant shrew
who refuses to get in the ark to save herself just because her husband wants her
to. She wants to sit in the tavern with her gossips and it takes a slanging match
and a knock-down fight to get her on board. The shepherds to whom the Angels

announce the birth of Christ are country lads who complain pointedly of the way the local gentry oppress poor people.

There is even more to this method of dramatizing the story than simply providing a refreshing variety by mixing burlesque with serious matters. It involves deliberate anachronism, that is, using the characters and mores of contemporary life to relate the story to its audience by showing them that the story is about people like themselves in a town and place like their own. For the same reason the dialogue of the Corpus Christi Play was always expressed in the local dialect of the town that produced the play. Pharaoh in Egypt was pictured as more like the Ottoman Turks who were threatening Europe at the time than as Ramses II, to whom the audience could make no imaginative connection. The soldiers who go about the difficult task of fastening the actor playing Christ to the cross and then raising and fixing it into place, seem to enjoy their gruesome work, insulting and torturing their victim with no more respect than the local hangman would give to a vicious traitor. Finally when the cross is fixed in place, the noise dies away, and Christ who all this while has said nothing speaks to the audience, inviting their contemplation of his cruel suffering. The familiar "Seven Last Words" and other such known themes likely to be rehearsed in sermons on Good Friday come through in stunning contrast. The whole tone and atmosphere shifts from gleeful violence to penitential pathos. Control like that can only be risked with an audience that is drawn into an action that seems to be happening now, right before their very eyes, not something that happened long ago and far way. Verisimilitude in historic drama can hardly achieve that degree of immediacy.

If we consider carefully the construction of the Corpus Christi Play—not the themes or argument of it, but the way it is put together—we can see that Shakespeare makes use of the same techniques. The Corpus Christi Play is a string of independent pageants; many of them could easily be performed as a kind of one-act play. And some of them were taken out of the cycle and performed separately. There is no fixed number of pageants in the cycle, which could be expanded or contracted, depending on the limits of time and money. A Shakespearean play is built on a series of scenes, each more or less an independent unit, dramatizing a particular event or action followed by a scene treating a later moment in the larger story. Eventually the separate scenes become part of the larger whole. The sequence of pageants, like the sequence of scenes in a play, is pretty much the heart of the design. Each part begins, rises in excitement and interest until the action is completed, then tapers off to make room for the next scene. Something that might be called a rhythm almost inevitably follows the steady alternation of scenes. Shifting focus from one group of characters to another provides variety, sometimes with a pointed contrast of one scene with another, and a quickened interest when characters reappear at a later point in their story.[47]

With this method of dramatization it is possible to show how characters change and develop in the course of time. This possibility seems not to have been exploited by the various adapters of the Corpus Christi Play, except for the series that involve the Virgin Mary, but it certainly was in Shakespeare's history plays. In the four plays dealing with the Wars of the Roses, he tells the story of Queen Margaret from the time she was just old enough to be married to King Henry VI until she became the cursing old crone in the time of Richard III. There are many others who appear throughout a series of plays, developing and changing, such as Prince Hal, Falstaff, Henry Bolingbroke, Mark Antony, to mention the most prominent examples. There are also those whose experiences in the course of a single play show a fascinating development, for example, Juliet, Hamlet, Othello, and Cleopatra.

Change of this kind is not a feature of Roman comedy or Greek tragedy. In classical comedy the characters seldom change; the fun is in their exhibiting the same characteristic behavior whatever the circumstances. It could be said that characters in tragedy only change, if at all, when they recognize the trap they have fallen into. It is obvious that Shakespeare could not have picked up his technique for serious drama from the grammar school study of Plautus and Terence or Euripides and Seneca. It is all the more obvious, I think, that his technique of designing a play derives from the Corpus Christi Play. Certainly in grammar school the ancient classics, not the medieval patterns, would have been held up as models to imitate, so that it would take a very strong influence from another source to suggest the Shakespearean form of drama. And that influence was surely from the popular form of drama, the Corpus Christi Pageants. One might also say Shakespeare's fellow dramatists followed the same native pattern, particularly in writing for the public theatre of their time.

Aside from the method of construction, another feature of Shakespeare's characteristic technique derives from the pageants' practice of introducing comic and satiric material from contemporary life. Shakespeare nearly always bases his plays on stories he read somewhere, in histories, romances, novels, or on plays he read or saw. The kind of story he likes to work with is nearly always traditional or legendary, set in a different time and country, almost never in the England of his own day. He usually complicates this traditional material by inventing a subplot where there is nearly always a comic contrast or parody of the traditional story that is reflective of contemporary life. The Falstaff subplot in the Henry IV plays provides a realistic picture of London life at the time Shakespeare wrote the play, although the main history of Henry IV and the rebel Hotspur is presumed to have happened nearly two centuries earlier. The history is serious and the subplot comic. A careful look reveals how the invented subplot, Falstaff's escapade in highway robbery, is a parody of Hotspur's rebellion. In the same way, in the Corpus Christi Play, the portrayal of Noah's wife as a shrew is a less serious treatment of the traditional cause, the stubborn willfulness of mankind.

Although only two pageants from the Coventry Corpus Christi Play have survived, this version was in its time probably the most famous in England. In fact "Coventry Play" was to some a synonym for Corpus Christi Play. "It was a national and not merely a local event, … a sacred entertainment which drew people from all over England."[48] And not unlike, I suppose, the attraction of going on pilgrimage in earlier times. It can hardly be doubted that William Shakespeare went to Coventry to see the Corpus Christi Festivals; there are too many indications in his plays that he had seen the pageants, if not at Coventry only eighteen miles from Stratford, then at least in one of the other towns where festivals very much like Coventry's were played.

Because of their common subject matter, it would be difficult to know whether Shakespeare used stories from the Bible directly or borrowed them from dramatizations he may have witnessed at Coventry. But he often visualizes the action in a manner that seems much closer to the way a story may have been staged than to the written record or to a redaction. When Henry V tries to terrorize the citizens of Harfleur, he describes the horrors that will follow if they don't surrender by reminding them of King Herod's slaughter of the innocents:

> Your naked infants spitted upon pikes,
> Whiles the mad mothers with their howls confus'd
> Do break the clouds, as did the wives of Jewry
> At Herod's bloody-hunting slaughter-men.

> (*Henry V* 3.3.38–41)

The picture of "infants spitted upon pikes" could derive from the scene as staged in the Coventry *Pageant of the Shearmen and Taylors*, where, I assume, the children were represented by rag dolls and carried off on pikes. The play includes the famous Coventry Carol: "Lully, lulla, thou little tiny child, by by, lully, lullay," sung by women just before the entrance of Herod's slaughter men. That is about as daring and rapid a contrast as can be imagined. The scene ends with a soldier saying after the killing is done, "Who heard ever such a cry / Of women that their children have lost."[49] And while we are speaking of Herod, it is in the same Coventry pageant that the famous stage direction occurs, "Here Herod rages in the pageant and in the street also," which recalls Hamlet's saying of acting that is all strutting and bellowing, "it out-Herods Herod" [3.2.13-14].

In his early history play, *Henry VI, Part II*, Shakespeare models his dramatization of the conspiracy against Humphrey, Duke of Gloucester, to be very like the conspiracy against Jesus as presented in the Wakefield Corpus Christi Play. And in *Henry VI, Part III*, Queen Margaret recalls the passion of Christ mocked with a crown of thorns and scourged by soldiers, as she describes the paper crown on the Duke of York's head and the napkin steeped in the blood of his murdered son. The night scene when Othello, betrayed by Iago, is arrested and brought before the Senate is patterned in many details on the story of Judas leading soldiers with swords and torches to capture Jesus. Even Othello's command that all put up their swords is reminiscent of the biblical story.

Finally, it should be noticed that the Porter's scene in *Macbeth* alludes to the Last Judgment in a way that could have been derived from the staging of Doomsday in the Corpus Christi Play.[50] The Porter imagines the gate of the Castle as Hell-Mouth, an elaborate device used to stage the Fall of Lucifer and the Rebel angels as well as for the Last Judgment. The sinners being pushed into Hell-Mouth are of all sorts and conditions of men and women, each representing a particular deadly sin. A painting of the Last Judgment on the wall of the Guild Chapel in Stratford once portrayed such a scene, although it was plastered over before Shakespeare was old enough to have seen it. In *Macbeth*, the porter breaks off his enumeration of sinners when the persistent knocking at the gate reminds him to get on with his job:

> But this place is too cold for hell. I'll devil-porter it no further. I had thought to let in some of all professions that go the primrose way to th' everlasting bonfire.

> (*Macbeth* 2.3.17–19)

Shakespeare would have had to have seen the plays before he was fifteen years old, for by then performances of the Corpus Christi Play were prohibited. The last performance of the York cycle was in 1574 and in Wakefield, 1576. The Mayor of Chester was summoned to answer to the Privy Council for permitting a performance in 1575. At Coventry the Cycle continued until 1579. It then seems to have been discontinued as much because of the high cost of production as for reasons of church policy. Queen Elizabeth's commissioners suppressed the performances because the Corpus Christi Play was too closely associated with Catholic traditions. In the Wakefield cycle, for example, pageants dealing with the later life of the Virgin Mary were cut from the cycle because the Reformers saw devotion to Mary as a form of idolatry. If plays featuring the Blessed Virgin could easily be cut, the remaining pageants might still have been used, but a more thorough objection to the Corpus Christi Play was set forth in 1576 when the Ecclesiastical High Commission of York decreed that a letter be sent to the bailiff, burgesses, and other inhabitants of Wakefield ordering:

> that in the said play no pageant be used or set forth wherein the Majesty of God the Father, God the Son, or God the Holy Ghost or the administration of either the sacraments of baptism or of the Lord's Supper be counterfeited or represented, or anything played which tend to the maintenance of superstition and idolatry.[51]

This amounts to a blanket prohibition of the dramatization of the story. The play is really about the actions of the Father, the Son, or the Holy Ghost and if those aspects of the Holy Trinity cannot be represented, the subject of the play is reserved exclusively for sermons or books of devotion. How far this command reached beyond the town of Wakefield is hard to tell, although it surely determined the fate of the York Cycle as well.

This movement toward suppression of dramatic representation illustrates confused thinking about truth and fiction, a preference for words over pictures, and the iconoclastic belief that all images are somehow idolatrous. Although the Corpus Christi Play was no longer produced by the time Shakespeare completed his grammar school education, it would have been well remembered by anyone with an interest in theatrical entertainment.

After Shakespeare had all the Latin grammar he could use, what he did after that cannot be traced with any certainty. Ordinarily the next step would have been for him to go on to a university. As he did not do that, something must have intervened. It could simply be that his father did not want to live a spare life at home while his son lived a spendthrift life at Oxford or Cambridge. There seems to be some evidence that John Shakespeare was running short of cash from time to time during the years following his son's schooling. In 1575 he bought property adjoining the house he already owned on Henley Street in Stratford. The next year he applied to the College of Heralds for a coat of arms, to which he would be entitled for his years of service as Alderman, Bailiff, and Justice of the Peace, but he did not pursue the matter. The following year he stopped regular attendance at the corporation meetings. He borrowed and leased some property for ready cash and was being sued for past debts and overdue loans. In various assessments made of the Aldermen, his portion was reduced or not levied at all.[52] His brother aldermen waited ten years before replacing him. All of these facts could be interpreted to mean that he didn't have a ready supply of money to meet the accustomed charges placed on Aldermen.

There is a temptation think of great writers as having overcome many obstacles, and this romantic image of an artist going through hard times is sometimes applied to the story of Shakespeare's youth: his father goes broke and William has to make his own way, like Dick Whittington who rose from poor orphan to Lord Mayor of London. The pattern makes for a good story, but there is no convincing evidence that it is true. The evidence is simply insufficient. Whatever John Shakespeare's difficulties may have been, he held on to most of his property and was not reduced to living on the charity of his neighbors.

John Shakespeare may have lost interest in his duties as an alderman for other reasons. Perhaps after nearly twenty years in various municipal posts he lost interest, or his energy may have been failing, or his business too frequently took him away from Stratford. But there is one possibility that deserves careful consideration. He may not have been in sympathy with government policies devised to get rid of the Catholic past and to force conformity to Anglican Protestantism. The suppression of the Corpus Christi Play is only one example of the steady efforts of Elizabeth's bishops to root out traces of the old religious practices. Other measures touched the pocketbook. Those who did not attend their parish church at least once a month could be fined. The rich paid up, the poor showed up for services. Those who steadily absented themselves were listed as "recusants" and—so that an eye could be kept on them—were reported to the authorities as persons who might be disaffected. The local authorities were especially to be on the look out for priests, largely of the Jesuit order, who began coming to England to proselytize, hear confessions, and celebrate Mass in private homes or other places away from the public eye. Anyone attending such events was in danger of fines, imprisonment, and torture. The priests who celebrated mass were regarded as traitors, especially if they came from the Catholic seminaries established on the continent. The authorities were convinced that English priests trained abroad were sent back to their native island to spy and plot against Elizabeth's government. If they were caught and would not renounce their faith after being examined and tortured, they were executed by the savage method of being hanged, drawn, and quartered.

As Catholic practice was driven underground, it became very difficult to tell who was living in conformity to the new ways and who was secretly practicing or in sympathy with the old ways. A disgusting aspect of this situation was that false intelligence could be given for favors, or a person accused could give names of others in exchange for leniency. Officials like John Shakespeare faced a dilemma. They could either turn a blind eye and a deaf ear to suspicious goings on or turn in their neighbors.

Stratford was a town divided between the conformists who favored Protestant practice and others who attended church as required by law but held on to the hope that traditional Catholic practices might one day be restored or at least tolerated. After all, men of John Shakespeare's generation grew up before there was a line dividing Catholics and Protestants. And as one historian writes, "After the abrupt religious reversals under Henry VIII, Edward VI, and Mary, Elizabeth's new reformation was widely anticipated to be an equally impermanent affair."[53] If Elizabeth died, the person to succeed her at the time would have been Mary, Queen of Scots. In that entirely plausible event, England might return to the Roman fold, at least to the point where some of the practices and institutions of traditional Catholicism might be tolerated. There is very good evidence that John Shakespeare was one who held on to that hope.

In 1580, a Jesuit mission came to England, headed by Edmund Campion and Robert Parsons. Although they were careful to conceal their identity and were protected by many who welcomed them, within a year Campion was arrested, examined, tortured, and finally executed.[54] Parsons escaped back to the continent. These Priests brought with them copies of a booklet known as a "Spiritual

Testament," a small declaration of faith to be signed by people who wanted a substitute for the last rites of the Catholic Church should they die without a priest in attendance. The wording of the fourteen articles of the Testament was devised by the Archbishop of Milan, Carlo Borromeo, when his city had a disastrous visitation of the plague. John Shakespeare signed a handwritten copy of the Testament, which he might well have gotten from Campion or another priest who visited the Midlands during their brief mission. John Shakespeare's signed copy was later found, hidden between the roof tiles and timbers of his house. It was discovered in the 18th century when the roof was being repaired. After some preliminaries, the first article of the testament reads:

> I will live and die obedient unto the Catholic, Roman & Apostolic Church, firmly believing all the twelve articles of the faith … with the interpretation, & declaration made thereon by the same holy church, as taught & declared by her.[55]

There follows a general confession, a promise to receive the Blessed Sacrament, the desire for the rite of extreme unction, and if a priest is not in attendance at the time of death, the testament is meant to cover that contingency. Other prayers and declarations cover the hope for forgiveness, a general pardon to others, the wish that friends will ease the soul in purgatory by having masses said, and that one's patron saint and guardian angel will support the soul at the Last Judgment.

Aside from the blank spaces at the beginning of each article where one's name would be inserted, the only other place where something personal could be added was the blank space for the name of a patron saint. John Shakespeare named Winifred, the patron of north Wales. Why did John name Winifred? Did the Jesuit missioner prompt him? Her shrine in Flintshire had been a place of pilgrimage since the 9th century. Margaret Beaufort, Countess of Richmond and the mother of Henry VII, restored and rebuilt St. Winifred's shrine and the well of healing waters beside it. Unlike the shrine of St. Thomas in Canterbury, that of Our Lady of Walsingham, and those of other popular places of pilgrimage, the reformers were never able to close St. Winifred's down. Perhaps it was too far from London Protestantism and too close to Lancashire Catholicism, where modern pilgrims still go. John Shakespeare's devotion to the Welsh saint may have begun on pilgrimage. In any case, his testament is a solemn document, and we should consider it seriously. There was something furtive about John. He didn't inform on the person who gave or the place where he got the testament, as his duties would have required him to do.[56]

Those who suppose that John Shakespeare was not inclined to Catholicism have noticed that when he was Chief Alderman of Stratford in September 1571, he and the Bailiff were authorized to sell the "Catholic vestments remaining in the Guild Chapel."[57] Selling the vestments could mean that John Shakespeare wanted to get rid of them or was only obeying orders. On the other hand, he could have known who might buy them for a private chapel. There he could get a better price than by selling them to a rag picker. It is quite true that during the reign of the boy King Edward, ornaments, rood screens, images and vestments considered superstitious by the reformers were banned. Some were hidden and brought back or replaced in Queen Mary's time and then hidden again after her death when the Elizabethan reforms were instituted.[58]

What all this had to do with William Shakespeare at this stage in his life is worth considering. It could explain why his father did not send him to a university. Shakespeare must have been an unusually intelligent fellow. There were scholarships for boys of that sort, so a shortage of cash in family funds would not have been much of a hurdle. Another difficulty was the graduation requirement at the Universities. One had to subscribe to the thirty-nine articles of the Anglican Church. It is surely possible that John Shakespeare spoke of these matters with his son. That would help to explain the unusual sympathy, appreciation, and understanding for Catholic ways and institutions exhibited in Shakespeare's plays.

Perhaps the most notorious example of his venturing on a matter of dispute occurs in *Hamlet* where the Ghost is shown to be undergoing punishment in purgatory. Another example that suggests bias toward the Catholic viewpoint is the sympathetic treatment of Queen Katherine in *Henry VIII*. An equally telling example is the characterization of the novice Isabella in *Measure for Measure*. There are many less obvious indications of this bias.[59] While Shakespeare is quite capable of portraying cardinals and bishops as politicians looking out for themselves and of mocking a village parson, he seldom speaks of nuns, friars, and priests, or of bells and beads, or of abbeys, convents, and chantries—"Bare ruined choirs where late the sweet birds sang"—except in tones of respect and appreciation.

Neither the grammar school nor parental example in Stratford nor an active imagination quite explains this conspicuous trait in his writing. To find the source of that, we need to look elsewhere. If Shakespeare did not go to a university, it is logical to suppose he once lived in circumstances where people were able to speak freely and at length of the old ways, and on occasion participate in the banned religious practices. Apparently the hotbed of Catholicism in those days was Lancashire. Perhaps his father arranged for him to go there. One historian has claimed that "Lancashire was to remain for centuries the most Catholic county in England."[60] In describing ways of avoiding fines for not attending the parish church, Antonia Fraser mentions that "Catholic parents often … dispatched their children at sixteen to a distant neighborhood."[61] Sixteen-year-olds became subject to fines for not attending the Parish Church. It is reasonable to consider that William went to Lancashire once he mastered all the Stratford grammar school had to offer.

Sometime in the mid-seventeenth century, the antiquarian John Aubrey began collecting curious notes about famous people, now usually published as *Aubrey's Brief Lives*. They are anecdotes and items of gossip, many of which turn out to be unreliable when they can be checked against other sources. Much of what Aubrey wrote about William Shakespeare has to be taken with a grain of salt. For instance, he says that Shakespeare's father was a butcher, but his last note on Shakespeare intriguingly reads as follows:

> Though, as Ben Johnson says of him, that he had but little Latin and less Greek, he understood Latin pretty well, for he had been in his younger years a school master in the country.

And on the margin of the manuscript, Aubrey wrote, "from Mr. ------Beeston"[62] It seems the note originated from William Beeston, son of Christopher Beeston, an actor who along with Shakespeare was a member of the Lord Chamberlain's Men, an acting company created in 1594. So in some sense the "school master in the country" statement may be true, since it comes from Christopher Beeston, a fellow actor of Shakespeare's. However the statement needs qualification.

The phrase "school master" could be read in several ways. It doesn't seem possible that Shakespeare in his youth could have been the master of an authorized

Latin grammar school. Such appointments would have been made by officials of the established church and would only be given to university graduates; since Shakespeare was not, that possibility is simply ruled out. But a Latin tutor in a private home would be called a schoolmaster—in fact Elizabethans very often called tutors, schoolmasters, and schoolmasters, tutors. The rich father in *The Taming of the Shrew*, hires two "schoolmasters," one to teach his daughters Latin and another to teach music. Tutors, if appointed as members of a large household, were often part of a large staff including musicians, jugglers, tumblers, and drummers, who supplied the material and personnel for Christmas revels and other celebrations. It should not surprise us to discover that the earliest English playwrights who were not professional clowns came from the ranks of schoolmasters.

A possible interpretation of the schoolmaster statement is that Shakespeare took service with a wealthy family as a tutor and with a sideline as a household musician and player. It would have been in a large household where the family was hanging on to their Catholic past and wished their own children and children-in-service to be tutored by someone of congenial views. Taking such a position would have provided valuable theatrical experience for a young man like Shakespeare, because tutors and schoolmasters were often the devisers and actors for household entertainments, especially for Christmas revels. Suzanne Westfall in her book, *Patrons and Performance: Early Tudor Household Revels* writes:

> Playwrights such as Bale, Skelton, Medwall, Heywood, and many whose names are now lost were closely associated with one and sometimes more than one noble patron. ... These men also served as schoolmasters (as John Skelton did for Prince Henry), enabling them to study and adapt classical structures used for school exercises.[63]

This was the case with Nicholas Udall, who wrote *Jack Juggler*, and with a long line of playwrights who were masters of St. Paul's School and of the Chapel Children. As we might expect, the character recruited to devise the "Pageant of the Nine Worthies" in Shakespeare's *Love's Labour's Lost* is the village schoolmaster. When we consider the theatrical opportunities available in the position of schoolmaster or tutor, Shakespeare's having been a schoolmaster in the country would seem a very useful way to gain access to a career in theatre.

This possibility has been explored in detail by E. A. J. Honigmann following suggestions made earlier by others that Shakespeare spent some time in the household of Alexander Hoghton, Esq. of Lea, and later in the service of Sir Thomas Hesketh of Rufford.[64] (Edmund Campion on his mission to Lancashire visited the households of those aristocrats.[65]) These men had their seats in Lancashire, near Preston, had players in their households, and had connections with the powerful Stanley family, the head of which was the Earl of Derby, Henry Stanley. The Earl and his heir Ferdinando, who had the title of Lord Strange, were patrons of playing companies and did pretty much as they pleased in their area of influence, Cheshire and Lancashire, where the Earl was the Lord Lieutenant. For example, on two occasions in paying a visit to Chester, the Mayor entertained the visiting Lords with a special performance of the "Shepherds' Play," presumably from the local Corpus Christi Cycle. That was in 1577 and 1578.[66] Although the Privy Council had put down performances of the Cycle in 1575, it seems the Mayor knew that the Earl of Derby would stand between him and possible punishment for the infraction. Evidence that the local authorities in Lancashire also allowed performances of the Corpus Christi Play, long after the plays were a thing of the past in other parts of England, is found in a book by John Weever, a native of Rufford in Lancashire. In his *Funeral Monuments*, published in 1633, he writes of the huge performance of the London cycle in 1409 and adds this note by way of explanation:

> They call this *Corpus Christi Play* in my country [Lancashire], which I
> have seen acted at Preston, and Lancaster, and last of all at Kendal, in the
> beginning of the reign of King James; for which the Townsmen were sore
> troubled.[67]

Weever was born in 1576, by which time performances of the Corpus Christi Play was banned. If he saw them acted as he was growing up, that is one more indication that in Lancashire the ban on the Corpus Christi Play was ignored with impunity and that that part of the kingdom was an enclave of the old ways.

The suggestion that Shakespeare spent some time in Lancashire comes from a statement in the will of Alexander Hoghton of Lancashire, proved in September 1581, in which, to quote E. A. J. Honigmann's summary:

he bequeathed his stock of play clothes and all his musical instruments to his brother Thomas, or, if he did not choose to keep players, to Sir Thomas Hesketh, and added, "And I most heartily require the said Sir Thomas to be friendly unto Fulk Gyllome and William Shakeshafte now dwelling with me and either to take them into his service or else to help them to some good master, as my trust is he will."[68]

The difficulty with this as evidence is obvious: William Shakeshafte doesn't strike us as being the same name as William Shakespeare. And this is particularly so because we have little familiarity with the haphazard spelling of the Elizabethans and tend not to recognize a word when it is right in front of us. The name of Shakespeare's wife was Anne, but in her father's will her name is spelled Agnes. Her last name, Hathaway, also appears as Whateley in the register of her license to marry William. The letters "th" were often pronounced simply as the "t" sound, so it wouldn't take a deaf clerk to hear "Hateley" for "Hathaway" and spell it "Whateley." Andrew Gurr suggested the phrase, "hate away," in Shakespeare's Sonnet 145 could be a pun on the name "Hathaway."[69] There are other instances of confusion in the spelling of the Shakespeare name. In the Snitterfield manor records the name of Richard Shakespeare, Shakespeare's grandfather, appears as "Shakeschafte" and "Shakstaff." Another man named Shakespeare is recorded as "Thomas Shakesmore," and in the accounts of the Revels Office in the time of King James, Shakespeare's name is recorded four times as "Shaxsberd."[70] A further example was uncovered by Leslie Hotson who found John Shakespeare's name in a record of the Court of Common Pleas, 1572 as "Shaxbere."[71] It is interesting to see such variations of the name as "Shakescene" and in the names of the hired murderers "Shakebag" and "Black Will" in the play *Arden of Faversham*, which I am persuaded Shakespeare had a hand in writing.[72] Additional evidence that connects Shakespeare to Hoghton and Lancashire is that the playwright was once employed by Alexander Hoghton as attested by a long-standing tradition that he worked for the Hoghton family for two years in his youth.[73]

In addition to accounting for Shakespeare's Catholic sympathies, the attractive thing about a "Lancashire period" in Shakespeare's life is that it explains how it happened that his earliest traceable connection with professional actors was with members of a company who had once been under the patronage of Ferdinando Stanley, Lord Strange, who later became the fifth Earl of Derby. After he died in

1594, a group of his players were recruited by the Queen's Lord Chamberlain to form a new company which included Shakespeare.

Both Lord Strange and his father, the fourth Earl of Derby, were patrons of playing companies that performed at court and toured to provincial towns, including Stratford, from the 1570's to the 1590's.[74] While there is much evidence of Shakespeare's later association with actors who were once members of the company known as Lord Strange's Men, there isn't any evidence of exactly when that association began. If it began soon after 1580 or earlier when he had finished study at the grammar school, it would be easier to understand how it was that he became such a prominent theatrical figure, as both actor and playwright, less than ten years later.

If there is a puzzle as to how Shakespeare managed to get into the professional theatre, another puzzle in his life occurred about the same time. He married Anne Hathaway when he was eighteen years old. Her father was Richard Hathaway, a prominent and wealthy farmer in the Stratford area who had died a year before. His holdings have been estimated to have been somewhere between fifty and ninety acres. John Shakespeare knew the Hathaway family from way back; in 1566 John stood sureties for Richard Hathaway and was called to pay debts for him.[75] It must be admitted that the marriage has had a bad press. It has been assumed more often than not that Anne and William were married under irregular circumstances, especially since the bride brought no special talents of jointure to the marriage. But contrary to the usual assumption, women in those days were active in trades and in managing affairs outside the home.[76] There are many aspects of the marriage that look unlike the way we think such things should be done. First of all, William was very young and still a minor.[77] Besides that, bachelors were not considered eligible if they didn't have the income to support a family. It is hard to understand how William Shakespeare, too young to have completed an apprenticeship to some craft or trade, would have had the money or prospects to take up the role of head of a family. Secondly, Anne Hathaway was twenty-six years old, about the right age for women to marry, but it seems odd for a marriage to be arranged with a youth eight years younger— except for the fact that Anne was pregnant.

It was the custom to publish the banns three Sundays running in the parish church before the ceremony could be performed. In this case, however, since weddings were not performed during the Advent season, William and Anne did not wish to wait till that season had passed. Therefore, to get it done before the four-week Advent season had passed, permission had to be granted by the Bishop of the diocese. This was done on November 27, 1582. Two friends of the Hathaway family, Fulke Sandells, a supervisor, and John Rychardson, a witness to Hathaway's will, journeyed to the Bishop's court in Worcester and posted a bond to pay £40 if impediments to lawful marriage should come to light. It was also stipulated that William should not marry Anne without the consent of her friends. Her father could not give his consent because he had died the year before. It was further stipulated that William would pay the costs if any legal action were brought against the Bishop and his officers for allowing the marriage.[78] The reason for going through all this in November, 1582 just before the Advent season began, if not clear at the time of the wedding, became obvious when their first child, Susanna Shakespeare was born and baptized only 6 months later, in May, 1583. It looks, to use the modern phrase, like a shotgun wedding.

Considering the customs of the times, we should recognize that the permission of parents would be needed for minors to marry. Thus, if Shakespeare's father objected to the match, both civil and canon law would have supported him in not letting the match go forward. The Church of England forbade a priest to marry any minor unless the father or guardian "shall either personally, or by sufficient testimony, signify to him their consents given to the said marriage."[79]

To put a better light on the situation, it might be reasonable to assume that the families involved had agreed to the match. Sandells and Rychardson, who went to Worcester to guarantee there was no impediment to the marriage, obviously wanted to see it carried out. Knowing their families approved the match, the couple gained a negotiated agreement to marry which included a financial settlement of some sort to support the new family. Richard Hathaway, Anne's father, in his will dated September 1, 1581, a year before the marriage, left ten marks to his daughter to be paid to her on the day of her marriage. That is about six and a half pounds, certainly not enough for Anne to be pursued by fortune hunters. The Hathaways were not poor, nor was John Shakespeare; thus it follows that if the marriage was properly negotiated, each family would have settled enough on the couple to make the marriage workable. William was not a callow youth with only sexual alacrity to recommend him. He was the eldest son and heir of John Shakespeare, a man of some substance. And if William was already under the patronage of Lord Strange, he was a man of some prospects of his own, and very likely not the least eligible bachelor among the Hathaway neighbors in Stratford.[80]

There was nothing secretive about the wedding, and the Shakespeares and the Hathaways were near neighbors, both alike in dignity. So much pressure from custom and law, family and friends went to make up the match, that it is difficult to see how William, although a minor, could shirk his duty without bringing on himself the charge of fornication and bastardy, and bringing disgrace on both families. There would have been no way out and divorce was impossible. Two years later, Anne gave birth to twins, a boy and a girl, baptized Hamnet and Judith, February 2, 1585.

Perhaps it has been too easily assumed that players lived on the edge of starvation and resorted to petty thievery to get on. The truth is that some players made fortunes. The best of them, Edward Allen, Richard Burbage, and William Shakespeare became very wealthy indeed.

Whether Shakespeare enjoyed his new status of married man or found it a drag of sorts, he seems not to have spent much time in Stratford. An unusual interest in the relationship of parent and child is however characteristic of his early plays. In the Henry VI plays there are many examples of this: young Talbot dies in the arms of his father; the murder of Young Rutland of the house of York and the murder of Prince Edward of the House of Lancaster are pivotal moments. And there is a double scene of a son who discovers he has killed his father and on the other side of the stage, a father discovers he has killed his son. In *King John* the role of Prince Arthur is carefully developed to emphasize his naïve goodness. In *Richard III*, the murder of the Princes in the tower is presented as the major turning point leading to Richard's downfall, and earlier in that play, the hapless plight of Clarence's children works on the emotions no less effectively.

In Shakespeare's early tragedy, *Titus Andronicus*, aside from the hero's suffering for his daughter and his sons, the villain of the piece reveals an unexpected tenderness toward his bastard son. Rather than dismissing Shakespeare's use of children as melodramatic claptrap—rather more appealing to Victorian taste than to ours—it seems to me that almost no other playwright of the period works on the emotions by using children in quite the same way.

It is hardly possible to know whether specific aspects of Shakespeare's private life and emotions are or are not directly mirrored in his plays. He is a storyteller, not a novelist. By that I mean, he does not make up the stories he dramatizes; he picks traditional materials which can amuse an audience. We cannot find much in the plays that is clearly illustrative of his biography. He remains a very elusive person, one who seems more a detached and bemused observer than a partisan. But when he uses the same emotional device again and again in his plays, some of his personal concerns may be revealed.

In the case of comedy, which by convention is almost always about courtship, the trials of young lovers, and so forth, Shakespeare uses his theatre to explore marriage, the relationship of husband and wife, as much as courtship, as in *The Comedy of Errors* and *The Taming of the Shrew*.

About the time of the marriage of William Shakespeare and Anne Hathaway, the town of Coventry made some effort to provide dramatic fare that would appeal to tourists as had their great Corpus Christi Cycle. They commissioned Master John Smythe of St. John's College, Oxford to write a new play, *The Destruction of Jerusalem*. On April 15,1584 Smythe was paid thirteen pounds, six shillings, and eight pence, "for his pains in writing the tragedy." R. W. Ingram comments that "This is an extremely generous reward."[81] The records suggest that neither expenses nor efforts were spared to make the new play an impressive success. Instead of the average of two rehearsals used in revivals of the Corpus Christi pageants, there were five rehearsals to prepare *The Destruction of Jerusalem*.[82]

Although the text of the play has not survived, the story probably derives from *The Jewish Wars* of Flavius Josephus who wrote the official account of the campaign of 70 A.D. by Vespasian and Titus to crush a revolt against Roman authority. The most terrible part of the campaign was the siege of Jerusalem. The city was surrounded, inside the inhabitants were fighting each other, were starving, reduced to cannibalism, and too weak to bury their dead. Finally the Roman army gained control. The city was looted and torched, the Temple treasures taken to Rome, and the building leveled to the ground. Eusebius, the early historian of the Church, added an anti-Semitic element to the story by saying the destruction came because the Jews did not accept Jesus as the Messiah.

Perhaps this interpretative addition to the story was used in *The Destruction of Jerusalem*, for Jesus is one of the characters in the play.

At any rate this horrible event from the past seems to have fascinated quite a few in Shakespeare's time. In the early 1500's a book titled, *The Destruction of Jerusalem by Vaspasian and Titus* was printed three times,[83] and a broadside ballad, first printed in 1586 (perhaps to take advantage of Smythe's play) was reprinted twice.[84] There were also several plays based on the story. Dr. Thomas Legge, a scholar-playwright who eventually became Vice Chancellor at Cambridge, was celebrated for his play on the destruction of Jerusalem, which has since disappeared but was well known at the time.[85] In 1591, the repertory of Lord Strange's Men included a play listed as *Q Jerusalem* (the "*Q*" perhaps stands for "Conquest"), and another called *Titus & Vespasian*, which could have been a similar play, or the same play with another title, was performed eight times in one season.[86]

Something of the familiarity of the Destruction story is shown by Shakespeare's allusion in *King John* to mutineers in Jerusalem. I include the allusion as an epigraph for this chapter. The obscurity of the allusion suggests that most in his audiences knew the story and were aware that mutinous conflict inside the city was the thing which made the siege so terrible.

The Destruction of Jerusalem attests to the diffusion of the story, although it is not likely that many people saw a performance of the Coventry version. After the 1584 performance, there is no record of a revival. However, it was on a list of plays the City Council gave the Commons permission to perform some seven years later. The wording from the Council Book, dated 19 May, 1591, is as follows:

> It is also agreed by the whole consent of this house that the Destruction of Jerusalem, the Conquest of the Danes, or the history of K[ing] E[dward] the 4, at the request of the Commons of this city shall be played on the pageants of Midsummer Day & St. Peter's Day next in this City and none other plays. And that all the May poles that are now standing in this City shall be taken down before Whitsunday next, none hereafter to be set up in this City.[87]

That last sentence about Maypoles is one more indication of how folk games and pastimes, not only those connected with the Catholic past, were being suppressed as part of the Puritan program of reform.

The significance of the Coventry play on the Destruction of Jerusalem for our sketch of Shakespeare's life is not that he may have seen the production. We can't be sure about that. It is significant, however, that the old play was designed to take the place of the Corpus Christi Play. It is not derived from legend or scripture, but from Roman history. The other plays which the Council permitted to be performed are also based on historical accounts. Their play about Edward the Fourth may have been very much like the kind of history play Shakespeare and Marlowe were to write a short time later. Shakespeare's history plays about Henry VI were in the repertory of Lord Strange's Men at the same as their *Titus & Vespasian*.

The other play permitted by the Coventry Council, *The Conquest of the Danes*, may have been adapted from the traditional "Hock Tuesday" play which the men of Coventry performed before Queen Elizabeth when she visited Kenilworth Castle some twenty years earlier in 1575. Apparently at that time there was some question as to whether the entertainment would be permitted. But as the good men explained, the play celebrated a defeat of the Danes in which the women of Coventry played a part, thus making it acceptable to Her Majesty. In his account of the citizens' view of the matter, Robert Laneham wrote to a friend:

> The thing, said they, is grounded on story, and for pastime wont
> to be played in our City yearly without ill example of manners,
> papistry, or any superstition, ... had an ancient beginning and a
> long continuance, till now of late laid down, they knew no cause
> why, unless it were by the zeal of certain their Preachers—men very
> commendable for their behavior and learning, and sweet in their
> sermons, but somewhat sour in preaching away their pastime. [They]
> wished therefore, that as they [the preachers] should continue their
> good doctrine in pulpit, so, for matters of policy and governance
> of the City, they would permit them, ... that they might have their
> plays up again.[88]

The revival of the Hock Tuesday play, suppressed earlier than the Corpus Christi pageants, was enjoyed by the Queen. In the city annals we read "Coventry men went to make her merry with their play of Hock Tuesday and for their pains had a reward and venison also to make them merry." As far as we can tell the play was a sort of mock skirmish with outlandish costumes and weapons, no doubt with drums, trumpets, banners and vaunting speeches, perhaps with some loss of blood on all sides, but the right side always won and the Danes were led off to captivity in a triumphal march by the women of Coventry. It could be that the preachers saw some atavistic fertility rite in all that. Further, if the women were played by men, the passage in Deuteronomy 22.5, which states that it is an abomination for a man to put on a woman's garments, would have been additional grounds for putting down the Hock Tuesday Play.

Earlier in 1565, Queen Elizabeth's first visit to Coventry is recorded thus in the city annals:

> And when the Recorder delivered the gift of the City which was
> a purse which cost 20 marks with one hundred pounds of angels
> in it. When the Queen received it her guard said to the Lords it was
> one hundred pounds in gold to whom the Mayor answered
> very boldly, "And it like your grace there is a great deal more in it."
> "What is that?" said the Queen. The Mayor answered again and
> said, "It is the faithful hearts of all your true loving subjects."
> "I thank you Master Mayor," said the Queen, "It is a great deal
> more indeed."[89]

As was customary then, the Corpus Christi pageants were on display at various places as the Queen passed through the city on her way to her lodgings in the White Friars. After her last famous visit to Kenilworth Castle in 1575, the Queen in her summertime progresses did not again venture that far north from London.

CHAPTER 4

THE SPANISH TRAGEDY
1585–1592

Majestical the order of their course,
Figuring the horned circle of the moon.
                                        (*The Reign of King Edward III* 3.1.71–72)

B Y 1592, when he was twenty-eight years old, William Shakespeare was
well enough known in London theatre circles to be the subject of an
envious attack in what might be called the Elizabethan equivalent of
tabloid journalism. It was in *Greene's Groats-worth of Wit, bought with a million
of Repentance*, a pamphlet by Robert Greene, written according to the title
page "before his death and published at his dying request." Robert Greene was
an accomplished playwright and pamphleteer. Much about his posthumous
pamphlet suggests that it was dolled up to seem like sensational hot stuff to catch
the eye of a variety of readers.

It appeared to be the deathbed repentance of a writer who had cultivated a
reputation for knowing the ways of the underworld by writing a series of lurid
pamphlets about card sharks, confidence men, pick pockets, and prostitutes.
He called them "Cony-catching" pamphlets; the word cony means rabbit, i.e.,
a foolish and gullible person. As the title page of *Greene's Groatsworth of Wit*
implies, these are the final words of a repentant sinner, dying in abject poverty!
He wrote that he was describing "the folly of youth, the falsehood of make-shift
flatterers, the misery of the negligent, and mischiefs of deceiving courtesans."
This description applies to a story, which takes up most of the pages, based
perhaps on Greene's life or a distorted version of it. The story goes like this: a
miser adept at sharp practice had two sons. The older son inherited only a groat

because he disapproved of his father's money grabbing ways. The younger son inherited everything because he was selfish and stingy like his father. With only a groat the older son was left to live by his wits. Accordingly he had a miserable life, often sinking to shameful ways to keep body and soul together. It is a bitter, rather nasty story.

There is added, in the manner of an appendix, an open letter from Greene to three gentlemen who were also playwrights, Christopher Marlowe, Thomas Nashe, and George Peele. In the letter Greene gives some not very helpful advice: Marlowe should quit flirting with atheistic ideas; Nashe should curb his satiric tongue; Peele should stop wasting his time supplying actors with plays. This advice is then broadened and turns into an angry attack on professional actors. He calls them puppets, antics, and rude grooms because they make a handsome living from the plays written by their betters and will do nothing to help poverty stricken playwrights, such as Greene himself. He goes on:

> Is it not strange, that I, to whom they all have been beholding: is it not like
> that you, to whom they all have been beholding, shall (were ye in that
> case as I am now) be ... of them forsaken? Yes, trust them not: for there is
> an upstart crow, beautified with our feathers, that with his *Tiger's heart
> wrapt in a Player's hide*, supposes he is as well able to bombast out a blank
> verse as the best of you: and being an absolute *Johannes fac totum*, is in his
> own conceit the only Shake-scene in a country.[90]

Two hints make it fairly clear that William Shakespeare is the "upstart crow" Greene is attacking. The phrase "Tiger's heart wrapt in a player's hide," echoes a line from Shakespeare's *Henry the Sixth, Part III*: "Oh tiger's heart wrapt in a woman's hide!"—part of a thrilling tirade by the Duke of York in Act I. Greene's sneer at such bombast leads to the give-away nickname, "Shake-scene."

There are many curious things about this letter to the three playwrights. As university graduates they were properly addressed as gentlemen, which allows Greene to remind his readers that players are not in the same class. Writing for them is an indignity such as might be suffered by a modern novelist reduced to writing advertising copy. And Greene is confused. He attacks Shakespeare for presuming to write like a university man, but parodies a rather unforgettable line as an example of bombast.

Although Greene's letter is the earliest surviving record of Shakespeare as an actor and as a playwright, it seems to me the most important thing about it is that Shakespeare is singled out as a player in London important enough to be the target of Greene's anger. It could be, as many commentators have suggested, that Shakespeare revised, or doctored, or plagiarized some of Greene's work. However, at that time people did not see much wrong in using a good thing from another writer. But we should not overlook the point of his letter. Unless he was striking out wildly, Greene's point is that the players refused to supply his desperate need for money. After all he had done for them, they deserted him as he lay dying. And the one player he singles out to be specifically named is William Shakespeare. This raises the question that cries out to be answered: why Shakespeare?

To answer this we need to consider a much broader question: what was Shakespeare's position among the players in 1592? In Greene's opinion, he's an upstart, perhaps not so much for being new to the theatre, as for not knowing his place, and a Jack-of-all-trades, but master of none. However, this can hardly be accurate, not even as the exaggeration of an angry man. The target of this anger cannot be an ordinary player; rather it is a man who was in a position to help Greene, but who turned his back on him. At least that is Greene's view of the matter.

At that time the standard practice had been that when a playing company paid a playwright for a script, it became their property. Without an author's copyright, the company was free to use the script in any way that suited its interests. The company's members were free to revise it to suit their particular staging and casting requirements. It could be in the repertory for years without any royalty payments being made. Once the play was no longer attracting audiences, the company was free to sell the script to a publisher who thought readers might want to buy it, or pass it on to another company. In England royalty payments were not required until a dramatic copyright act was passed in 1833.

Obviously playwrights like Greene might sometimes feel cheated by this system, even if they could earn a steady income by continuing to write because new scripts were in great demand. It is known, by his own confession, that Greene tried to beat the system by selling his play *Orlando Furioso* to the Queen's Players, and while they went on tour, sold the same play to the Lord Admiral's Men! All this came out in a pamphlet, *The Defense of Conny-Catching*, published by Greene some months before his death.[91] The leader of the Admiral's Men was Edward Alleyn, and Orlando was one of his big roles. By bragging about his trick, Greene was burning his bridges. Having invested in the play, the Queen's Men

would consider it part of their stock, an investment made for the exclusive right
to produce the play, and here was Alleyn taking advantage of Greene's double
dealing. Although Alleyn got the best of the bargain, neither he nor the Queen's
Men could be easy about dealing with Greene in the future.

Why then did Greene attack Shakespeare? How would Shakespeare be in
a position to relieve Greene who was dying in poverty? Perhaps as has been
suggested Shakespeare may have been a moneylender.[92] But I think it probable
that Shakespeare had some leading position in a playing company.

Gerald Bentley has carefully researched the organization of playing companies
in Shakespeare's time. He argues that there were three categories of personnel in
the companies: sharers at the top, apprentices at the bottom, and in the middle,
hired personnel—actors, stage hands, costumers and assistants of various kinds.[93]
The sharers were the ones who owned the company stock, made decisions about
expenses, the wages paid to hired personnel, trained the apprentices, provided
costumes, properties, scripts, rented the theatre, made decisions about casting,
rehearsals, touring, and collected the receipts for public performances and the
rewards for private ones. After expenses were paid, they shared the profits. If
Greene expected some bonus or charitable donation to relieve his wants, it would
be from those who made the profits from the enterprise, that is, the sharers
of one of the companies he had sold scripts to, not from the ordinary actors
who worked as hired men and who probably were paid by performance. This, I
think, implies that Shakespeare was indeed a sharer in one of the London playing
companies. But which? There are two likely possibilities, Lord Strange's Men or
The Earl of Pembroke's Men.

From about 1589 to 1594, Lord Strange's Men and the Admiral's Men
were playing together at The Rose Theatre on the Bank Side. According to the
court records, as studied by E. K. Chambers, "the company seems to have been
regarded as Strange's. But the leading actor, Edward Alleyn, kept his personal
status as the Lord Admiral's servant."[94] This "combined" company was so much
in favor that it gave a record of six performances at Court in the Christmas
season of 1591-1592. The company was enjoying this success during the winter
of Greene's death. In the few surviving documents Shakespeare is not mentioned
as one of the sharers, but his early plays were in their repertory. However, the
company was split in two sometime early in 1592, and some of the players,
principally Richard Burbage, whose father owned The Theatre in Shoreditch,
found a new patron in the Earl of Pembroke. Pembroke's Men took with them

some of the plays that were earlier in the repertory of Lord Strange's Men. This
suggests that the plays in their repertory were divided as a settlement for claims on
their common stock. At least two of the plays that went to Pembroke's Men were
by Shakespeare: *Titus Andronicus* and *The True Tragedy of Richard, Duke of York*,
now known as *King Henry the Sixth, Part III*. It could well be that Shakespeare
owned his own scripts; Alleyn personally owned some of the plays he starred in,
such as *Orlando* and *The Jew of Malta*. If so, then Shakespeare's scripts may have
comprised part of his investment to become a sharer in the new company, or he
may have bought a share with cash.

Aside from the question of which company Shakespeare may have been
connected with as a sharer, there are two other points which I think can be
inferred from Greene's angry attack. The first is that Shakespeare was singled
out because as a sharer he had access to company funds or exercised some of the
functions of a manager, as he briefly did later for The Lord Chamberlain's men.[95]
It is pertinent to note here that John Shakespeare was keeper of the accounts of
the Stratford Corporation for several years. The second point is that Greene's
attack indicates that Shakespeare was a more accomplished actor than has been
suspected. At the time neither playwrights nor investors were, as far as is known,
made sharers in acting companies. Only actors capable of playing substantial roles
in the repertory were taken on as sharers. Even the best playwrights like Marlowe,
Jonson, Dekker, Middleton, and Fletcher were never made sharers in a playing
company. There was, of course, no reason an actor could not write plays for the
company, but also no reason for a playwright to be made a sharer. They got their
money for writing, not for acting. Considering the case of two playwrights who
were sharers as well as actors, Gerald Bentley writes, "William Shakespeare and
Thomas Heywood were valuable to their companies as writers, but certainly a
share was not the common way of paying a devoted playwright."[96]

The reaction to Greene's attack was such that Henry Chettle, the printer of
Greene's *Groats-worth of Wit*, was moved in his next publication, a writing of his
own called *Kind-Heart's Dream*, to add an apology for not softening Greene's
words which he could easily have done as editor of the pamphlet. It seems that
both Marlowe and Shakespeare took offense. Here is part of Chettle's apology:

> With neither of them that take offense was I acquainted, and with one of
> them I care not if I never be: The other, whom at that time I did not so

much spare, as since I wish I had, ... that I did not, I am as sorry as if the
original fault had been my fault, because myself have seen his demeanor
no less civil than the excellent in the quality he professes: Besides, divers
of worship have reported his uprightness of dealing, which argues his
honesty, and his facetious grace in writing, that approves his art.[97]

Chettle regretted he had printed Greene's attack on Shakespeare because of
his admiration for the work of an actor "excellent in the quality he professes."
Hamlet, for example, asking a player for a speech says, "Come give us a taste of your
quality." And Chettle mentions "divers of worship," meaning "diverse noblemen"
who had spoken of Shakespeare's honesty and his artistry as a playwright. It
is likely that "honesty" still carried its Latin meaning of "honorable," another
indication that Shakespeare was a sharer in a theatrical company, not simply one
of the journeyman actors. Further, we must not overlook the fact that being a
sharer is additional evidence of his being a good actor. From what little is known
about the casting of plays in the Elizabethan-Jacobean theatre, Gerald Bentley
concludes, "Sharers are generally assigned what appear to be the major roles."[98]

There were sharers who were leading actors, who took nearly all the big roles.
In Lord Strange's Men and later, the Lord Admiral's Men, the leading player was
Edward Alleyn. He played Faustus, the Jew of Malta, Tamburlaine, Orlando, so
many that it is likely that whenever he acted, he played the lead. In the Earl of
Pembroke's Men and later, in the Lord Chamberlain's Men, Richard Burbage
was the same kind of actor. He played Richard III, Romeo, Hamlet, Othello,
and Lear. It is possible that Shakespeare was not a lead player, because unlike
Alleyn and Burbage, there is no evidence of his being identified with a particular
leading role.

Aside from the leading player, companies had actors who specialized as the
principal clown or comic. They were likely to be identified with a personal style
of banter and were allowed moments for playing off an audience, some of it
improvised. Richard Tarlton had that specialty in the Queen's Company, William
Kemp in Lord Strange's Men, and Robert Armin in the Lord Chamberlain's Men.
These were much talked of, and joke books of their jests were printed from time
to time. If Shakespeare had played the clown, it is likely that we would also have
books of his routines and merry pranks, such as were published about Tartlton,
Kemp, and Armin.

If neither the leading player nor the clown, then what kind of roles did

Shakespeare take? The question, however, is misleading because it is based on an assumption that actors in Shakespeare's time could always be identified with a specialty, or a restricted range of roles. Such was not the case, which explains why the few anecdotes written down over the years telling a bit about the roles Shakespeare played add up to so very little and give the impression that acting was not a very important part of his career. Before reviewing the anecdotes about Shakespeare the actor, some idea of the operations of a theatre company in his time should be taken into account. This will help to explain why it is we know so little about the particular roles Shakespeare may have played. For while we know a lot about the roles of the lead players and the clowns, very little is known about actors who did not have one of those two specialties.

Possibly the greatest difference between performances by an Elizabethan company and a modern one is that after a production opens in one of our theaters, it usually runs as long as the reviews are good and audiences keep coming. Night after night the same play is on stage. In the Elizabethan theatre, on the other hand, it is nearly accurate to say each afternoon a different play was presented. They had a huge repertory; fifteen or twenty plays if they were performing in London. On tour to smaller towns there weren't enough theatregoers for more than three or four performances, so a smaller repertory would meet the demand, which could be repeated in town after town. In London, on the other hand, a much larger repertory was required to keep audiences coming. When Lord Strange's Men played at The Rose Theatre, a surviving record of their performances from February to June in 1592 shows that with a repertory of twenty-three different plays, they gave 105 performances. Some plays were performed only once, while the popular ones were presented a dozen times or more, and at least four days elapsed before a play was repeated.[99] They apparently needed a sufficient number of plays to keep up with the demand of the playgoers in London. With so large a repertory, it would not be easy to identify any actor with a specific role unless it was a lead role in a very popular play that remained in the repertory year after year.

For a small company to sustain such a repertory within the newly hatched English theatrical context is very remarkable, but that is only half the story of what these actors were able to do. They were not solo entertainers, nor amateurs, but professional actors, that is, men who made a living by acting, a new phenomenon. When a town put on the Corpus Christi Play, they could easily find as many amateurs as could be used for the annual festival. But once the actors had to earn enough for living expenses all year long, their number necessarily had to be kept to a minimum. To make do with fewer, plays designed for an Elizabethan acting company were so organized that by doubling, tripling, even quadrupling roles, little more than a dozen players were needed to fill out the cast. Plays were written with that practice in mind.

A compelling essay by William A. Ringler, Jr., comes very close to demonstrating that Shakespeare's early plays were designed to be performed by sixteen actors if doubling is used to the fullest extent.[100] That this was the number of players, or something very close to it, regularly used by the company is confirmed by the fact that crowd scenes almost never require more than sixteen players. Further, such scenes are placed widely enough apart to allow for costume changes. That limit holds not only for the smaller number of roles in comedies like *Twelfth Night* and *Much Ado*, where sixteen can do the play almost without doubling, but also for large-cast dramas like *Julius Caesar*, where many of the senators can double as the mob, and reappear as soldiers in the final scenes. Considering all this in planning a script for production, a playwright would have to be familiar with the acting company he hoped would buy his script. The notion that some aristocrat could work on a play while living in a palace, instead of in the neighborhood of a commercial theatre, seems very unlikely.

This limitation of the size of the company to a precise number would have been efficient and practical. If, instead of thinking of Shakespeare's company as a flexible group, enlarged or diminished depending on the variable needs of the performance of the day, we think of it as a company of a fixed size, their extensive repertory seems much more manageable. But if the repertoire included many plays requiring a varying number of actors, the book-holder would have to send messengers all over town to assemble the right number of actors for each play. When the lead player is called to sustain the great tragic roles, the rest of the company are doing bits, swelling processions, fighting battles, appearing as one character in early scenes, and as another in later scenes. And when comedy makes less strenuous demands on the lead player, the subordinate roles are longer, and doubling less likely. In either case the physical work of the performance would be more fairly and evenly divided among the sixteen actors. With the size of the acting company limited in this way, the actors would necessarily have played all sorts of roles. There would not have been one group for comedy and another for tragedy, like a football team split between defensive and offensive players.

In his analysis of the casting in *A Midsummer Night's Dream*, Ringler suggests that the roles of the five "mechanicals," Quince, Flute, Snout, Starveling, and Snug, could double as the fairies attending on Titania, namely Peaseblossom, Cobweb, Moth, and Mustardseed. Of course, since the actor playing Bottom the Weaver appears in scenes with both the mechanicals and the fairies, he cannot be double cast. This goes against our imaginative view of the Fairies as tiny, flitting critters and the mechanicals as bulky stumblebums. But imagination is controlled by what the dialogue suggests, not simply by the physical size of the actors. In these circumstances where one man played many parts, even by going often to the theater, playgoers would not have been able to remember a particular role an actor had played, unless he appeared several times in a commanding role, such as Hamlet, Lear, or Othello, roles for which Burbage was remembered.

The point is illustrated in *The Taming of the Shrew*. A Lord welcoming a traveling company of actors remembers a performance he enjoyed, but cannot recall either the role or the name of the actor who played it:

> *Lord.* This fellow I remember
>   Since once he play'd a farmer's eldest son.
>   'Twas where you woo'd the gentlewoman so well.
>   I have forgot your name; but sure that part
>   Was aptly fitted and naturally perform'd.
> *1st Player.* I think 'twas Soto that your honor means.
>
> (Induction 83-88)

Doubling was standard practice, not as it is in the modern theatre, where it is sometimes used to point to an underlying similarity in roles, or when there are not enough actors to fill all the roles. In discussing the effect of the Elizabethan practice of doubling, Bernard Beckerman describes the situation succinctly:

> This tradition of doubling gave the Elizabethan no opportunity to
> develop a specialty. He could not concentrate on a specific genre, for
> he was called upon to play courtly men, villains and saints.[101]

This required an actor to be a flexible and versatile performer, and eventually, if he remained in the profession, a highly accomplished one. The actors thus had little opportunity to specialize in particular roles, and they would be prized, as they were able to transform themselves quickly into something new and strange.

This is the opposite of the practice today of casting according to type. In film, for example, the actor is expected to look like, or even supposed to be, the character. The modern audience comes to identify an actor with a certain character-type and expects to see a version of that type at every appearance the actor makes. In the theatre of Shakespeare's day an actor could be well known, but as he shifted roles at a protean pace, the audience would have learned to overlook the improbabilities, rather than try to rationalize the dizzying display. All this made for a different kind of work for the actor and provided a different kind of pleasure for the audience.

The modern convention that an actor must look the role is part of a broader range of realistic expectations. The contrast between the kind of stage the Elizabethan actor used and a modern theatre also points to a difference in acting techniques. The public arenas designed for theatrical performances in Shakespeare's time were huge, capable of holding an audience as large as 3,000. The front of the stage was practically in the middle of a yard open to the sky. Thus, the actor was surrounded by spectators, many below the stage level staring up, others seated in a gallery at eye level looking straight on, and still others gazing down from two higher galleries. Some were seated behind the actor's back. In the outdoor public theatres performances were all done in daylight. Commanding an attentive audience in such circumstances requires direct awareness and contact with the audience as much as with other actors in the scene.

Bearing in mind the conditions Elizabethan actors learned to exploit in their everyday work, stories about Shakespeare as an actor can be more readily understood, especially with a better sense of why information about his acting amounts to so little.

In 1610 John Davies published an epigram entitled, "To Our English Terence, Mr. Will. Shakespeare." Three lines allude to Shakespeare's acting:

> Had'st thou not played some Kingly parts in sport,
> Thou hadst been a companion for a *King*;
> And, been a King among the meaner sort.[102]

This has been taken to mean that Shakespeare made some sort of specialty of playing kings. But that possibility tells us very little. Consider the saintly Henry

VI, the politician Claudius of Denmark, or the patriarchal Duncan of Scotland. The possibilities are many, and the characterizations of kings are so varied that Davies' epigram tells us only that Shakespeare sometimes played the king, as did many other actors. By the way, to be knighted and made a "companion for a king" was an honor not granted to players until 1895 when Henry Irving was knighted by Queen Victoria. King James I promoted the sharers in his company to be grooms of the chamber, but that hardly made them "companions."

In 1709, almost a hundred years after Shakespeare left the scene, Nicholas Rowe added a sketch of Shakespeare's life to his edition of the plays. In it he reported his efforts to gather information about the roles Shakespeare may have played. He consulted Thomas Betterton, the leading actor of the Restoration theatre. Betterton's celebrated Hamlet was said to be based on instructions by Sir William Davenant, who had "seen Mr. Taylor of the Black-Friars Company act it, who being instructed by the author, Mr. Shakespeare, taught Mr. Betterton in every particle of it."[103] Betterton had other sources of information. As a young man, during Oliver Cromwell's time when the public theaters were closed, he was apprenticed to a bookseller, John Rhodes, who had been Wardrobe Keeper for the King's Men. If anyone might have known about Shakespeare's roles as preserved in stage tradition, it would likely be Betterton. But for all that, he knew little and Rowe had to confess:

> I could never meet with any further account of him [Shakespeare]
> this way, than that the top of his performance was the ghost in his
> own *Hamlet*.

That tidbit of theatre lore is not to be lightly dismissed and it certainly is of interest. The ghost is a portentous figure dominating the opening of the play and capping the climax of the drama by intruding in the scene between the Prince and his mother. A first-rate performance of the ghost can be memorable. The role demands an actor who can command attention as much as the role of Hamlet. If we were to guess what roles may have been doubled by the actor playing the ghost, we can come up with a large list: Rosencrantz, Guildenstern, the Player King, the Grave Digger, Fortinbras, and others.

There is another story about Shakespeare's acting, though versions of it were not written down until the 18th Century. The story is that actors from the London stage went to Stratford to see an old man; supposedly a brother of Shakespeare who as a young man had seen Will act during a trip to London. On being asked what he remembered of Shakespeare's acting, the brother could only recollect:

> having once seen him act a part in one of his own comedies, wherein being to personate a decrepit old man, he wore a long beard, and appeared so weak and drooping and unable to walk, that he was forced to be supported and carried by another person to a table, at which he was seated among some company, who were eating, and one of them sung a song.

That is a fascinating picture, and those who know *As You Like It* will recall the scene in the Forest of Arden [2.7] where Orlando carries Old Adam to the Duke's table. Then too, the story is affecting in its suggestions of a dim, distant, and vanished past. But the details are not right in one important circumstance; Shakespeare had no brother who survived him. In another version of the story, however, the questioners were from Stratford, not London actors, and the old man is said to be only a relative of Shakespeare, not his brother. Thus the story, passed on and reworked in the process, may be true in its main point that Shakespeare played Adam in *As You Like It*. It is a highly sympathetic role, that of a loyal servant. With exemplary generosity, he rescues Orlando from a murderous plot and helps him escape but in style of speech and quality of action, it is a big jump from that to the ghost in *Hamlet*. Adam disappears from the scene after being brought to the Forest, so the actor playing him could double with characters making their first entrance after that.

Possible doublings in speaking roles would be Sir Oliver Martext in Act III, William in Act V, and Hymen or the Second Brother in the final scene. William M. Jones made a case for Shakespeare playing Adam, and then doubling as Audrey's country swain, William.[104] Much of the brief scene between William and Touchstone gains point, according to the argument, if the audience recognizes Shakespeare as William. For example, when he says he has a pretty wit and to the question, "Art rich?" replies, "'Faith, sir, so, so." Actors of the best quality were notorious for their wealth, and perhaps Shakespeare was considered especially so.

There is an Elizabethan joke that tells us who played Richard III. The joke, recorded in the diary of John Manningham, 13 March 1602, goes like this:

> Upon a time when Richard Burbage played Richard III, there was a citizen's wife who grew so in liking with him, that before she went from

the play she appointed him to come that night unto her by the name of Richard the Third. Shakespeare overhearing their conclusion went before, was entertained, and at his game ere Burbage came. Then message being brought that Richard the Third was at the door, Shakespeare caused return to be made that William the Conqueror was before Richard the Third.[105]

It makes a good story, one that Manningham heard from a fellow Middle Templar, named William Towse. And it may be a better and more informative story than has been suspected. Suppose Shakespeare were as well known for acting William the Conqueror as Burbage was for Richard the III?[106] It so happens that a play once ascribed to Shakespeare contains this very role. The title page reads:

> A Pleasant Comedy, of fair Em the Miller's daughter of Manchester: with the love of William the Conqueror: As it was sundry times publicly acted in the honorable city of London, by the right honorable the Lord Strange his servants.[107]

Manchester was then a very small village in Lancashire, but it was a place where the welcome mat would be out for Lord Strange's Men, Manchester being in the area of their patron's greatest influence, and the play supposedly about a local character. There is another play in the repertory of the Earle of Sussex' Men listed as "william the conkerer," when they played at The Rose Theatre early in 1594.[108] It may simply be another name for *Fair Em*.

There are two stories in this "pleasant" comedy. One relates the way Em the Miller's daughter is able to hold off her silly suitors. As it has so little to do with the other story about the Conqueror, we don't need to review it. This other story tells of William the Conqueror's travels to Denmark, disguised as Sir Robert of Windsor, to have a look at Blanche, the Danish Princess. She falls for him, but he on seeing Mariana, a lady betrothed to the Marquis of Lubeck, decides to court her instead of Blanche. The women find this out and devise a plan whereby William thinks he is eloping back to England with Mariana, but the lady he escorts is really Princess Blanche in disguise. When the King of Denmark discovers the Princess is gone, he follows after in hot pursuit with an army to invade England. Then, and it is hard to imagine why it took so long, William discovers that Blanche has fooled him. He is furious and vows to have nothing to do with women. At that point the other story dealing with Fair Em, the Miller's daughter of Manchester, is joined to the William story. Events too complicated to untangle here show William that not all women are false; so he accepts marriage with Blanche and the war with Denmark is called off.

The play, although it uses the names of characters from history, as do many others written in the late 1580's and early 1590's, is a combination of history and romance, mostly romance. It is the kind of play that could be called a comical history or an historical comedy. A king or prince is shown as infatuated with a woman he eventually has to give up. Robert Greene wrote two of the best plays that exploit this situation, *Bacon and Bungay* and *James the Fourth*. A more interesting example of the type is found in *King Edward III*, an anonymous play, although some scholars have recently come to believe that Shakespeare himself wrote a good part of it.[109] According to a commonly held belief, when the passions of kings or princes are thwarted, violent and tragic events are likely to explode, generating much excitement. The characterization of the Conqueror is no exception. However tense these plays become, there is always a rather abrupt turn toward a happy ending. Such plays probably became old fashioned after Shakespeare developed the history play and showed how historic themes and figures could be given a serious as well as a popular treatment on the public stage.

When Ben Jonson published his "Works" in 1616, although without naming the roles Shakespeare played, he lists him as one of the principal comedians in the first performance of *Everyman in his Humour* and as one of the principal tragedians in the first performance of *Sejanus*. Shakespeare could easily have played several of the roles. Jonson seems to have listed the principal actors according to their rank in the company, not necessarily according to the importance of the roles they played. Shakespeare appeared as an actor with the leading companies of his day, so we can be sure he was a versatile performer who played a wide range of roles. Given the facts of the repertory system then in use, we could hardly expect to know more. Indeed, it has to be admitted that what we know at this late date about the roles Shakespeare may have played amounts to very little: the solemn ghost in *Hamlet*, the gentle Adam in *As You Like It*, and possibly the lusty William the Conqueror in *Fair Em*.

This survey of Shakespeare's acting must include a bit of stage gossip written in the 1680's in John Aubrey's brief notes on Shakespeare:

This William being inclined naturally to poetry and acting, came to
London I guess about 18 and was an Actor at one of the Play-houses and
did act exceedingly well…. He was a handsome well shap'd man: very
good company and of a very ready and pleasant smooth wit.[110]

A handsome, shapely body, and a lively mind—just what an actor needs!

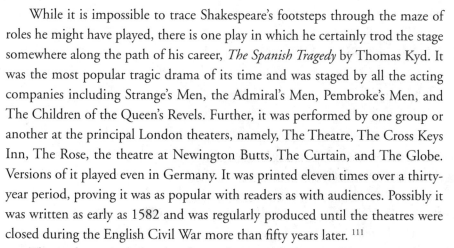

While it is impossible to trace Shakespeare's footsteps through the maze of
roles he might have played, there is one play in which he certainly trod the stage
somewhere along the path of his career, *The Spanish Tragedy* by Thomas Kyd. It
was the most popular tragic drama of its time and was staged by all the acting
companies including Strange's Men, the Admiral's Men, Pembroke's Men, and
The Children of the Queen's Revels. Further, it was performed by one group or
another at the principal London theaters, namely, The Theatre, The Cross Keys
Inn, The Rose, the theatre at Newington Butts, The Curtain, and The Globe.
Versions of it played even in Germany. It was printed eleven times over a thirty-
year period, proving it was as popular with readers as with audiences. Possibly it
was written as early as 1582 and was regularly produced until the theatres were
closed during the English Civil War more than fifty years later. [111]

The prologue includes the ghost of a murdered Spanish courtier and the
figure of Revenge. He describes with appropriate classical and gruesome allusions
his journey after death through the underworld. Finally we learn that he has
been allowed to return to our world to watch his mistress take revenge on his
murderer. The play proper begins with a war in which the Spanish have defeated
the Portuguese and annexed their territory. As the story unfolds, it is proposed
that the captured Prince of Portugal be married to the niece of the King of Spain,
who happens to have been the mistress of the murdered man whose ghost we met
in the prologue. She in the meantime has fallen in love with Horatio. When this
is discovered, her brother, who wants the Portuguese marriage to go forward, has
Horatio secretly murdered. The body of Horatio is found hanging in an arbor
by his father Hieronymo. Now the focus goes to the old man, mad with grief for
the loss of his son, and we follow his efforts to discover who murdered the boy.
Once he finds out, he plots a gruesome revenge that involves a play within the
play where all the principals are killed and Hieronymo commits suicide.

The Spanish Tragedy exemplifies what has been named a revenge tragedy and which kept its popularity all through the Elizabethan-Jacobean era. Shakespeare's *Titus Andronicus* and *Hamlet* are cut from the same pattern. In *Titus* a father goes mad with grief for the rape and mutilation of his daughter and the murder of his sons, but finally manages to pull off an atrocious revenge at a cannibal banquet. In Shakespeare's version of the Hamlet story, the son goes mad with grief for the murder of his father, and the tragedy uses a ghost for a prologue and a dueling match instead of a play or a banquet for the final bloodletting sequence.

The atmosphere of a revenge tragedy is defined by a setting in a foreign and corrupt court, where vice is pampered, murder buys promotion, and as in the tragedies of Seneca, the career of crime engulfs everyone. Finally the avenger, frenzied with grief and frustration, unable to get justice, sets a trap for his enemies, which works because his enemies think they can humor his madness. Thus he sweeps to his revenge. Perhaps much of the appeal of the play lies in that conclusion. Even today, when other revenge plays are no longer popular, *Hamlet* remains a favorite. I have heard audiences cheer when Hamlet finally stabs the incestuous usurper to death with a poisoned sword and pours the poisoned wine down his throat. Certainly the play is liked for the sheer variety of its incidents, its fascinating characters, and the introspective hero. Moreover, I think the long wait for the revenge to be carried out remains part of its appeal.

The Elizabethan revenge play is in some ways like modern espionage films with spies, counter agents, devilish plots, and strange instruments of death. The biggest difference is that modern undercover agents always win; Elizabethan avengers die. Both the revenge play and the modern spy film appeal to audiences by exploiting fears of a foreign enemy. All the years *The Spanish Tragedy* held the stage, London audiences were wary of one more move whereby Spain might gain control over England or insure in some way that a Catholic prince would succeed on the death of Elizabeth. By setting the play in Spain and Portugal, Kyd was taking advantage of the recent takeover of Portugal by Philip II in 1580, which brought Portuguese shipping under his control and made harbors on the Atlantic available as staging areas should an invasion of England be undertaken. In a rather odd interlude in *The Spanish Tragedy*, Kyd included a pageant where the court was entertained by a dumb show of three English lords who had in years long past defeated the kings of Portugal and Spain [1.4]. Aside from these Portuguese-Spanish current events, a more obvious reason for a London theatre audience to be interested and excited about the Spanish threat came when the

United Provinces in the Netherlands revolted from Spanish rule. Their leader William the Silent was assassinated in 1585.

After the discovery of the "Babington Plot," a plan to assassinate Queen Elizabeth so that Mary of Scotland could inherit the throne, Elizabeth was persuaded to sign the warrant for Mary's execution that was carried out in 1586. Those who at home and abroad hoped for a Catholic monarch in England now saw Philip II as next in line and urged him on to the "enterprise of England." Elizabeth sent troops to aid the insurgents in Holland under the command of Robert Dudley, Earl of Leicester. The English and Dutch were no match for the large and efficient Spanish troops commanded by one of the most skillful generals of the time, Alexander Farnese, Governor of the Spanish Netherlands and Duke of Parma. As it became clear that Parma was assembling a large army just across the Channel and would gain control of the seacoast, dread of the Spaniard worked on the popular mind. In 1587, Sir Francis Drake raided the harbors of Cadiz and Lisbon, "singeing the king's beard." The war with Spain flared into the open, and Philip launched his "invincible" armada to escort Spanish troops from Flanders into England. The English navy engaged them as they entered the Channel and harassed them into the stormy North Sea. The rendezvous with Parma's army never occurred. Although his armada was largely destroyed, Philip nevertheless went on to plan a second attempt, and the English correspondingly planned an invasion of Portugal in support of Don Antonio of Crato, pretender to the throne. This latter attempt ended in failure, and the "war" with Spain continued for fourteen years.[112]

The Spanish Tragedy was so enormously popular that anyone who frequented the theatre would probably have seen it. The play begins with this solemn speech by the Ghost of Don Andrea:

> When this eternal substance of my soul
> Did live imprisoned in my wanton flesh,
> Each in their function serving other's need,
> I was a courtier in the Spanish court.

(1.1.1-4.)

The lines were burlesqued in Francis Beaumont's *The Knight of the Burning Pestle* where Rafe, a grocer's apprentice, improvises a death scene:

When I was mortal, this my costive corps
Did lap up figs and raisins in the Strand,
Where sitting I espied a lovely dame....

                                        (5.3.124-126)

As Beaumont's play was written about 1607, audiences would still have been able to pick up its echoes from *The Spanish Tragedy*.

In the play within the play in Shakespeare's *Dream*, when Pyramus discovers the body of Thisbe he cries out:

O wherefore, Nature, didst thou lions frame,
Since lion vile hath here deflowered my dear?
Which is—no, no—which was the fairest dame

                                        (5.1. 274-276)

—lines which might evoke Hieronymo's lament over the body of his son:

Alas, it is Horatio, my sweet son!
Oh no, but he that whilom was my son.

                                        (2.4.14-15)

Another line open to parody comes when Hieronymo discovers the body of his son hanging in the arbor. His entrance line is:

What outcries pluck me from my naked bed....

                                        (2.5.1)

Shakespeare echoes the line when Titania in *A Midsummer Night's Dream* is roused from her slumbers by the singing of Bottom the weaver:

What Angel wakes me from my flowery bed?

                                        (3.1.107)

When Shakespeare began writing plays and the chronology of his works are both matters of conjecture. It can usually be known when a play was printed, although that typically happened some time after the play was first performed. Sometimes there is a hint in the dialogue of a current event or excitement that would help in dating the play's writing. Allusions to topical events, however, are not entirely reliable in dating, because they could have been added at a later time to give an old play a new sparkle. Whole scenes might be inserted for the same reason. For example, Ben Jonson was paid to add several scenes to *The Spanish Tragedy.*

Students of the chronology of Shakespeare's plays agree in the main as to which plays were written early in his career and which ones came later, although they are by no means in agreement when they come to fine points and doubtful cases. They seem to agree that by the time Robert Greene attacked him in 1592, Shakespeare had written at least ten plays counting his possible collaboration on *King Edward III.* For a twenty-eight-year-old that is a surprising number, considering their scope. Except for *Two Gentlemen of Verona* and *The Comedy of Errors,* they are three-hour dramas with large casts. Shakespeare's output by 1592 is especially impressive when we consider its quality and variety: three comedies, one tragedy, and six histories. The three Henry VI plays when produced in practically uncut versions by the Oregon Shakespeare Festival in the 50's and 60's revealed an unexpected theatrical result. I was fortunate enough to take part in the festival productions of *Part III* in 1955 and *Part I* in 1964, and I directed *Part II* in 1965. Those performances attracted less than full houses, and the Festival has since resorted to producing heavily cut adaptations of the Henry VI plays. It is to be regretted, I think, that productions by other theatres have often adopted the same practice of cutting lines and roles as well as altering the sequence of scenes in Shakespeare's scripts.

Be that as it may, it is probable that many will agree that the dramatic skill displayed in Shakespeare's early works suggests that he may have written other plays—what we might call beginner's stuff—which have since disappeared. Certainly the plays that survived by being printed were both stage worthy and popular, but they could hardly have been the first ones he wrote. Beginner's luck doesn't seem a probable explanation. We are dealing with the work of a practiced and sophisticated playwright. And it is possible that some of the plays we have were revised and polished before they were published.

Of the plays we have written before 1592, most were history plays. Four were linked together in a continuous thread following the major events and important characters of the wars of the rival houses of Lancaster and York: the three parts of

King Henry VI and *King Richard III*. The challenge of threading so much material into a coherent fabric is one that few dramatists would have the audacity to take up or the understanding and skill to carry out. It is as if someone took on the American Civil War and told the story from the time of President Buchanan through General Grant in a series of plays reviewing the political and ethical issues of that great epoch in a fully articulated dramatic form.

During this same period in his career, Shakespeare worked in the same style on two other history plays: *King John* and *King Edward III*, which indicates his new kind of drama was popular. We must admit however, that this type of play has little appeal in the modern theatre. The reason may simply be that the names and events are unfamiliar to us and that we are not much interested in ancient dynastic squabbles. Shakespeare's early history plays are rather like newspapers; characters make the headlines for a while and then disappear. So when we look for a central figure to dominate and define the action, we discover that he or she just isn't there. The exception is found in *Richard III*, where that royal scoundrel seems to create and sustain the action. Whatever reservations we may have about these plays, scanty as the records are, it is clear that Shakespeare's success in his own theatre was immediate.

Greene's parody of a line from *Henry VI, Part III*, "Oh tiger's heart wrapp'd in a player's hide!" shows how popular that play was, or the hit would have gone unrecognized. And *Henry VI, Part I* stirred the excited praise of Thomas Nashe who described the effect of Shakespeare's treatment of Lord Talbot:

> [It would have] joyed brave Talbot, the terror of the French, to think that after he had lain two hundred years in his tomb he should triumph again on the stage, and have his bones new embalmed with the tears of ten thousand spectators at least (at several times) who in the tragedian that represents his person imagine they behold him fresh bleeding.[113]

Nashe's estimate of "ten thousand spectators at least" is supported in the records of performances given by Lord Strange's Men at The Rose Theatre from March to June in 1592, a season cut short by an outbreak of the plague. The play listed as "Harey the vj,"[*1] which I take to be *Henry VI, Part I*, was performed fourteen times; the play coming nearest to that record was the old, ever popular

---

[*1] vj = VI (edd.)

Spanish Tragedy, which had twelve performances. At the first performance of "*Harey vj*," when the price of admission was customarily doubled, the theatre receipts were a record, 3 pounds, 16 shillings, 8 pence. At the second performance three days later, another record of 3 pounds was set.[114]

It is often repeated without much evidence that the popularity of Shakespeare's history plays in his own time can be explained by an outburst of patriotism and pride following the destruction of the Spanish Armada and the evaporation of the threat of invasion. An interest in England's history was no doubt stimulated by this event. However, there is—with a few possible exceptions—very little in Shakespeare's history plays that could be called flag waving or some sort of idealization of the heroes of England's past. He handles the matter of history in a realistic, almost sardonic vein. His kings and nobles are a bunch of wrangling pirates, factious, devious, and cruel. When Shakespeare portrays an honest man in high place, like the Protector Humphrey of Gloucester in *Henry VI, Part II*, he also shows the good man's enemies setting him up for a fall. In a loyal and valiant soldier, like Lord Talbot in *Henry VI, Part I*, we see that politicians, envious of each other, allow him to be slaughtered on the field. In addition, when that virtuous and humble king, Henry VI, is depicted, we see that he is too naïve for this wicked world. The fascinating king who crowns the final play in the series, Richard III, is quite simply a monster able to have his way because so many supported him for their own ends.

In *Henry VI, Part I*, Shakespeare does his bit to denigrate the French, particularly Joan of Arc, the Dauphin, and to some extent, Margaret, the Amazon from France who later marries Henry VI. And there are digs at the French like Joan's jibe after she has persuaded Burgundy to break his alliance with the English, "Done like a Frenchman: turn, and turn again" [3.3.85]. But Shakespeare's ridicule of the French is not counter-balanced by an idealized picture of the English. They do not lose their French territories because of the Dauphin's dumb luck or Joan's witchcraft; rather they lose because the English are disloyal, rebellious, and factious.[115]

The stirring final speech in *King John* could be read as a brag, suiting the mood of an English audience after the Armada sank into its watery grave:

> This England never did, nor never shall,
> Lie at the proud foot of a conqueror,
> But when it first did help to wound itself.

Now these her princes are come home again,
Come the three corners of the world in arms,
And we shall shock them. Naught shall make us rue,
If England to itself do rest but true.

(*King John* 5.7.112-118)

However, that speech closes a play where the disastrous reign of John has been surveyed: his surrender of territories, his attempts at murder, his dismal submission to the Papal Legate, capped by a French army landing on his island. Instead of a note of cocky triumph, the speech is the moral of the piece: united we stand, divided we fall. Unity is hardly possible when the ruler is a wicked man surrounded by disaffected nobles. These history plays are serious, not playful. And if there are scenes that can only be played for a laugh, they reinforce the serious political and ethical issues the dramatist asks his audience to entertain.

However much attention Shakespeare gave the Muse of History during these years, the Comic Muse always dealt him her best cards. At the same time that he developed the history play, he worked up three comedies: *The Two Gentlemen of Verona*, *The Comedy of Errors*, and *The Taming of the Shrew*. They are, of course, quite unlike the histories, but each is also noticeably different from the others. If they could be called experiments, they yielded positive results that are still affecting. It is true that *Shrew* has been having a difficult time on stage recently. An assumption about the "role" of women, presumed to be expressed in the play, has brought the appropriateness of producing it in the modern theatre into question. *The Taming of the Shrew*, however, displays contrasting ways of courtship and marriage in the Elizabethan age. One way is to go about the business directly, without fancy talk and rituals; the other is to approach the business indirectly, to follow conventional forms while attempting to circumvent them. The fun comes in noticing that neither way works as might be expected.

The Two Gentlemen of Verona is a much different kind of comedy; indeed it is not like other Shakespearean plays and comes off badly if we imagine it is an early attempt to do something more ambitious. It is more like a vaudeville sketch with master and clown routines of banter and choplogic, and a slight, romantic story sketched largely through monologues and predictably complicated by headstrong fathers and rivalry between two suitors who were once best of friends. But it does illustrate a feature of Shakespeare's playwriting that is worth considering. I am thinking of the way he mixes modes and dramatic styles.

We are accustomed to hearing that a play should be either a tragedy or a comedy, although much of modern realistic drama contains comedic moments, and heroes who are not heroic. But the question of whether a comedy or a tragedy is intended is a less than helpful question to resolve considering a play by Shakespeare. They never quite fit a regular pattern.

In *The Two Gentlemen of Verona,* for example, when Valentine flees into the forest and becomes the leader of a gang of outlaws in the manner of Robin Hood, the playwright has switched from the mode of regular comedy to the mode of pastoral tragicomedy by changing his landscape from a court to a forest and his characters from city folk to rustics. Following the conventions of a pastoral setting, the attempted rape of Sylvia is interrupted at the last moment, and Proteus, upon his repentance, is immediately forgiven. Shakespeare is seldom a fastidious or consistent writer. Apparently an Elizabethan audience was more willing than we are to go along with whatever works.

In *The Comedy of Errors,* however, the switch in modes is not quite so noticeable. Here Shakespeare has reworked the classical farce of twins mistaken for each other and framed it with material from the medieval romance of Apollonius of Tyre. Despite the fact that both stories are tales of separation and reunion, they remain incongruous if we are looking for a consistency of mode. The dominant farce material seems to survive whatever outrageous gimmicks are tossed in to enhance its absurd elements. Shakespeare is so inventive in this comedy that he stimulates this quality in actors and producers who work on it. We see two sets of twins separated at birth strolling about town and not bumping into each other until after the whole town is confused, angry, and at loggerheads. This situation is not written off as absurd because the audience is in on the trick and quite willing to be part of the practical joke as long as the playwright can keep coming up with new characters to entangle in the errors. When the boiling point is reached, the resolution is beautifully managed as the twins finally are on stage together, and the father and mother of the twins, also separated at the birth of the sons, are reunited, and the whole cast on stage is lost in the wonder of their bewilderment.

Finally about the same time, perhaps even during the same year Shakespeare wrote *Errors,* he came up with a tragedy, *Titus Andronicus.* A work in such contrast to the comedy, so full of inventive, extravagant, and appalling situations that some readers have wished the tragedy had not been written by the gentle Shakespeare idolized by their teachers. He was, the critic of *Titus* could say, a poet, not a contriver of monstrous spectacles. The truth is that he did write most of *Titus*, although George Peele has been credited with the opening scenes. [116] Titus was as popular as *The Spanish Tragedy*. In 1614 Ben Jonson poked fun at the continued popularity of those two old-fashioned plays by having one of his characters say: ·

> He that will swear *Jeronimo* [*The Spanish Tragedy*] or *Andronicus* are the best plays yet, shall pass … here as a man whose judgment shows it is constant, and hath stood still these five and twenty or thirty years.[117]

Titus is not all that different from the history plays. If we count the number of severed heads paraded or tossed across the stage in them or the atrocities of child murder, bloody napkins, or Cade's rebellion, *Titus* won't seem very different.

The history plays are tragic dramas in many respects. There are, however, a few conventions that seem to have been followed to make them distinct. In the history play the incidents are taken from English history with a few adjustments of fact to make the flow of history fit the stage. They tend to be realistic and follow a theme exploring political matters rather than the fate of a dominating figure. In Shakespeare's tragedies, on the other hand, the incidents are taken from legend and ancient history, usually centering on a heroic figure. Somewhat greater liberties are taken with the traditional materials to intensify the passions and to get out of the ordinary world into a place of extraordinary suffering and violence. There is pleasure in tragedy, not every kind of pleasure, but a pleasure peculiar to it, as Aristotle suggests. *Titus Andronicus* is, I think, straight tragedy. There is almost no comic by-play.

The play moves with unrelenting energy from one horror to the next, human sacrifice, rape, chopped off hands and arms, and a cannibal feast. Despite that, it is a play where the tragic hero Titus is a marvelous and contradictory figure resembling Lear. For Titus is as childish as brutal, as wrong-headed as devoted, destroyed by his love of his daughter as much as by his terrible drive toward revenge. Unexpectedly the driving emotion of the play emerges from deep feelings of familial love among the characters, both the Romans and their Gothic enemies.

Titus Andronicus has often been excused as the early work of an exuberant and inexperienced playwright who didn't quite know what he was doing. One who had all the right instincts, but lacked skill. It could just as well be said that he knew exactly what he was doing, did it very well and, unwilling and uninterested in repeating himself, went on to invent what we know as Shakespearean tragedy, a somewhat different sort of thing.

One of the pleasures in reading Shakespeare's plays is to notice how consistently he enhanced or reinvented the forms of drama he used. If he studied Plautus and Seneca in school, he bettered their models in *The Comedy of Errors* and *Titus Andronicus*, especially in making them fit the theatre he worked in. His history plays were yet another distinct species of drama. But those forms of drama, so carefully differentiated as he began work as a playwright, were melded as his career progressed. The modes of both comedy and tragedy are more fully integrated into historical drama. Tragedy mixed with comedy evolved into the romances or tragicomedies that were his final works. There are powerful arguments to be made in praise of his hybrid dramas, which make nonsense of the conventional theory that a play should be either a tragedy or a comedy.

CHAPTER 5

SIR JOHN OLDCASTLE
1592–1599

Note as an instance, this one perilous fray,
What factions might have grown on either part?
To the destruction of the King and realm,
Yet, in my conscience, Sir John Oldcastle
Innocent of it, only his name was used.

(Sir John Oldcastle 1.1.127-130)

ALTHOUGH we look back on the destruction of the Spanish Armada as a decisive moment in history, Englishmen of the time could not feel that danger had passed. Nor was Philip II about to give up on the "Enterprise of England." Expecting a second invasion attempt, the government of Elizabeth tried to forestall the threat by a variety of measures. Spanish ports and shipping were raided, troops were sent to try to clear the French and Flemish coasts of Spanish control, and repressive actions against suspected Catholic sympathizers at home were intensified.

Commissioners in the various counties were appointed to examine and report the names of all persons who were shirking the obligation to attend their parish church, a sign of recusancy, that is, a refusal to accept the authority of the national church. The recusancy returns for Warwickshire in 1592 included the name of John Shakespeare. His answer was that he did not go to church for fear of being arrested for debt, an excuse that has never seemed very plausible.[118] Being on the list would put him in fear of having his house searched. Perhaps that is when he hid the "Spiritual Testament" in the rafters of his house (see Chapter 3). In any case his excuse seems to have been plausible to officials in

Stratford, or they pretended it was. As far as we know nothing more was done about it. Perhaps officials hesitated to look too closely into the affairs of such a prominent townsman.

In crowded London town the situation was altogether different. Being closer to areas of the coast where Spanish troops might land and be welcomed ashore by underground supporters, the Lord Mayor and Aldermen, who had no regular police force, were fearful of any large gathering of people. Under this cloud of fear and paranoia, theatrical enterprise in England was bound to be affected. The London Council of Aldermen was never very hospitable to performances on public stages, because they encouraged idleness in workers and apprentices, and the crowds assembled for afternoon performances sometimes became unruly. So the city authorities were consistently on the look out for an excuse to close the theatres. And for all practical purposes they had banned public performances inside the city limits. The Rose Theatre, which was the big attraction in the 1590's, was located in the suburb of Southwark, on the south bank of the Thames and outside the usual control of London officials. On June 11, 1592, a crowd protesting the arrest of an apprentice rioted near the site of the theatre. As Midsummer Eve was approaching, often an occasion for unruly gatherings, the Queen's Privy Council was persuaded to forbid public performances in London and the suburbs until Michaelmas on September 29. However, when that time came around, the city council had an even better reason to close down the theatres. An outbreak of the bubonic plague continued the prohibition indefinitely. One way to break the spread of infection was to forbid all public assemblies except church services. The belief that theatrical performances were sinful was so strongly held in some circles that a sermon preached at Paul's Cross included this seemingly logical statement: "the cause of plagues is sin … and the cause of sin are plays: therefore the cause of plagues are plays."[119] The severity of the plague brought the anti-theatrical prejudice into full swing. The playing companies were forced to disperse or go on the road.

Public playing in London was resumed briefly in January 1593, but was prohibited again in February when the plague returned. The plague did not abate until June of the following year, 1594, resulting in an almost complete interruption of performances in London and the suburbs for two years. Possibly the players who went on tour were able to sharpen their acting skills, but they did not return richer. Country towns could not have been all that eager to entertain visitors from an infected city.

There were other matters that made the London theatre world of 1593 a discouraging place. One problem developed from the hostility London craftsmen felt toward foreign Protestant refugees who came to escape persecution as the Catholic armies extended their control over larger areas of the continent. English official policy was to welcome the refugees, but as these "strangers" began practicing their crafts and trades in London, the native English felt increasingly hostile to them. Just as this issue became a matter of concern to the government, William Shakespeare finished working on a play for Lord Strange's men on the life of Sir Thomas More.[120] In it he wrote a sequence showing how More succeeded in dispersing a mob about to attack French tradesmen in London, an event that became known as the "Evil May Day" riot of 1517. The play was never printed, but the manuscript survives and on the cover written in large letters was a note from the censor, Edmund Tilney, Master of the Revels, who ordered the players on their peril to cut the riot scene, to report it briefly, but not to show it.[121]

There is nothing in the riot scene that would ordinarily stir up an audience to take to the streets, but in this instance the scene came too close to echoing what was happening at the moment the play was submitted to the censor. Tilney's order to cut or rewrite the scene was in response to a series of libels posted in various parts of the city warning strangers to get out of the country or face violence from a mob of apprentices. The authorities felt they had to defuse a dangerous situation. Censoring the play may have seemed helpful, but their real task was to find out who wrote and who posted the libels. In the hunt for clues, various places were searched including the lodging of Thomas Kyd, author of the famous *Spanish Tragedy*.

What the searchers found, shuffled among the papers on Kyd's writing table, was a shocking series of notes outlining arguments against the divinity of Christ. Arrested on May 12th and called before the Privy Council to answer the dangerous charge of atheism, Kyd was thrown in prison and probably tortured for information. Kyd made the excuse that he had once shared lodging with Christopher Marlowe and that the papers were not his but Marlowe's. If Kyd made that up, his story would still have seemed plausible. Marlowe, as well as being the author of brilliant plays filled with magic and marvels and flavored with a dash of sardonic and cruel humor, had a reputation for expressing a preference for boys, tobacco, and opinions that in his day were publicly unacceptable. Some were disturbing, some skeptical, and some simply annoying. Investigators were already on to Marlowe's case. One of the most hostile libels against the strangers was posted at the Dutch Church on May 4th. It was a doggerel poem signed "Tamburlaine," the name of the hero of Marlowe's two-part play, and included allusions to his *The Jew of Malta* and *The Massacre at Paris*. Marlowe was arrested, brought before the Council on May 18th and then, instead of being put in prison, as was done with Kyd, was let go and ordered to appear when summoned. Perhaps the investigators let him go to watch his movements, or perhaps Marlowe was given preferential treatment as a University graduate. Marlowe went out of town, no doubt to escape the plague. By the end of the month, and before any charges were heard, he was killed in Deptford. He had been dining with companions, and after supper, according to the coroner's report, there was a quarrel about paying the "reckoning," or bill. In a scuffle, Marlowe died from a dagger thrust in his brain. His attacker pleaded self-defense.

The circumstances suggest that there is a real detective story here. This is not the place to reveal more of Marlowe's demise, a story that has been recently treated by David Riggs and earlier by Charles Nicholl.[122] We might note in passing, however, that one scholar had built a case to demonstrate that Marlowe was not killed, but kidnapped to a secret castle abroad where he wrote all the plays now assigned to Shakespeare! [123] There are, however, three interesting threads to our story. One is that the notes found shuffled among Kyd's papers were heretical, although not exactly original with Marlowe since they were copied from a Unitarian tract in circulation for over forty years. Thread number two is that Thomas Kyd died within the year, possibly from being tortured in prison. Finally, thread number three has to do with the fate of Shakespeare's play about Thomas More. Since the theatres were closed, the play had to be set aside. A decade later, when the fear of riots against strangers had evaporated, other writers revised it for a new production. The riot scene was retained and seems to be the only part remaining from Shakespeare's earlier work.

After the deaths of Greene, Marlowe, and Kyd, the London theatre would certainly need the work of Shakespeare more than ever, but the ban on performances made writing and rehearsing new plays a pointless exercise. Shakespeare set his work as playwright aside. The actors, except those who tried their luck touring to towns untouched by the plague, had to decide whether to wait for better times or find other things to do. Apparently Shakespeare did not go on tour. His name does not appear in any surviving documents granting companies and their chief members license to travel. And we can be pretty sure that he took an enforced vacation to write two narrative poems: *Venus and Adonis* and *The Rape of Lucrece*. He greatly enlarged the slim story materials from Ovid and Livy with a virtuoso display of rhetorical and poetic devices. He was, I think, showing off. The stories were very well known, as is evidenced not only by the number of versions or allusions to the stories made by other writers, but also in the number of pictures by painters who created their versions of Venus trying to get Adonis onto her saddle, or of Lucrece, weeping tears and looking toward the heavens, pointing a dagger to her naked breast.

Shakespeare's *Venus and Adonis* was a great success. And, although it is not exactly popular today, it is deliciously erotic, nicely skirting short of being obscene. No wonder some students at Cambridge had fun characterizing a Shakespearean enthusiast by having him exclaim in a Christmas revel:

> O sweet Master Shakespeare! I'll have his picture in my study at the court…. Let this duncified world esteem of Spencer and Chaucer, I'll worship sweet Master Shakespeare, and to honor him will lav his *Venus and Adonis* under my pillow.[124]

Venus and Adonis was more than a student favorite; mature women and men must have liked it too, for it was reprinted sixteen times in the 17th century, more often than any work by Shakespeare at that time[125].

Shakespeare's *Lucrece* was nearly as successful, being reprinted eight times. Writing about 1600, Gabriel Harvey noted:

> The younger sort takes much delight in Shakespeare's *Venus & Adonis*: but his *Lucrece*, & his tragedy of *Hamlet, Prince of Denmark*, have it in them, to please the wiser sort."[126]

Harvey had in mind a real difference. In *Lucrece,* Shakespeare displays the same rhetorical and versifying skills as in *Venus* but adds a world of moral tirades, reflections, and sentiments.

However successful the two poems may have been for the printers and booksellers, Shakespeare's chance to enhance his income as well as his reputation lay in the expectation of a reward and possibly service from a rich patron. As Jonathan Bate has written, *Venus* and *Lucrece* "had made their author into a modern reincarnation of Ovid, someone who would have been an addition to any sophisticated and ostentatious nobleman's coterie."[127] With dedications to the right man, the poet might win a place in a noble retinue. In this regard, Shakespeare seemed to have picked a winner. *Venus and Adonis*, printed in the spring of 1593 was dedicated: "To the Right Honourable Henry Wriothesley, Earl of Southampton, and Baron Titchfield." Wriothesley—his name was pronounced either "Risley" or "Rosely"—inherited the Earldom when eight years old on the death of his father, and as a minor became the ward of William Cecil, Lord Burghley, the Queen's principal secretary. In 1592 Southampton was about to come of age and would assume control of large and wealthy estates belonging to the earldom. The young Earl found *Venus and Adonis* very much to his taste and had given a welcome reward to the new poet. Shakespeare, it could be said, returned the compliment the next year in presenting *The Rape of Lucrece* to Southampton. The words of his dedication, compared to the one written for *Venus and Adonis*, suggest that Shakespeare was delighted with his patron. It begins, "The love I dedicate to your Lordship is without end"; and continues in phrases expressing complete devotion.

There are reasons to believe the relationship between Shakespeare and Southampton was, however, more complicated than we can infer from the dedications. Professor Akrigg, in a thoroughly researched biography of Southampton, begins his exploration of the relationship by frankly admitting, "We have no evidence as to when, where, or under what circumstances William Shakespeare first met the Earl of Southampton."[128] Or, we could add, any evidence that they ever did meet. But of course they did. It is unlikely that a messenger was simply sent round with a note of thanks and a purse. Having come of age and into his own, Southampton was out to cut a figure in the world, to win a following among poets and artisans, as well as a place among soldiers and courtiers. He would have sent for the poet or met him when he came to his London residence to present the first copy.

About the same time he was working on *Venus* and *Lucrece*, Shakespeare began writing his sonnets. There are good reasons to regard some of them as autobiographical, rather than simply as exercises in imaginative writing, and to regard some of them as a response to a close relationship to Southampton.[129] For one thing, the sonnets go up and down the scale between joy and sorrow, ranging from exalted praise to caustic reprimand, from preamble to epilogue. Such a variety of emotions rings true to experience, unlike the usual songs of one in love about being in love. Perhaps the overriding consideration for their autobiographical relevance is that the sonnets imply an unconventional story involving three people, we might say a love triangle.

Writing sonnets became something of a craze or game among English poets in the early 1590's. Anyone who wanted to try a hand at making verses tried their luck with sonnets or similar verse forms. Very often they were published in a sequence that implied the course of a courtship or an affair ending in marriage as in the case of Spenser, or in disappointment as in the case of Sidney. These sequences are not controlled by a story told in chronological order; there are too many pauses for reflection and too many variations on repeated themes. There is, however, an implied and traceable story-outline.

Shakespeare's sonnets tell a story which strikes me as an oddity. The poet, or the speaker of the sonnets, is a man devoted to a younger man of higher rank whom he idolizes and praises, principally for his youthful beauty. There are two persons that come between them: a "rival poet" who also writes in praise of the beloved boy and a "dark lady," the poet's mistress who also seduces or is seduced by the young man. The odd part comes when the poet finds this out and talks himself into forgiving the man he loves [Sonnet 42].

Generally speaking, the sonnets were arranged for printing in two sections: in the first 126 sonnets the poet writes to or about a young man. There may have been several young men who momentarily infatuated the poet and inspired him to write poems on the same themes, although the poems were printed in a sequence that implies the same young man inspired them all. Many of them reflect the experience of being in love; others are meditations on mortality and the unceasing movement of time. The second group, comprising twenty-seven sonnets, is about—but not to—the poet's mistress, whom he comes to despise. She could hardly take pleasure in them. They are insulting and bitter poems. Perhaps the poet is angry with himself for finding his mistress as faithless as he himself was to his wife back in Stratford.

There is no reason to suppose the love for the young man was "Platonic." Clearly the poems profess an erotic fascination and love for the young man the poet calls "my lovely boy" [Sonnet 126] and "the master mistress of my passion" [Sonnet 20]. Nothing is in the closet, except the names of the persons Shakespeare is writing about.

If the Sonnets are considered personal and autobiographical, a question is raised to which there seems to be no answer: "Who were these people mentioned in the sonnets?" As I have already suggested, the rival poet, the dark lady, and the lovely boy may have been conflations of several persons who figured in Shakespeare's emotional life. After all, he certainly began his sonnets in the early 1590's when he was making a bid for the patronage of the Earl of Southampton. It is also at the same time when he was writing *Venus* and *Lucrece* as well as the plays *Love's Labour's Lost, Romeo and Juliet, A Midsummer Night's Dream,* and *Richard II*, plays which display a special poetic fascination with rhyming dialogue and verse patterns. But, as far as we can tell, some of the sonnets could have been written as late as 1609, the year they were arranged for publication, long after Southampton could have had any close relationship with Shakespeare. To make the matter more confusing, when the sonnets were published, Thomas Thorpe, the printer, not the author, wrote a dedication to one "Mr. W. H." No one now knows whom those initials stand for. Perhaps someone Shakespeare never knew. It seems to me more than likely that other young men, and mistresses, and rivals may have driven Shakespeare to explore his feelings and write in a similar manner. The collection which seems to be about a single trio of people, is really about many.[130]

The ban on theatrical performances in London from 1592 to 1594 put so great a strain on the acting profession that the playing companies were practically broken up. There survives an interesting correspondence between Philip Henslowe, owner of The Rose Theatre and his son-in-law, Edward Alleyn, the famous actor, who was traveling with Lord Strange's Men when plague closed the London theatres. One of Henslowe's letters from London, September 1593, reports the plight of Pembroke's Men who went broke on the road:

> as for My Lord of Pembroke's which you desire to know where they be, they are all at home and have been this five or six weeks for they can not save their charges with travel as I hear and were fain to pawn their apparel.[131]

From this we should not infer that Pembroke's Men were a second-rate company. It simply suggests that touring provincial towns did not pay enough.

While the London theatres were closed and Shakespeare was bidding for service with the Earl of Southampton, the Earl of Derby died and in due course the Earldom passed to his son, Ferdinando Stanley, who earlier had the title of Lord Strange and was the patron of the celebrated company that Alleyn was leading on tour. Thus his company took his new title as the Earl of Derby's Men. Unfortunately Ferdinando Stanley was Earl of Derby very briefly. Within the year he died unexpectedly. And not without suspicion of foul play.

The Stanley family was much in favor with the house of Tudor. In his play, *Richard III*, Shakespeare shows young George Stanley held hostage by Richard and shows George's father, Lord Stanley, at the final battle handing the crown to Henry Tudor, who was, incidentally, a child of his second wife, Lady Margaret of Beaufort. Henry Tudor became King Henry VII. Thus Lord Stanley was made the first Earl of Derby and wealthy as well. Further, Ferdinando Stanley's mother, Lady Margaret Clifford, was a descendant of Henry VII, which made the new Earl a possible candidate for the throne if Elizabeth should die. That may explain as well why Shakespeare has a Lord Clifford and his son play such an important part in the Henry VI plays as partisans of the house of Lancaster. However much in favor with Elizabeth the Earls of Derby may have been, there were other members of the Stanley family who needed wary watching. The most notorious was Sir William Stanley, who in 1587, while serving in Holland under Leicester, betrayed the town of Deventer and took his regiment over to the Spanish side.

In 1593 Sir William Stanley sent another self-exiled Catholic on a dangerous mission to Ferdinando Stanley, the new Earl of Derby, to sound him out on no less a question than this: if Elizabeth should die, would he allow his claim to the throne to be put forward? The assumption in back of the question was that he might grant his Catholic subjects more freedom to practice their religion. Derby immediately reported this to the Privy Council. The unfortunate messenger was executed for high treason. The unexpected death of the Earl followed. Some, then and now, who believe Elizabeth's ministers were monsters entertain the idea that Derby was poisoned to remove him as a claimant whose followers might cause trouble; others who believe that Jesuits and Spaniards were monsters entertain the idea that he was poisoned for having denounced their messenger.[132]

Returning to the plight of the London acting companies, it is striking to notice that Shakespeare had some connection with three companies of that time. The title page of his play *Titus Andronicus,* printed in 1594, reads:

The Most Lamentable Roman Tragedy of Titus Andronicus: As it was
Played by the Right Honorable the Earl of Derby, Earl of Pembroke, and
Earl of Sussex their Servants.

This outlines a series of companies that performed the play and probably
indicates Shakespeare's acting career as well, from Lord Strange's—there by their
new title of Derby—to the Earl of Pembroke's, and finally to the Earl of Sussex's.
All three companies were in trouble.

Sussex's Men were also on tour during plague time, but as the plague relaxed
its grip on London, they were able to mount a brief run of performances in
February of 1593. At that time *Titus* was their big hit. Unfortunately the plague
returned, and the London theatres were again shut down. By the time the theatres
were reopened, the acting companies were in such disarray that something
had to be done to get the enterprise going again. In May of 1594, The Lord
Chamberlain, Henry Carey, Lord Hunsdon, and The Lord Admiral, Charles
Howard, each a member of the Privy Council, decided to grant patents to players
recruited from the remnants of the old companies. The new arrangement placed
Edward Alleyn as lead player of the Admiral's Men, presumably to perform in
The Rose Theatre owned by Alleyn's father-in-law Philip Henslowe, and Richard
Burbage as lead player of the Chamberlain's Men, presumably to perform in The
Theatre owned by his father James Burbage. This arrangement may have been
worked out to assure the theatre owners, Henslowe and Burbage, of the income
to maintain their theatres, as they were in some sense respectively servants of the
Lord Admiral and the Lord Chamberlain.

The arrangement was a piece of good fortune for the newly organized
companies. For both enjoyed the protection of Lords on the Privy Council who
could provide the opportunity to give performances at court during the Christmas
season, the advantage of limited competition, and the use of a playhouse for
public performances with some assurance of not being arbitrarily closed by the
Lord Mayor and Aldermen of the City.[133]

Shakespeare was one of the original members of the Lord Chamberlain's
Men. The company first appeared at court with two plays as part of the Christmas
festivities in 1594. The payees for those performances were Richard Burbage,
the lead player, Will Kemp, the chief comic, and William Shakespeare. This is
some indication that Shakespeare had a special standing in that company. Gerald

Eades Bentley, in his survey of the duties of sharers, points out that one of them must have acted as a sort of "manager" who actually kept track of company funds, signed for receipts, and saw to it that payments were made according to agreements made by the sharers as a body.[134] At that time Shakespeare was probably performing some of those managerial functions, or he would not have signed as a receiver of the reward for court performances along with Burbage and Kemp.

Although the court records do not list the plays they presented at court on that occasion, it is likely that some old plays were refurbished, since the new company scarcely had time to be up and running, let alone rehearse new scripts.

Shakespeare's plays written shortly after public playing resumed were probably *Love's Labour's Lost*, *A Midsummer Night's Dream*, *Romeo and Juliet*, and *The Merchant of Venice*. *Love's Labour's Lost* was not printed until 1598 and the title page announced that it was presented before Queen Elizabeth "this last Christmas" and "Newly corrected and augmented by W. Shakespeare." If the printer had copy of a revised play as shown at court, of course he would advertise it; in this case he felt there was also some advantage in using Shakespeare's name. The printings of *Venus and Adonis* and *The Rape of Lucrece* had his name on the title page. Although other plays of his were already in print, this was the first time a printer used Shakespeare's name to help sell a play. It should be pointed out that it was in the company's interest to see their plays in print. It was simply a form of publicity. That explains why the producing company was usually named in the title page of a printed play, although the author was seldom mentioned. It has often been said that having a play in print would bring it into the public domain which would allow rival companies to produce it as well. Peter Blayney has argued convincingly that whether a play got into print was a decision that had to be made by a publisher, not by a company or a playwright.[135] Although we can't know when *Love's Labour's Lost* was first presented, nor to what extent it was "corrected and augmented"—presumably to bring it up to date—we can nonetheless guess it was popular enough to stay in the repertory for more than one season. There was even a performance before Queen Anne during the Christmas season of 1604, possibly ten years after the play was first produced.

As arrangements were being set up for that performance, Burbage is reported to have touted the play by saying

> there is no new play that the Queen hath not seen, but they [the players] have revived an old one, called *Love's Labour's Lost*, which for wit and mirth … will please her exceedingly.[136]

Love's Labour's Lost has a pastoral setting, and the story develops at a leisurely pace around a highly artificial arrangement of incidents satirizing current fashions, affectations, fruitless learning, and courtship, rather than using a strong sequence of incidents driven by a suspenseful plot. It mixes country folk and aristocrats in the traditional manner of pastoral. Another mark of the pastoral mode is the use of a variety of verse forms, songs, sonnets, and rhyming dialogue. There are in addition—and here is where topicality presents problems—characters that seem to be caricatures of contemporaries as in the comedies of Gilbert and Sullivan or Aristophanes. There have been attempts by various scholars to demonstrate that the roles of Don Armado, Holofernes, Nathaniel, Moth, and Costard are takeoffs on people the original audiences would easily recognize. But all have been no more successful in pinning labels here than in identifying who was the lovely boy, or the dark lady, or the rival poet of Shakespeare's sonnets. Sir Walter Raleigh, George Chapman, Antonio Perez, and Gervase Markham have all been argued as the model for Don Armado, although the original is the braggart soldier from classical comedy.[137] The King of Navarre and his circle of courtiers who begin the play pledging themselves to an austere program of studies, may be a spoof of the Earl of Essex and his companions, or of Sir Walter Raleigh and his so-called School of Night, a group devoted to esoteric studies. Perhaps each group is a target at one moment or another of the comedy.

Despite the fact that scholars today can't build a convincing case as to who or what is being ridiculed, modern audiences, even without explanatory footnotes, find the play lively, interesting, and fun. My guess is that this kind of comedy depends as much on the audience sensing the playfulness of the performance as on their recognizing all the targets of the lampoon. Certainly Shakespeare's characters here are both ridiculous and appealing.

Although the topicality of *Love's Labour's Lost* can be overlooked, it would be a mistake not to consider the way contemporary events were worked into the fabric of *The Merchant of Venice*. The memorable character is not Antonio, the merchant, but Shylock, the Jewish moneylender. Shakespeare's play imitates in several ways Christopher Marlowe's old play *The Jew of Malta*, written before the London theatres were closed and recently revived to feed interest in a sensational treason trial.

In 1592, Don Antonio, a claimant to the throne of Portugal, came to London hoping to get English support against their common enemy, Philip II of Spain. At the time Roderigo Lopez, a converted Jewish refugee from Portugal, had become physician to Queen Elizabeth. The Earl of Essex denounced him as a traitor who sought to poison both Don Antonio and Queen Elizabeth. Lopez was tried in February of 1594 and executed in June.[138] Almost as soon as the news broke, Marlowe's old play *The Jew of Malta* was re-staged by the Lord Admiral's Men. It was probably reworked in places to reinforce the cruel and anti-social character of the starring role, a fabulously wealthy Jewish merchant. He is an entertaining monster, although the grotesque anti-Semitism of the play—a quality that made it timely and popular then—would be difficult for modern sensibilities to accept.

The Lord Chamberlain's Men were not going to allow the rival company to get all the advantage of public interest in a sensational trial. It was in these circumstances that Shakespeare wrote *The Merchant of Venice*. There is much evidence that rivalry between the two companies played an important part in the decisions they made about the kind of plays they wanted in their repertory. Like modern film and television producers, they noticed what was drawing the crowds and tried to find something similar to attract viewers. If one company had success with a play about Richard III, or a lurid revenge tragedy, or a romance of adventure in exotic places, the other company would come up with one too. They didn't so much strike out on their own to find new material as they followed the lead to where the money was.[139]

Incidents in Marlowe's *Jew of Malta* were certainly imitated by Shakespeare as he wrote out his version of a folktale of a bond carrying the penalty of a pound of flesh as a forfeit. Shylock, Shakespeare's Jew of Venice, like Barabas, Marlowe's Jew of Malta, is an alien in his own town; he is resentful and secretly plots to damage or destroy his Christian neighbors. He has a daughter who becomes a Christian. Shylock has asides fashioned out of the same sharp, sardonic humor. However, in contrast to the Jew of Malta, Shylock is not entirely devilish; we can't laugh off his cry for revenge, because we are made to sympathize with his resentment. And if, as I would maintain, Shakespeare's play is less powerful than

Marlowe's, its anti-Semitic bias is perhaps more disturbing, because the story of the pound of flesh is interwoven with a romantic tale of how a spendthrift aristocrat, a very unlikely pretty boy, manages to solve a riddle to win the hand of a fabulously rich heiress. She is a very good girl, but a very unlikely student of the law, yet she manages to untie a legal knot to save the bosom friend of her lover from the hands of the cruel Jew. We want to sympathize with the lovers, but are disturbed by the desolate figure of Shylock at the end of Act Four.

There are other features of Marlowe's play that Shakespeare adopted, such as the moment when the Jew's daughter filches money from a nunnery and throws it down to her father from "above," that is, from a balcony [2.1]. In *The Merchant of Venice*, the Jew's daughter greets her Christian lover from a balcony and then steals money from her father before she elopes with her lover [2.6].

Scenes resorting to the use of a balcony for a meeting of lovers are quite common in Elizabethan drama. Such moments would almost inevitably have a touch of clandestine romance because, according to the culture of the times, the chance for them to meet without supervision would seldom occur. They might meet by accident at a dance, as Romeo and Juliet did, or be formally introduced in the course of marriage negotiations, but using a balcony was almost the only way lovers would have of meeting privately to arrange an assignation or an elopement. It is not surprising that many playwrights used a balcony scene to move love stories along. Artists illustrating *Romeo and Juliet* use the balcony scene more than any other to recall the emotional impact of the play. The scene is skillfully placed, i.e., surrounded by elements that bring out its luster. Like a pearl placed on black velvet, the love story develops against the background of a city made dangerous by outbreaks of violence from the idle followers of two feuding families. At night in a quiet moonlit orchard, the young lovers are gradually lifted upward in a sweet swell of feeling, expressed so exquisitely we wish the scene would never end. Shakespeare's balcony scene in *Romeo and Juliet* is so memorable, however, that it would be easy to suppose Shakespeare was the first to write such scenes.

There is, of course, more to the play. The balcony scene is only one of many breakthroughs that Shakespeare made as a dramatist in writing *Romeo and Juliet*. It is at heart a domestic tragedy, one dealing with the lives and loves of a private family rather than with tragic doings among kings and queens. In accord with the nature of that kind of story, there is a comic side in nearly all the roles. Romeo's name has become synonymous with a first time lover who suffers the emotional turmoil of despised love, followed by the reckless joy of being loved, and then by the violent despair of knowing he cannot realize his dream. The pattern is so recognizable that it becomes amusing until his reckless violence raises a deeper concern. On the other hand, Juliet is steady in her devotion. The principle of contrast operates all through the cast of characters, just as the fighting in the streets by idle young men is a foil to the lovers' meetings. The lovers are given contrasting confidants: Juliet's nurse, a garrulous chatterbox, is set against Friar Lawrence, whose ineffectual wisdom no one is prepared to recognize. The brawlers Mercutio and Tybalt are both swordsmen, but one is a witty daredevil and the other a humorless hothead. Juliet's father, warm, sympathetic, then outrageously angry with his daughter, is quite the opposite of her mother, proper, cold, and withdrawn.

Brilliant as all this is, it is easy to find fault with the improbabilities of the play. We tend to think that people have a right to love, marry, and separate to suit themselves. If the family objects, too bad for them. So it seems rather arbitrary and irrational that the secret marriage of Romeo and Juliet eventually leads to their double suicide. However, it is also easy to imagine the world Shakespeare is picturing. Children were expected to follow the wishes of their parents. Marriage involved the whole family and could not be regulated by the whims of inexperienced children. No doubt some of the appeal of the play for Shakespeare's audience was that it is a fantasy response to wishful thinking. The strict rules that kept boys and girls separated until a marriage was arranged provide a foreboding excitement to the story. The courtship pursued outside the conventions of the time might even have made the play shocking.

An intriguing comparison can be made by noting that Shakespeare wrote *A Midsummer Night's Dream* very close to the time he wrote *Romeo and Juliet*. One point of comparison is that both plays treat love as madness. In *Dream* the lovers are made wacky, first by love and then by a magic spell, one being a kind of metaphor for the other. In *Romeo,* madness makes the lovers desperate and destructive. Another comparison is that both plays tell a story of secret lovers driven to suicide by a chain of coincidences. In *Dream*, this story comes into sharp focus only in the final scene when Ovid's "Pyramus and Thisbe" is burlesqued in a play-within-the-play staged as part of a wedding celebration. These comparisons invite us to speculate on whether *Romeo* or *Dream* displays the finer dramatic technique. From the point of view of inventing a variety of speech to suit varied speakers, both plays display a masterful control. In *Dream* there is a special elegance in the rhyming dialogue, fine tuned to suit the greater variety of character types: the fairies, the working men, the lovers, and the nobles, each has its own style of language.

Another interesting line of speculation develops when we notice that Shakespeare is making fun of his own profession as well as the characters he presents. His company was created by the Lord Chamberlain to entertain distinguished visitors, to provide entertainment at court during the Christmas season and on other ceremonial occasions such as weddings. In *Dream*, the play-within-the-play is performed to celebrate the wedding of the Duke. This has led to speculation that Shakespeare may have been commissioned to write *Dream* for some aristocratic wedding. That could be, although the play fits the repertory of public theatre just as well, and no one has found strong evidence for a particular wedding the play was designed to decorate.

Many parts of *Dream* are treated in a mock-heroic vein. The lead characters have the names of ancient Athenians, but they seem all to come out of an English country village. The warrior Theseus is more like a lord of the manor than an ancient hero; Hippolyta, the warrior Queen of the Amazons, is a lady solicitous for the welfare of the villagers; the fairy king and queen, Oberon and Titania and their retinue are diminutive creatures, not the powerful figures of pagan mythology they are named for. Indeed, some modern directors and critics notice this and take *Dream* to be a play about sexual torment, as much as about giddy love. Shakespeare allows us to have it both ways.

In 1596, Shakespeare's eleven-year-old son, Hamnet, died. He was buried on August 11th, and that is all we know about that sad event. Shakespeare was living in London and could only have visited Stratford and his family irregularly considering the demands of his work as producer, player, and playwright. So the sad news of the death of his son may have been quite unexpected. It would have been shocking in any case, because it meant he had lost a male heir and was not likely to have another. His wife was nearly forty years old, and their marriage could not have been a close one.

There is an irony in that two months after the boy was buried, a grant of arms was finally made to John Shakespeare who applied nearly twenty years earlier when he was entitled to it for his service as the High Bailiff of Stratford.

Thus he was no longer a yeoman, but a gentleman whose arms and title could be passed on to his son, William.[140] In that society where the obligations of rank were more strictly observed and the obligation to keep up position was most keenly felt, Shakespeare's next move was to live up to his rank.

Early in 1597 he purchased a great house in Stratford, called New Place, on the corner of Chapel Street and Chapel Lane. Several wings, presumably servant quarters, faced the street and surrounded a small courtyard. Beyond that lay the main house and a large garden. Although the house was in disrepair and probably was bought at a bargain, Shakespeare repaired it and had it made into a showplace.[141] It seems likely that he had the family arms carved over the doorway. During the Civil War in July 1643, Queen Henrietta Marie kept her court there for three days when she joined Prince Rupert's royalist forces. Unfortunately, a later owner, the Reverend Francis Gastrell, refusing to pay a new assessment for relief of the poor of Stratford or annoyed by the increasing curiosity of tourists, tore New Place down in 1759. Thus the only pictures we have are early 18th-century sketches.

Although it is not likely that Shakespeare could have spent more than passing visits to New Place in Stratford, his purchase of a large house is one of several indications that he was accumulating cash and looking for places to spend or invest it. The London theatre world of the late 1590's was, however, far from being in a settled state, and Shakespeare had a large financial interest in what was going on there. To get part of the picture, we have to realize that the large London playhouses, especially "The Theatre" and "The Rose," when playing to capacity could generate considerable wealth. And wealth breeds quarrels and lawsuits. One has only to look at the modern reconstruction of The Globe Theatre in London to sense how expensive it would have been to build the original playhouse. Certainly the men who financed construction could only have been willing to invest heavily in them because they knew there was money to be made in the enterprise. The records of Philip Henslowe, builder and owner of The Rose Playhouse, give a rather lavish picture. The Rose was built south of the Thames in Southwerk in an area called the Bankside. Henslowe's income as a theatre owner came from half of the money collected for admission to the galleries; the other half went to whatever company of players would be renting the theatre. The pennies collected for admission to the pit, the standing room area below the stage, went entirely to the players. It has been estimated that Henslowe's accounts show a landlord's income from rents and admissions was something like this:

> From an initial investment of some 500 pounds and an additional 100 pounds every five years or so in maintenance, a landlord's return from his playhouse in a moderately successful year might be 250 pounds. That was a weekly income of some 5 pounds. By statute, the wage of a skilled tradesman—a joiner, say, or a dyer—was fixed at 5 pounds *per annum*. In some years, Henslowe's playhouse would earn him over 400 pounds.[142]

With that kind of money at stake the theatre owners had to be sure the facilities they provided for spectators were spiffy, gorgeous, and impressive. To make money they had to do what they could to support an exciting program of plays and players.

In 1576 James Burbage, an actor with the Earl of Leicester's Men, built the first theatre in London, or to put it a better way, the first building designed especially for use as a playhouse. It was called "The Theatre" to suggest it was a reconstruction of a classical theatre as was described by Vitruvius, the ancient Roman architect.[143] It was built in a country setting north of the city walls in an area called Shoreditch. To finance it, Burbage went heavily into debt and took on John Brayne, his brother-in-law, as a partner, which generated a series of lawsuits and cross-suits over who owed what for ground rent, maintenance costs, and to repay the loans.

The most colorful squabble is recorded in testimony given in 1590 when Burbage and his sons, Cuthbert and Richard, attacked Robert Miles and Nicholas Bishop, who came with the now widowed Mistress Brayne to stand at the gallery entrances to collect her share of the admissions which she had been granted by court order:

> James Burbage "looking out at a window upon them," joined his wife in reviling them as a murdering knave and whore, and expressed his contempt for the order of Chancery; Cuthbert, who came home in the middle of the fray, backed him up; while Richard Burbage, the youngest son, snatched up a broom-staff, and as he afterwards boasted, paid John Miles his moiety [i.e. his share] with a beating.

He also threatened Nicholas Bishop, scornfully and disdainfully playing with this deponent's nose. James said at their next meeting his sons should provide pistols charged with powder and hemp seed and shoot them in the legs.[144]

Old man Burbage had similar quarrels with playing companies. However, his big problem developed because he had taken a twenty-year lease on the land where he built the Theatre. By 1596 when time drew near to negotiate a new lease, the landowner seemed unwilling to renew on the old terms. He may even have been refusing or delaying renewal so he could take possession of the playhouse once the ground lease expired, or perhaps he planned to develop several rental properties in the suburban area. Burbage may well have quoted Master Page in *The Merry Wives of Windsor*, "I have lost my edifice by mistaking the place where I erected it" [2.2.216-217].

However James Burbage was a resourceful man who managed to evade eviction through tedious attempts to negotiate a new lease. The Theatre stood vacant while that was going on. About the same time, February 1596, Burbage got a lease on the Parliament Chamber in an expensive residential district of London, the Blackfriars, so named because the district belonged to the Dominican order before the Reformation. Burbage immediately started to convert the chamber into an indoor playhouse that could take the place of his outdoor theatre. Unfortunately when word got about of what he was doing, the inhabitants of that fashionable district objected to such an intrusion in their quiet neighborhood and persuaded the Privy Council to forbid the opening of a common playhouse in the Blackfriars.[145] Before anything could be done about that, in late January 1597 James Burbage died, although he had probably not yet begun to fight. As the lease for the ground where the Theatre stood was still not settled, negotiations for a new lease passed to his elder son Cuthbert as well as the lease of the Parliament Chamber in the Blackfriars, which the Chamberlain's Men were forbidden to use. The result of all this was that the company of Richard Burbage, Will Kemp, and William Shakespeare had to find a new place to perform.[146]

There is another piece of evidence suggesting that Shakespeare may have had some managerial position in the Lord Chamberlain's Men. By a curious coincidence near the same time Burbage's lease expired, a newly erected playhouse called The Swan was about to be opened on the Bankside. Johannes de Witt, visiting from Utrecht made a brief note about the London theatres with special praise for The Swan, capping his praise with a sketch of the interior. Part of his note goes like this:

> There are four amphitheatres in London of notable beauty, which from their diverse signs bear diverse names. In each of them a different play is daily exhibited to the populace. The two more magnificent of these are situated to the southward beyond the Thames, and from the signs suspended before them are called The Rose and Swan ... Of all the theatres, however, the largest and most magnificent is that one of which the sign is a swan, ... for it accommodates in its seats three thousand persons, and is built of a mass of flint stones, ... and supported by wooden columns painted in such excellent imitation of marble that it is able to deceive even the most cunning.[147]

Some of this may seem exaggerated, but John Orrell made a careful study of the capacity of The Globe Theatre and concludes that the figure of three thousand could not be far wrong.[148] The man who financed The Swan Theatre was a man who made a fortune by sharp practice. His name was Francis Langley. He purchased the Manor of Paris Garden on the Bankside and as Lord of the Manor set about making his purchase a source of new wealth by developing tenements. The Swan was planned to be his big money maker.[149]

There are several reasons to suppose the Lord Chamberlain's Men were the initial occupants of The Swan. They needed a playhouse, and The Swan being new would be fresh and attractive. We know, for instance, that sometime after October 1596 William Shakespeare moved from St. Helen's Parish, located near the Theatre, to the Bankside, where The Rose and The Swan were located. Then on November 29, 1596, one William Wayte petitioned for sureties of the peace for fear of death against four persons: William Shakespeare, Francis Langley, Dorothy Soer, wife of John Soer, and Anne Lee. By this action the persons named were required to post a bond to keep the peace, usually for a year, or forfeit a penalty. This remarkable information was unearthed by Leslie Hotson.[150] Perhaps Shakespeare was guarding the interests of the company using The Swan and Francis Langley the owner, but we can only guess that Dorothy Soer and Anne Lee may have been servants of the playhouse or of the acting company. Hotson also found out that earlier in the same month, Langley sued for sureties of the peace against William Wayte and William Gardiner, which suggests that Wayte was returning the favor when he asked for sureties against Shakespeare, Langley,

Soer, and Lee. From what we know of Langley, he was determined to keep his own. Like Burbage, Langley, backed up by Shakespeare, might have brandished a pistol charged with hemp seed while the two women shouted threats and obscenities. Wayte was the son-in-law of William Gardiner, a Justice of the Peace for Surrey with jurisdiction over the Bankside area where The Swan stood. It looks like this was a fight about money, perhaps extortion for licensing fees or bribes. Shakespeare was either defending the interests of the acting company or had some kind of financial stake in The Swan playhouse itself.

In any case, William Shakespeare's involvement with Langley and The Swan did not last very long. The Chamberlain's Men once again were operating in the Shoreditch area, this time in The Curtain, a playhouse built about the same time and close to the Burbage Theatre. The owner seems to have had some agreement with the neighboring playhouse. There is evidence that *Romeo and Juliet* and some of Shakespeare's history plays were performed there.[151]

In the meantime a reorganized company under the patronage of the Earl of Pembroke began using The Swan. Their stay was a fiasco. In July of 1597 Pembroke's Men produced a satiric play called *The Isle of Dogs*, written by Ben Jonson and Thomas Nashe. As we have no script of the play, it is hard to know why those in authority took offense at the play. They closed down the theatre, imprisoned several of the actors, including the actor-playwright, Jonson. Nashe, the other playwright, said he realized the play would get him in hot water so he skipped off to Yarmouth in Norfolk. Although the imprisoned actors were released about three months later, The Swan was not immediately permitted to reopen. When it did, Pembroke's Men had scattered to join other companies, so Langley had a playhouse, but was without a regular acting company to use it.

To return to the fortunes of the Chamberlain's Men, Shakespeare's second group of English history plays entered their repertory from about 1595-1599. They were *Richard II*; *Henry IV, Parts I* and *II*; *Henry V*, and perhaps between the last two in the series, *The Merry Wives of Windsor*, a domestic comedy disguised as a history. The new sequence explores the origins of the interminable civil strife, now called the War of the Roses, which Shakespeare so successfully presented ten years earlier in his histories covering the period from the reign of Henry VI to the downfall of Richard III.

The first in the new series, *Richard II*, has an unusually well unified plot, at least for a Shakespearean history. The conflict is easily defined as between King Richard and Bolingbroke. Richard believes his right to the crown by inheritance is the right to follow his whim or will wherever it leads. Bolingbroke is a powerful noble sent into exile who returns in arms to regain his inheritance confiscated by the King. Richard is forced to grant Bolingbroke's demands, is deposed, and sent to prison. Bolingbroke becomes King Henry IV by right of conquest, but nothing is settled. Many nobles, either dispossessed or merely disgruntled by the new regime, plot a counter-revolution. Richard, likely to become the unifying figure in any such plot, is murdered in prison by a partisan of Henry's. In some ways, *Richard II* is a sad and nostalgic play—sad because both Richard and Henry are caught in a tangle of circumstances where neither can do right nor be right, and nostalgic because an ordered and sheltered kingdom is torn apart and all the king's horses and all the king's men cannot put the pieces back together again.

The next three plays in the series follow the trying times of Henry IV and the fortunes of his son, who becomes Henry V. In addition to consulting books of English history, Shakespeare planned the series by expanding and enriching an old play called *The Famous Victories of Henry the Fifth: Containing the Honorable Battle of Agincourt.*[152] As the title of the old play implies, its main story line is about the Prince of Wales, whose madcap ways make a rather incongruous prelude to the ways of victorious kingship. But he was an English king, and whether remembered through fable or history, audiences loved the bully boy who kept the common touch. Shakespeare was out to keep all the good stuff, at least as much as would remind the audience of the story they knew. And know it they did, for there were at least three plays on the life of Henry V staged before Shakespeare began his version.[153]

In *Henry IV, Part I*, Prince Hal's escapades in highway robbery and riotous living are developed in the context of a serious political situation during the reign of Henry IV. The northern earls, who supported Henry's usurpation of the throne, as developed in *Richard II*, turn against him and form an alliance with lords in Scotland and Wales to get rid of Henry and divide the kingdom among them. Therefore the story of the prince who is out to have fun is shown in striking contrast to the story of the rebels who are out to spoil a kingdom. And though Hal seems at first a very unpromising Prince of Wales, it is finally shown that when the crisis is at hand, he comes up to the mark. If at first the rebels seem very likely to win, their rebellion finally fails because rebels will not be ruled, and so can neither compromise nor coordinate their efforts.

The play's subplot is dominated by the character we know as Falstaff, an old, fat, witty ruffian who is the best drinking buddy of the Prince and the seeming leader of his youthful riots. Falstaff's refusal to take things seriously and his agility in talking his way out of tight corners sets him off as the perfect foil to the tough characters in the main plot who are so serious and honor bound to win at all costs.

Henry IV, Part I is Shakespeare's best combination of serious political history and comic by-play. The political materials concern matters of great consequence, which are neatly resolved by a royal victory in which Hal is recognized as the true prince. In contrast, the comic escapades could be said to be of much less importance, having no influence on the course of events in the realm of politics, and that, I think, allows a holiday spirit to have full play.

On the other hand, *Henry IV, Part II* is a disappointment, as sequels often are. Shakespeare goes back to the same situations. The King again mistrusts the Prince who prefers life in the tavern to life in the palace. Again a rebellion threatens King Henry's hold on the crown. If there is a new area to explore, it is the passing of one generation to make way for another, brought into strong focus in the scene of Hal's interview with his father, where the crown becomes the emblem and symbol of the passing. In the character of Prince Hal, we catch his reluctance in saying farewell to youth, which finally plays out in the final scene where he rejects the companions of his wilder days. There is a decidedly elegiac, autumnal shading cast over the play. Falstaff is ill, the King is dying, the rebels have little zeal, and the royalists defeat them by a shocking betrayal. The scenes from common life are inhabited by folk who fall asleep. Finally the old king dies, and the play's closing is enlivened by the coronation procession of King Henry V. Falstaff is dismissed with a stinging rebuke.

While *Henry IV, Part I* in Shakespeare's time as today was immensely popular—there were five printings of *Part I* compared to only one printing of *Part II*—it could also be those audiences looked forward to the sequel in *Part II* with special curiosity because the play was expected to continue using the Falstaff character to lampoon an important nobleman, William Brooke, Lord Cobham.

To tell the tale we must go back to July 22, 1596. On that day Henry Carey, Lord Hunsdon, died. He was Lord Chamberlain, the patron of Shakespeare's company. His son, George Carey, inherited the title of Lord Hunsdon and took over as patron of his father's players, who thus became Lord Hunsdon's Men. However, the office of Lord Chamberlain passed to William Brooke, Lord Cobham, who apparently had small interest in players. The players of course had great interest in any Lord Chamberlain of the Queen's Household, for in large measure that officer regulated the theatrical enterprise. It seems that Shakespeare had a peculiar animus against Lord Cobham, but before examining the matter in detail, it should be pointed out that Shakespeare was not long troubled by the situation because Cobham died after only eight months as Lord Chamberlain. In March of 1597, George Carey, the new Lord Hunsdon was appointed to the vacancy once held by his father, and his players again took the name of the Lord Chamberlain's Men.

When Shakespeare's *Henry IV, Part I* was first performed, the character we know as Falstaff was named Sir John Oldcastle. It so happens that an ancestor of Lord Cobham was the historic Sir John Oldcastle, a soldier and friend of King Henry V, who was cast off by the king and suffered a martyr's death because he was a Lollard, i.e., one who accepted the early Protestant teachings of John Wycliffe. Shakespeare certainly knew who Oldcastle was, and one of the things he knew was that while Catholics regarded Oldcastle as a heretic, Protestant historians reworked the record to present him as a martyr. To make his mockery quite evident, Shakespeare's Falstaff character lards his talk with biblical citations and snippets of moral maxims like a precise Puritan hypocrite.[154] Shakespeare must surely have been aware of Lord Cobham's descent from Sir John Oldcastle, and to use the name as he did was surely a retort to those who wanted to make a martyr of the man. Further, a way of getting one up on Lord Cobham was to place Oldcastle in the company of the Prince Hal's unruly gang. His trick worked too well. Even after Henry Brooke, the new Lord Cobham, stepped in to force the players to change the name of the character, the cat was out of the bag. The name Oldcastle stuck, and the printer of that old play *The Famous Victories of King Henry the Fifth* decided to bring his copy up to date by changing the name of a character named Jockey to Oldcastle.[155]

To comply with orders from above, Shakespeare chose to rename Oldcastle, "Falstaff," which I take to be a variant spelling of the name Falstolfe. That could be taken as almost as impudent as using the name Oldcastle because the historic

Falstolfe was a Knight of the Garter who was disgraced and degraded for fleeing from the enemy, as dramatized by Shakespeare in *Henry VI, Part I*.[156] If that seems too obscure a point, notice that Falstaff implies an unreliable person, so the implication could hardly satisfy Oldcastle's descendants. The family name of the Lords Cobham was Brooke, which provided Shakespeare with another dig when he wrote *The Merry Wives of Windsor*. In that play Master Page, the jealous husband, goes disguised to Falstaff, giving his name as Brooke, which Shakespeare later had to change to Broome. There are other personal affronts in the original text of *Henry IV, Part I*. The members of the Falstaff gang we know as Bardolph and Peto were first named Russell and Harvey. Those names could have been associated with Lady Elizabeth Russell and Sir William Harvey. The Lady's London residence was in the Blackfriars precinct, and she was probably a backer of the petition to prevent the Chamberlain's Men from using the Parliament Chamber as a theatre. Sir William Harvey was courting the widowed Countess of Southampton over the objections of the young Earl, perhaps because his mother's marriage to Harvey could jeopardize part of Southampton's inheritance. We can follow this path a bit farther by remembering that Southampton's great friend was the Earl of Essex, a political enemy of Henry Brooke, the new Lord Cobham. At the time, Essex wanted the post of Lord Warden of the Cinque Ports to go to Sir Robert Sidney, a man he desired as an ally. However, Cobham wanted the post for himself.[157] It is easy to believe that Shakespeare may have been encouraged to lampoon Lord Cobham and Sir William Harvey because he knew Essex and Southampton would enjoy the jest. But quite aside from the immediate situation, Shakespeare had an old dislike of the Brooke family and its titled relatives, the Lords Cobham. In writing *Henry VI, Part II*, he portrayed Eleanor Cobham, the wife of the good Duke Humphrey of Gloucester, as an ambitious woman who made use of witches and wizards to promote her dream of becoming queen. She is easily recognized as similar to Lady Macbeth.

The York Herald, Ralph Brooke, who claimed relationship to the Lords Cobham, raised a fuss about the work of his colleagues in The College of Arms for granting arms to certain unworthy persons. He listed some twenty-three names including "Shakespeare, the player."[158] It looks like he was stretching to make a point, for it was John Shakespeare, not William who received the grant.

When *Henry IV, Part II* was printed there were no tracks in the text suggesting that Falstaff was once named Oldcastle, except for a slip. A speech heading [1.2.120] is printed as *Old.*, a mistake for *Fals.*, which Shakespeare made in his script even after he apparently decided to try to stop the confusion of Falstaff with Oldcastle. For the final paragraph of the epilogue, he wrote:

> One word more, I beseech you. If you be not too much cloyed with fat meat, our humble author will continue the story, with Sir John in it, and make you merry with fair Katherine of France; where, for anything I know, Falstaff shall die of a sweat, unless already a be killed with your hard opinions; for Oldcastle died a martyr, and this is not the man.
>
> (Epilogue, 26-32)

This apology comes at the end of a traditional bid for applause and is out of key with the rest of the epilogue. My guess is that it was added after the initial performances. "Oldcastle died a martyr" is possibly a concession to the partisans of Lord Cobham, but it is also an admission that confusion about Falstaff and Oldcastle had to come to a halt. How can the possibilities of the complex character of Falstaff be realized if any remark can be suspected as a sly dig at Oldcastle or Cobham? Shakespeare had to get out of that rut by not using him in *Henry V*. So instead of going to France to die of a sweat—that is of a venereal disease—Falstaff dies off-stage. We are told the King's rejection broke Falstaff's heart and Mistress Quickly describes his death as his body growing cold from the feet upward, suggesting the way Plato recorded the death of Socrates. The similarity seems far-fetched until we consider a side of Falstaff's character worth noticing. Like Socrates, accused of misleading the youth of Athens, Falstaff stands in opposition to conventional morality and notions of honor, which shocks those who suppose they know more than they do. He is like Chiron the Centaur who raised Achilles, a wild man whose influence goes to the making of heroes. After all, heroes have to get out from under the influence of their fathers. Many readers suspect that Prince Hal's graduation into leadership owes something to his early associations outside court circles. In dropping out he learned to go in disguise among the common folk and came to know himself as much as to know them.[159]

Shakespeare's farewell to Falstaff leads into a joke in *Henry V*. In one scene Fluellen, the Welsh Captain, praises the King for

> being in his right wits and his good judgments, turned away the fat knight with the great belly doublet. He was full of jests, and gibes, and knaveries, and mocks—I have forgot his name.
>
> (4.7.46-50)

Gary Taylor suggests the line gave the actor a chance to play on the problem of which name to use, Oldcastle or Falstaff?[160] Believing that Elizabethan audiences were used to being prompted and welcomed a chance to participate, I can imagine that in the pause both names "Falstaff" and "Oldcastle" were called out from the audience before Captain Gower could pick up his cue and say, "Sir John Falstaff."

My review of the Oldcastle lampoon may give too much prominence to a small part of the Falstaff character and distract us from noticing the complexity of the play. The allusion to Socrates is an example of that complexity. In reviewing the life of Shakespeare, however, the matter of Oldcastle is important. It may not tell us much about the play, but it does tell us something of what was going on in Shakespeare's life. It also tells us something of his character, namely his assurance and his willingness to use the special power of a playwright to sway opinion by expressing his own.

There is more to be said of Shakespeare's Oldcastle. *Henry IV, Part I* was such a success for the Lord Chamberlain's men that the rival company, the Lord Admiral's men, decided that they needed to cash in on the hot topic. Thus they paid for a new script, printed as *The first part Of the True and Honorable Historie of the life of Sir John Old-castle, the good Lord Cobham.* Their company records show that four playwrights collaborated on the play: Anthony Munday, Michael Drayton, Robert Wilson, and Thomas Hathway. While many plays produced in the Elizabethan public theatres were written in collaboration, in this case the use of four co-authors suggests a rush order was put out to get the script ready as soon as possible. A second part of the history was also completed, although it never got into print. Perhaps they had no more success with their part two than Shakespeare had with his. *Sir John Oldcastle, Part I* is rather well knit and exciting, especially the serious part, although the comic stuff is a patchwork of old routines. The prologue says right out that our Oldcastle is the true one:

> It is no pampered glutton we present,
> Nor aged counselor to youthful sin,
> But one, whose virtue shone above the rest,
> A valiant martyr, and a virtuous peer,
> In whose true faith and loyalty expressed
> Unto his sovereign, and his country's weal....[161]

Oldcastle is presented as a follower of John Wycliffe. In efforts to suppress this threat to ecclesiastical authority by the early Protestant movement, the Bishop of Rochester is cast in the role of the villain who works to undermine the King's trust in Oldcastle, blaming him for any demands for reforms in the Church or for any signs of discontent. Near the end of *Part I*, Oldcastle is trapped by his enemies and placed in the tower. He manages to escape and is on the run for the rest of the play, meeting interesting country folk in adventures along the way. At the end of *Part I*, he sets out for Wales. While it is clear he is headed for martyrdom in Part Two, it is hard to imagine how a play could be developed to end with a description of his death, a rather horrible one, for he was roasted on an iron grill.

There are many scenes in the play of *Sir John Oldcastle* that are written in imitation of moments in Shakespeare's *Henry V*. The incident where Henry discovers the treachery of Cambridge, Scroop, and Grey [*Henry V* 2.2] is also dramatized in *Sir John Oldcastle* in a slightly different way. Oldcastle traps the conspirators [3.1] and reveals their treachery to the King [4.2], turning the tables on his enemies just when they thought they had him. Several times the King goes into disguise to meet the common folk, and there is a series of scenes featuring a village priest who is a robber and thief. He is called Sir John and he is companioned with a village girl called Doll, echoing Sir John Falstaff and Doll Tearsheet from *Henry IV, Part II*.

Two final notes on the tangled relationship of Oldcastle and the Henry IV plays. At the second printing of the Oldcastle play, 1600, the same year as the first, these words were added to the title page, "Written by William Shakespeare." If the publisher knew enough about the play to want it on his list, he would have known Shakespeare wasn't the author. But Shakespeare, at least in the popular imagination, stirred up the dust in the "old castle" and on that topic his name sold books. About 1603, the Jesuit, Robert Parsons, director of Roman Catholic missionary activity in England and Rector of the English College in Rome, attacked the Protestant view of history in John Fox's *Book of Martyrs*, by writing of Sir John Oldcastle:

> A ruffian knight as all England knoweth, and commonly brought in by
> comedians on their stages: he was put to death for robberies and rebellion
> under... King Henry the Fifth.

This was countered some years later by John Speed in his *History of Great Britain*, where he attacks Parsons for making Oldcastle a ruffian, a robber, and a rebel, and "his authority taken from the stage players, is more befitting the pen of his slanderous report, … being only grounded from this Papist and his poet."[162] Speed implies that Shakespeare made up slanders about Oldcastle and was a poet in the pay of Father Parsons.

Nicholas Rowe published the first sketch of Shakespeare's life in 1709. In it he recorded this story:

> Queen Elizabeth… was so well pleased with that admirable character of Falstaff, in the two parts of *Henry the Fourth*, that she commanded him to continue it for one play more, and to show him in love. This is said to be the occasion of his writing *The Merry Wives of Windsor*.[163]

Whether the story is credible or not, the Falstaff of *Merry Wives* is neither in love nor is he the same fascinating person as the Falstaff in the Henry IV plays. But he is very funny in a very new way, particularly when he describes his failures. In three attempts to make love to the Windsor wives, thinking they might give him access to ready cash, Falstaff is thrice interrupted by the return of the supposedly absent husbands. The comedy is unusual in that it is placed in the English town of Windsor. Shakespeare usually prefers foreign locales for his comedies. None of his other plays so carefully mentions the landmarks of a specific town. Here he mentions the Thames, Windsor Forest and Castle, taverns, streets, meadows, and other areas of Windsor, including the Chapel of St. George, home of the Noble Order of the Garter.

Mention of the Order and the traditions associated with it are so frequent that *Merry Wives* could be called a Garter play.[164] If we ask why all these allusions are worked into the fabric of the play, the answer is not hard to find. In March of 1597 George Carey, Lord Hunsdon, was made the Lord Chamberlain, and in April the Queen named him to the Order of the Garter. He made great preparations for the Garter Feast held in Whitehall and for the ceremony of installation held in the Garter Chapel in Windsor. It was reported that the Lord

Chamberlain "will have 300" to accompany him as he entered Windsor castle, and a herald's description is fabulous:

> my Lord Chamberlain [came] with a brave company of men and gentlemen his servants and retainers, in blue coats faced with orange colored taffeta, and orange colored feathers in their hats, most part having chains of gold; besides a great number of knights and others, that accompanied his Lordship.[165]

Shakespeare was in that fellowship, blue coated with orange taffeta facings and capped with orange feathers, perhaps even a gold chain. With this in mind it seems likely that the *Merry Wives* was written as a contribution by the Lord Chamberlain's Men to their patron's celebration of his installation as a Knight of the Garter. The play is in many places rather too topical to be entirely clear to modern readers, and in fact parts of it are quite obscure. However since most modern productions cut the obscurities, the play works very well without them. In the theatre the play has usually been heavily adapted, and nine or more operas have been derived from it, the most notable being Verdi's final work, *Falstaff*.

Completing this series of history plays, Shakespeare's *Henry V* was probably staged in 1598. A special feature of the play is the use of a character called the Chorus to tell the parts of the history that are not acted out and to describe place, time, and atmosphere. More importantly, he appeals to the audience to admire King Henry as he takes on the ominous risks of attempting the conquest of France. Although the Chorus always speaks in adoring praise of Henry, the action of the play does not overlook Henry's faults—his dubious claim to the French crown, his foolhardiness, and his brutality when cornered. The details of soldiering in this and in Shakespeare's other war plays so well reflect the attitudes and behavior of common soldiers as well as officers that it has been seriously speculated that Shakespeare himself may have seen service in the Lowlands or France.[166] It is highly unlikely that servants of the Lord Chamberlain would be picked by a local Justice to fill up a muster, unless the Lord himself were campaigning abroad, something Shakespeare's patron was not called to do. I rather think such knowledge of soldiering as Shakespeare displays would be easy enough to acquire. There were many campaigns in 1580's under Leicester and in the 1590's under Essex, so it would not be difficult for outsiders to pick up from the talk of insiders what military service was like. Shakespeare tells us the tricks of it when he has Captain Gower explain how Pistol, the braggart soldier in *Henry V*, might pass for a true soldier:

> And such fellows are perfect in the great commander's names, and
> they will learn you by rote where services were done—at such and such
> a sconce, at such a breach, at such a convoy; who came off bravely, who
> was shot, who disgraced, what terms the enemy stood on; and this they
> con perfectly in the phrase of war, which they trick up with new-tuned
> oaths; and what a beard of the general's cut and a horrid suit of the camp
> will do among foaming bottles and ale-washed wits, is wonderful to be
> thought on!
>
> (3.6.69-79)

In 1599 the printer William Jaggard published *The Passionate Pilgrim*, a collection of poems he labeled as "by William Shakespeare." The miscellany contains twenty poems, but only five are by Shakespeare. These included two of his privately circulated sonnets, which were inaccurately printed, and three passages from *Love's Labour's Lost*, which was published the year before. The rest are by Marlowe, Raleigh, Griffin, Barnfield, and others that can't be identified. It must be understood that there was no such thing as author's copyright in those days. Publishers might pay for copy, but if copy were found or filched that seemed likely to sell, they were free to bring it on the market without payment or permission. To judge William Jaggard by the standards of modern publishing would be naïve. He had to have supposed there was a demand for Shakespeare's work. In a later printing of *The Passionate Pilgrim*, he took "by William Shakespeare" off the title page, admitting that not all the poems were by Shakespeare.[167]

As the sixteenth century came to a close, Shakespeare became the subject of praise from poets and versifiers who wanted to cut a figure among the wits of the town. One of the most interesting tributes came from Francis Meres, a graduate of Cambridge, who set himself up as a sort of critic. In 1598 he published a treatise called, *Palladis Tamia: Wits Treasury*, a compilation of chatter about literature. In one section he mentions Plautus and Seneca as being the best of the Roman comic and tragic dramatists and cites Shakespeare as the best of the

English in both kinds of drama, mentioning six comic and six tragic plays. His list includes only plays well known in the late 1590's, naming *Love's Labour's Lost* and a play called *Love's Labour's Won*. There seems to be no trace of *Love's Labour's Won*. That may have been an alternate title for a play we have, possibly *Much Ado About Nothing*, as a way of capitalizing on the popularity of *Love's Labour's Lost*. If there is a puzzle about which play Meres had in mind, it may be best to skip trying to solve it and assume that *Love's Labour's Won* is lost.

About the same time as he wrote *Henry V*, Shakespeare wrote *Much Ado About Nothing*, a very witty and polished comedy of courtship. Beatrice and Benedick begin their courtship by teasing each other with cutting remarks and retorts. Their roles exploit the manner of high comedy. Although they never shout or knock each other about, in many ways they reprise the roles of Katherine and Petruchio in *The Taming of the Shrew*. As the play develops their friends trick them into realizing that they love each other. This unconventional pair steals the show from Hero and Claudio, a proper young couple in the main plot who follow the ways of polite society and have their marriage arranged by their friends.

There is a villain in the piece who slanders Hero so that Claudio brutally rejects her publicly when he arrives at church to be married. This dramatic surprise releases a lot of emotional turmoil, in the midst of which Beatrice and Benedick realize and admit their love for each other. The plot of the villain is overheard by the town watchmen, and when that is revealed the play ends in a double wedding.

Shakespeare's control of language in *Much Ado* is extraordinary. Beatrice and Benedict say the most outrageous things of a sort one expects should be followed by a "just-kidding" disclaimer. Up to the crisis in the church, all the characters, in their own way, use the same style of banter. It is obvious these people are having fun. But when the explosion comes in the climactic scene, they speak under such emotional turmoil that wit flies out the window. There seems to be no way that comic dialogue could be brought back into play. But it does come back when Master Constable Dogberry discovers the dirty work of the villain. He is so full of self-importance and so sure he is making sense, when he obviously does not understand what he has discovered and is so tangled in malapropisms reporting it, that he turns on laughter when none of the other characters could. His discovery restores everyone to their former witty ways.

In the same work mentioned above, *Paladis Tamia,* Francis Meres uses the phrase "honey-tongued Shakespeare" referring to *Venus and Adonis, Lucrece,* and Shakespeare's sonnets "among his private friends." We can infer from this that Meres knew friends who knew Shakespeare, or knew Shakespeare himself, or had at least seen some of the privately circulated sonnets. I suspect he was dropping hints that he belonged to the inner circle of those who knew the latest and best.[168]

A lot of Shakespeare's fans liked to use the word "honey" to describe his work, not so much for sweetness as for eloquence, for being mellifluous, i.e., "honey-flowing," suggesting a good land "flowing with milk and honey." The same sense of "sweet" as something fresh and inspired, moved the King James translators of the Bible to render an obscure phrase by referring to David as "the sweet psalmist of Israel" [2 *Sam.* 23:1]. In 1598 Richard Barnfield published a collection which included a poem that begins, "And *Shakespeare* thou, whose honey-flowing vain,/ (Pleasing the World) thy praises doth obtain."[169]

Another who made similar claims to know the latest was John Weever. Also a Cambridge graduate, he echoed Meres' phrase "honey-tongued Shakespeare" in a book of epigrams published in 1600. Significantly his epigram "Ad Gulielmum Shakespear" was the only one in his collection that was written in the form of a Shakespearean sonnet, suggesting that he too knew about the privately circulated sonnets. His epigram begins, "Honey-tongued *Shakesepeare* when I saw thine issue / "I swore *Apollo* got them and none other," which is about as extravagant a tribute as could be paid to the creator of the characters Weever mentions in the epigram: Adonis, Venus, Lucrece, Tarquin, Romeo, and Richard. Weever was a Lancashire man, twelve years younger than Shakespeare, and they may have met when both were living in that part of the country.

Despite his early life in Lancashire, Weever was clearly a Protestant, at least in his published writings. Weever published *The Martyr's Mirror, or the Life and Death of Sir John Oldcastle,* about the same time as his epigrams, where he versified the story of Oldcastle from the Protestant point of view, exploiting interest in the topic stimulated by *Henry IV, Part I*. In it he alluded to Shakespeare's latest tragedy, *Julius Caesar*.

> The many-headed multitude were drawn
> By Brutus' speech that Caesar was ambitious.
> When eloquent Mark Antony had shown
> His virtues, who but Brutus then was vicious?
> Man's memory with new forgets the old,
> One tale is good until another's told.[170]

The orations of Antony and Brutus at the funeral of Caesar are both powerful and strongly contrasted statements, one formal and reasoned, the other seemingly impromptu and emotional. They are superb examples of Shakespearean eloquence, his honeyed tongue that could so dominate the stage and so sway his contemporaries. Considering the rhetorical training in Elizabethan schools, Shakespeare's audience, at least those who had a Latin grammar school education, would be likely to have a keen appreciation of his skill and could respond more directly to its spell. It is not surprising that Weever had to comment on the funeral orations in *The Tragedy of Julius Caesar*.

Another memorable sequence is the quarrel scene between Brutus and Cassius in Act IV. The movement from tension to blazing anger, then to shame and reconciliation, is surprising and unforgettable. We might well ask, where did all this come from and what is it doing in the play? It is as if the play has been left behind and we are seeing something real. It is a great scene for the actor playing Cassius, as the earlier scene is for the actor playing Antony. The Stoic control of Brutus in each sequence is nicely at odds with the emotions of Antony and Cassius.

Shakespeare's *Julius Caesar* is very much like his history plays based on English chronicles, only here he uses Plutarch, translated into English by Sir Thomas North as *The Lives of the Noble Grecians and Romans*. Although Shakespeare's play is called a tragedy, it takes the form of a history play—the main characters are well differentiated and are in conflict because they pursue their own version of the good. And from the audience's point of view, the major characters all have some qualities we can admire and some we can't. They lack what we think of as the traditional heroic virtues. Caesar is powerful but sick, a phantom, even before he appears as one. Cassius is an envious devil, but devoted to Brutus; Antony is ambitious and ruthless, but as attractive as an Olympic athlete. Brutus is perhaps as noble as they get, but so coldly logical he can't be right, and so boring! They are all murderers. The play seems at moments restrained and classical, at other moments bloody and soiled by mob violence, war, suicide, and assassination disguised as ritual murder.

As Cuthbert Burbage came to realize he could not get favorable terms for a new lease from Giles Alleyn, the owner of the ground in Shoreditch where The Theatre stood, he believed that under the terms of the lease he could dismantle the playhouse and move it to another location. In those days, and like log houses today, the large timbers were cut, fitted, and pegged together in a lumber yard and then taken apart and reassembled at the building site. The same process could be reversed in dismantling and moving the building without losing the large and expensive oak timbers that made up the frame. Burbage decided to move his playhouse.

The fact that he relied on terms in an expired lease and was technically a trespasser made his actions questionable. At least Giles Alleyn thought so and took him to court. Alleyn's testimony asserts that Cuthbert Burbage with Richard Burbage, Peter Street, William Smyth and twelve other persons about the Feast of the Nativity, 1598:

> [did] riotously assemble themselves together and then and there armed themselves with divers and many unlawful and offensive weapons, as namely swords, daggers, bills, axes and such like. And so armed did then repair unto the said Theatre and then and there ... in a very riotous, outrageous, and forcible manner and contrary to the laws of your Highness realm attempted to pull down the said Theatre ... and having so done did then also in a most forcible and riotous manner take and carry away from thence all the wood and timber thereof unto the Bankside ... and there erected a new play house with the said timber and wood.[171]

It sounds like a peasants' revolt, as if a drunken, destructive, and defiant mob armed with makeshift weapons did all this in one gaudy day. Perhaps no court could fail to see that passionate feelings rather than the facts created that description. Surely taking the theatre apart, carefully preserving boards and timbers, took days or weeks. The landlord may have been out of town while all this was going on and came to the site when the salvaged materials were already carted and shipped to the Bankside on the south side of the Thames. Maybe it would be enough to enrage anyone who wanted the timbers for himself. After reviewing several claims in various courts made by Alleyn, E. K. Chambers writes, "Although the conclusions of these suits are not on record, it is not likely that he succeeded in obtaining a favorable decision." [172]

The Burbages, the other party to the dispute, were also saddled with losses and new expenses: the cost of leasing a new site, of hiring skilled workmen and laborers to dismantle, transport, rebuild, and refurbish the new playhouse. So they called in partners to finance the enterprise. Cuthbert and Richard Burbage retained half the shares, and William Shakespeare, John Heminges, Augustine Phillips, Thomas Pope, and Will Kemp, five members of the Lord Chamberlain's Men, bought ownership of the other half. These seven men became the owners or "housekeepers" of the new playhouse, responsible for the ground rent and repairs, but sharing the gallery receipts and the playhouse rent paid by the acting company. Two Londoners, William Leveson, a merchant adventurer, and Thomas Savage, a goldsmith, helped in making financial arrangements so the playhouse would remain in the hands of members of the company. Thomas Savage was a native of Rufford in Lancashire who probably knew Shakespeare from his time there.

Shakespeare's theatrical career was by this time producing income in four ways: as actor, as playwright, as sharer in the company, and as one of the owners of a playhouse. The reassembled Theatre was renamed The Globe, perhaps to suggest the new world of the explorers and astronomers. The sign was of Hercules holding the globe with the motto, *Totus mundus agit histrionem*, "The whole world plays the actor," or as the point was expressed in *As You Like It*, "All the world's a stage." It was open and ready by September 1599 when Dr. Thomas Platter, a visitor from Switzerland, saw a performance of *Julius Caesar* and wrote this note in his Journal:

> After dinner on the 21ˢᵗ of September, at about two o'clock, I went
> with my companions over the water, and in the strewn roof house saw

the tragedy of the first Emperor Julius with at least fifteen characters very well acted. At the end of the comedy they danced according to their custom with extreme elegance. Two in men's clothes and two in women's gave this performance, in wonderful combination with each other.[173]

Like the tourist Dr. Platter, visiting 16th-century London from the continent, we too would find it noteworthy to see a tragedy concluded by a dance of four men, two straight and two in drag. But I think we have to notice the dance was "with extreme elegance," and on that note see The Globe Theatre well launched on its impressive career as the finest public theatre in Europe.

CHAPTER 6

THE MALCONTENT
1599–1606

Nym. My humor shall not cool. I will incense [Page] to
   deal with poison; I will possess him with yallowness,
   for the revolt of mine is dangerous – that is my true humor.
Pistol. Thou art the Mars of malcontents. I second thee; troop on.
                              (*The Merry Wives of Windsor* 1.3.100–105)

A NOTABLE feature of the role of the Chorus in *Henry V* is that he is both narrator and presenter who plays directly with the audience rather than with other characters on stage. He can easily refer to current events as well as to events in the play. Using this possibility, Shakespeare has the Chorus invite the audience to imagine the triumphal return of Henry V to London after his campaign in France:

> How London doth pour out her citizens!
> The Mayor and all his brethren in best sort,
> Like to the senators of th'antique Rome,
> With the plebeians swarming at their heels,
> Go forth and fetch their conqu'ring Caesar in.
>
> (Chorus 5.24–28)

He then compares that welcome to the one the Earl of Essex will receive when he returns from his campaign in Ireland to put down the insurrection led by Hugh O'Neill, the rebel Earl of Tyrone:

As by a lower but by loving likelihood,
Were now the general of our gracious Empress,
As in good time he may, from Ireland coming,
Bringing rebellion broached on his sword,
How many would the peaceful city quit,
To welcome him!

(Chorus 5.29–34)

Unfortunately the return Shakespeare anticipated as a triumph was rather the opposite. In 1599, after some delays in getting started, Essex arrived in Ireland in April with 15,000 men. Then after some alarms and excursions that accomplished very little, he negotiated a truce with Tyrone, left his command, and returned unexpectedly in September without the Queen's permission. He impulsively broke into her private chamber before she was properly dressed, hoping she would forgive his actions if he explained the situation in Ireland and how his efforts were frustrated by his enemies at court—Secretary Cecil, Lord Cobham, Lord Grey de Wilton, and Sir Walter Raleigh.

Whatever he said had little effect. Elizabeth was tired of her once favorite courtier. In the course of the Irish campaign, he had appointed Southampton his General of Horse, an appointment she forbade him to make. Although she had ordered the young Earl of Rutland to stay at home, he took off and joined Essex, who appointed him Lieutenant General of Infantry. As a commander, Essex was in the habit of creating knights right and left; he made some 170 while in Ireland. Such actions seemed alarming to the Queen. It appeared that Essex was building a large following among nobles, captains, and common soldiers. Such doings were as troubling as his fruitless forays into rebel territory.[174]

The Privy Council reviewed the situation, and Essex was placed under house arrest. His principal source of income was a lease on a monopoly of the import duties on sweet wines. The lease expired in November, and the Queen neglected to renew it; Essex was headed for ruin. Believing, as does the Chorus in Shakespeare's play, that the citizens of London loved him, Essex brooded on a plan to call them out, capture the Queen at Whitehall, and force the removal of his enemies on the Council. While the pot was simmering, large numbers of his followers gathered near Essex House waiting to see what might be done to help their disgraced Lord. Southampton and his friend Rutland were reported passing "away the time in London merely in going to plays every day."[175]

Several of the malcontents approached the Lord Chamberlain's Men to arrange a performance of Shakespeare's *Richard II* at The Globe. The play was not in the current repertory, but they were promised a reward to revive it. They accepted and performed the play with only a day's notice on February 6, 1601. Twelve days later, when Augustine Phillips, one of the actor-sharers of the Chamberlain's Men was examined before the Privy Council, he explained how several men approached the company "to have the play of the deposing and killing of King Richard the Second to be played the Saturday next, promising to get them 40 shillings more than their ordinary to play it."[176] The play had taken on a new meaning in this context. Although the performance was arranged to remind the citizens that a monarch's favorites could be removed, it didn't have the intended effect. When Essex made his move, the citizens did not rise up, and he and his followers were trapped. At the trial, speaking to Southhampton, who with Essex was charged with treason, Attorney General Coke aggravated the charge:

> I protest upon my soul and conscience I do believe [the Queen] should not have long lived after she had been in your power. Note but the precedents of former ages, how long lived Richard the Second after he was surprised in the same manner? The pretense was alike for the removing of certain counselors, but yet shortly after it cost him his life.[177]

A jury of their peers condemned Essex and Southampton, and the sentence was the usual one for traitors—to be butchered by the hangman—but Essex was sent to the block and beheaded, while Southampton was spared and sent to prison in the Tower.

While Essex's return and rebellion, trial and execution kept the town awake and fearful, Shakespeare's version of the Hamlet story held the stage at The Globe. Since the play sounds the deep notes of mysterious ambiguity and foreboding anxiety, it is tempting to theorize that Shakespeare was reacting to the fall of Essex and Southampton while writing the play. But *Hamlet* was being performed well before Shakespeare was aware of the deep waters the two earls were treading.[178] If The Globe Company had any idea the Privy Council was building a case for a charge of treason, it seems very unlikely they would have agreed to stage *Richard II*. About the same time Shakespeare had more personal matters to think about. His father, John Shakespeare, died in September 1601. Again it has been suggested that this experience prompted the moving expressions of grief at the loss of a father found in *Hamlet*. However, the play was written well before John Shakespeare died. There is no question that personal experiences inform a playwright's work, but also no question that imagination is just as rich a source of material. The best we can say is that Shakespeare probably surmised the way things would go with rash politicians like Essex and with old men like his father. John Shakespeare would have been in his seventies, an age that few men or women attained in those days. He had given his son a taste for the theatre, a serviceable education, experience in business affairs, an appreciation of the religious practices of the past, and, let us not forget, real property in Stratford. Additionally, William may have picked up from his father a liking for the roving, somewhat furtive life of a man not often at home. However affecting the loss of his father may have been, or the fall of Essex, Shakespeare wrote two of his most cheerful comedies around the same time as *Hamlet*, *As You Like It* and *Twelfth Night*.

Briefly, this is the story of Hamlet. His father, the king, had been secretly murdered by Hamlet's uncle, Claudius, who then married Hamlet's mother and usurped the throne. The ghost of Hamlet's father appears and tells Hamlet how he was murdered and charges him with the task of revenge. Both Hamlet and Claudius spy and plot against each other through a long middle section of the play. Then a rapidly changing series of events drives the play to its inevitable conclusion. Plans to trap Hamlet fail. Accidental, mysterious, and violent deaths engulf all the major characters in the tragedy. There are broad hints that vengeance is really designed by providence, sometimes aided and sometimes hindered by human agency. Hamlet may be grieving for the death of his father, but the play is more about his hostility and suspicions of two father-figures: Claudius, his uncle/stepfather, and Polonius, who might become his father-in-law. Hamlet cherishes his impotent rage by insulting Polonius and by telling himself how wonderful his deceased father was and how loathsome his uncle is. And that isn't all. Hamlet feels betrayed by his mother Gertrude for her marriage to his uncle and betrayed as well as by those who went along with the new regime. Hamlet is a malcontent deprived of his rights and surrounded by enemies. Consequently, he drifts into the melancholy notions of suicide and homicidal paranoia.

Perhaps what is most tantalizing about *Hamlet, Prince of Denmark*, is the liveliness of its action, despite the solemn key many actors affect in the role and many directors impose on the play, and a forward drive that moves the play into emotional high gear. Critics too have done their part in making the play seem more solemn than it is, particularly when they set out to find some consistency in the characterization of Hamlet, who was made essentially inconsistent. It is much more satisfying to note that every time Hamlet reenters the stage he appears as a slightly different person. I guess that Shakespeare did not make the character consistent because he felt it more important to give the lead actor a chance to display the full range of his abilities, to surprise the audience one moment after another as new aspects of the prince are revealed. Hamlet is by turns high strung, hostile, homicidal, grief stricken, playful, paranoid, conniving, considerate, and the brooding prince of malcontents.

Shakespeare didn't make up the story; he rewrote an older play of revenge, which in turn was derived from a French version of Danish legend. Many in his audience would have known the old play. Thus favorite situations and highlights had to be reworked into something fresh and more compelling. The process of melding an older version with a new vision may account for some of the rough edges of Shakespeare's *Hamlet*, but also for some of its fascination.

Shakespeare's *As You Like It* was written about the same time as *Hamlet*. Although vastly different in tone, it too develops a story of family betrayals. A duke is forced into exile when his brother usurps the dukedom. He takes refuge in a forest where several lords join him rather than put up with the regime of the tyrannical duke. Nobody talks about revenge or plans a rebellion. They wait patiently for the turning of the tide, when providence will disperse the storm clouds and all shall be restored. At the center of the play is an analogous story about another set of brothers: the elder mistreats the younger and plots to destroy him, but the young fellow escapes to the forest to join the banished duke.

These stories are rapidly sketched and seem to drop out of sight when the action switches to the Forest of Arden. We leave a place of envious power plays for a locale of apparent pastoral simplicity. Time is spent leisurely discussing love and the folly of lovers, the pleasures of leading a simple life in companionship, as opposed to the pains of competing in the court with malcontents and satirists.

In large part the scenes in the forest are a series of dialogues, as these topics are discussed by a variety of humorous characters, shuffled and rearranged in fresh combinations. Rather than following a strong narrative line where one event creates the next, as in formal tragedy and comedy, *As You Like It* has been described as "Shakespeare's pastoral comedy." After the setting changes to the forest, it becomes "like many pastoral poems ... lacking in event or action," but is "mainly a play of talk and song."[179] A switch to pastoral scenes from the court to the open country occurs in many of the later plays of Shakespeare, and is a regular feature of tragicomedy, the dramatic form he pursued after writing his major tragedies.[180]

There seems to have been a renewed interest in pastoral poetry when Shakespeare wrote *As You Like It*. *England's Helicon*, an anthology of 150 poems was published in 1600. Hugh Macdonald, who edited a modern reprint, observed

> "Whoever was responsible for the book had a very definite object in view. He wished to make it a pastoral anthology.... [He] frequently made small changes in the poems themselves to give them the desired pastoral character."[181]

Shakespeare's lyric, "On a day, (alack the day)," from *Love's Labour's Lost* [4.3.99–118] was included and titled, "The passionate Shepherd's Song," probably taken from the play published in 1599.

Escaping the watchful eyes of tyranny by going to the forest is a perennial motif in folklore. In England the tales of Robin Hood and his merry men, clothed all in green, coursing the deer, and carousing under the greenwood tree, are prime examples of the type. Shakespeare used that material for the final scenes of *Two Gentlemen of Verona*, but in *As You Like It* he used it to the full. He was also supplying the Lord Chamberlain's Men with a script to rival a production of the Lord Admiral's Men, *The Downfall of Robert, Earl of Huntington* (Huntington being Robin Hood). Shakespeare certainly had that play in mind when he wrote *As You Like it*. There is a suggestion in *The Downfall* that nearly everyone on arrival in the forest becomes a better person. Shakespeare picks up that idea and develops it much further. Everyone, the refugees as well as their pursuers, arrive in the forest exhausted. Then as if by magic they are transformed into people who give up anger and fear and enjoy the company of others. There are other points of similarity, enough to suggest that Shakespeare hinted in the title of *As You Like It* that he was dishing up more of the latest theatrical hit as well as responding to an interest in pastoral poetry.

The rival company could hardly resent Shakespeare's copying ideas and situations to challenge their success, for they were copycats too, whose version of the Oldcastle story capitalized on the interest in Falstaff. Apparently *The Downfall* was such a success that they contrived *The Death of Robert, Earl of Huntington* to look like a sequel, but after two or three scenes, the play becomes a rehash of situations, themes, and characters from Shakespeare's *King John*.[182]

One of the few examples of an Elizabethan playgoer's response to a Shakespearean play is to be found in the *Diary* of John Manningham (the same Manningham mentioned in Chapter 4, who jotted down the story of Shakespeare as William the Conqueror beating Burbage as Richard III at an assignation). Here is his entry for February 2, 1602, describing a feast held in the Middle Temple, the Inn of Court which was his London residence while he studied law:

> At our feast we had a play called "Twelve Night, or What You Will," much like the Comedy of Errors, or Menaechmi in Plautus, but most like [one] … in Italian called *Inganni*. A good practice in it to make the Steward believe his Lady widow was in love with him, by counterfeiting a letter as from his Lady in general terms, telling him what she liked best in him, and prescribing his gesture in smiling, his apparel, &c., and then when he came to practice, making him believe they took him to be mad.[183]

We can infer a great deal from this entry. The feast was held on Candlemas Day, a traditional time when the Inns of Court often engaged players for private performances to enhance their own high jinx during the Christmas season. There is also a record of the *Comedy of Errors* being performed at Gray's Inn on Innocents Day, December 28, 1594, and ten years later at Court on Innocents Day 1604. Apparently Manningham had just seen his first performance of *Twelfth Night*, but has a lively memory of *The Comedy of Errors*, knows a similar play in Italian, and remembers from school days, Plautus' *Menaechmi*, the Latin comedy about twins. I would guess that many educated persons in Shakespeare's audience knew many plays and could easily recognize a reworking of a traditional comic formula.

Twins are separated by shipwreck, eventually cross paths in a strange city and finally are reunited. Usually one is entangled in some sexual pursuit which takes the introduction of the other twin to untangle. Manningham sees this part of the play, the story of Olivia, Viola, Orsino, and Sebastian, as so familiar he can tick off names of plays like it. However the new material that Shakespeare introduced as his sub-plot, a story of the gulling of the steward, Malvolio—involving as it does the whole household of the Countess Olivia, Toby, Maria, Sir Andrew, and Feste—is so fresh and funny that Manningham puts his finger on the device of tricking the steward by a practical joke as the heart of the comedy.

This part of the play, based on contemporary life in a great Elizabethan household, is in contrast to the story of the separated twins and their love affairs, which has the feel of happening in fantasyland. The story of the household tricking the Steward places the audience inside an elaborate practical joke that is happening in the here and now. By recalling the school drama of Shakespeare's youth, *Jack Juggler*, we note that Shakespeare's counter-plot in *Twelfth Night* has the quality of a playground impromptu, and the sport goes on until all kinds of twists are exhausted and the tricksters are ready to call it a day.

One other detail in the entry from Manningham's Diary should be noticed. He mentions the subtitle of the comedy as, *What You Will*. This catch phrase was popular at the time, and it may not be unusual that it was remembered. However, it may have gotten Manningham's attention because about the same time as *Twelfth Night*, a young playwright, who also lived in the Middle Temple, wrote a play titled, *What You Will*. His name was John Marston,[184] and it was produced by Paul's Boys. In the Induction it is asked "what kind of a play is to be performed comedy, tragedy, pastoral, moral, nocturnal or history?" The character Philomuse responds: "Faith perfectly neither, but even *what you will*, a slight toy, lightly composed, too swiftly finish'd, ill plotted, worse written, I fear me worse acted, and indeed *what you will*."[185]

We can't be sure which play, Shakespeare's or Marston's, came first, but they had a similar source in some variation of the Italian play that Manningham mentioned. The similarities go further. David Riggs reviews the similarities very succinctly in this sketch:

> In the main plot, a noble suitor pursues a reluctant gentlewoman; in

the subplot, a crew of courtly mischief-makers plays a practical joke on a graceless social climber who tries to compete with the Duke for the gentlewoman's affections. Marston assigned the latter role to Lampatho Doria, alias Ben Jonson; Shakespeare gave it to Malvolio, a surly ill-wisher who has a number of traits in common with the twenty-nine year old Ben Jonson.[186]

This would not be the only time Marston and Shakespeare drew water from the same well. James Bednarz goes so far as to write, "Marston imitated Shakespearean themes, characterization, plot, and diction *in every play he wrote for Paul's.*"[187]

Manningham jotted down an anecdote about Marston when he danced with a lady at the same Christmas season the performance of *Twelfth Night* was given in the Middle Temple. After Marston complimented her wit and beauty, the lady told him she thought he was a poet. "'Tis true," said he, "for poets feign and lie, and so did I when I commended your beauty, for you are exceeding foul."[188] Shakespeare used the same joke in *As You Like It*: "For the truest poetry is the most feigning, and lovers are given to poetry; and what they swear in poetry may be said as lovers they do feign" [3.3.19–22]. It may have been an old joke, or another instance of Marston's imitating Shakespeare.

A number of plays were written to lampoon the plays and playwrights of rival theatres. It is particularly interesting that Marston's *What you Will* lampooned Ben Jonson by carrying on a "Poet's Quarrel," which some scholars refer to as the "War of the Theatres." Jonson, being a great satirist and as quick to take offense as to dish it out, gave Marston a run for the money—that is, for the cash of customers in the theatres who enjoyed the scrimmage and were eager to egg them on. The situation is aptly described in a speech from Marston's *What you Will*:

> This is the strain that chokes the theatres,
> That makes them crack with full-stuff'd audience.
> This is your humour only in request,
> Forsooth to rail; this brings your ears to bed,
> This people gape for.[189]

Eventually Jonson and Marston quit squabbling, although Jonson continued to have a difficult time with anyone who aimed to rival him.

Marston was twelve years younger than Shakespeare. After study at Oxford, he lived in the Middle Temple with his father, who was a prominent and prosperous lawyer. Records show that in the 1590's the elder Marston was counsel for the corporation of Stratford-on-Avon. John Marston was a friend of Thomas Greene, Shakespeare's "cousin, whose great-grandfather and Shakespeare's grandfather were brothers. When Greene entered the Middle Temple in 1595, both Marstons went sureties for Greene, a guarantee in case of default."[190] Greene became solicitor for Stratford in 1601, served as town clerk from 1603–1617, and for a brief time his family lived at Shakespeare's New Place. Greene named two of his children William and Ann, both Shakespeares possibly serving as their godparents.

Leslie Hotson writes, "The role of Middle Templars in Shakespeare's time from the neighborhood of Stratford is an impressive one." And he suggests that "Shakespeare had a special interest in the Middle Temple and the Middle Temple in him."[191] The Inns of Court were both residences of lawyers who needed to be in London when the courts were in session and were also schools where young gentlemen could become familiar with the legal system. They studied with experienced lawyers and were able to observe the tangles of court procedures. The Inns operated somewhat like private clubs or university colleges. They also were something of a stimulating hotbed for literary endeavors and private theatricals. While at the Middle Temple, John Marston caught the fever of writing snarling, biting, and bitter verse satires, which had become very fashionable in the 1590's. In *As You Like It,* Shakespeare used the role of the melancholy Jacques to comment on the nature of satirists and satire and to provide a dash of vinegar for the scenes in the forest. It has been plausibly suggested that Marston was Shakespeare's model for the melancholy Jacques.[192] It is difficult for us to understand this craze for satires. The victims, or imagined victims, of the satires naturally took offense. There was some meddling in church politics with the result that the Bishops were so disturbed that in 1599 they ordered no more satires would be allowed and unsold copies of certain satires were to be burnt. Marston's satires went into the conflagration along with others of the same stripe.

Marston continued writing satire, however, but now in the form of plays for Paul's Boys, a company made up of children who performed once a week in St. Paul's School. The playing space was similar to the hall of the Middle Temple, probably smaller, unlike the great outdoor amphitheatres used by professional players, but with a clientele who could pay more to be part of a private performance. Marston wrote at least five plays for them, *What you Will* being one of the first.

One of his plays that still causes a stir is *Antonio's Revenge*. It parodies and echoes situations and characters from Shakespeare's *Hamlet* and such relics from the older tradition of the revenge play as *The Spanish Tragedy, Titus Andronicus*, and material copied from the Roman tragedian, Seneca. But Marston's biggest debt is to *Hamlet*. What causes the stir is the difficulty of knowing how to take it; at times Marston seems to be lampooning by parody, at times praising by imitation. It seems disjointed because of all the switches in topics and tones. Bernard Harris aptly describes this quality as "shifts from philosophic reflection to bawdy abuse, from pathetic description and virtuous sentiment to serious invective."[193] John Marston knew a lot about theatrical fireworks. He certainly reinvigorated the revenge play, pushing the idea that revenge has to be more than just paying back; it requires more gore, more horrendous and appalling deeds.

Although it may seem odd that he would write such "adult" stuff for a company of children, it is understandable that he wouldn't let a Bishop's bonfire stop him, since satire was Marston's forte. We should remember, however, that Elizabethans were not Victorians. There had been a long tradition of child actors among choristers in the great cathedrals, the chapels of great nobles, and the town grammar schools. All were trained in acting as well as in singing. As they invariably took part in revels celebrating the Christmas season, their plays were expected to include some mockery of the audience and of authority in the spirit of a Winter Saturnalia. And because their performances were in some sense private theatricals, they were less badgered by censorship. Censors worry much more about what happens in public and less about what goes on in private parties.[194]

About this time Shakespeare wrote his own most satiric play, and one that is also, like Marston's, somewhat disjointed and rather difficult to know how to take, *Troilus and Cressida*. The story is based largely on Chaucer's *Troilus and Criseyda* and picked up through renewed interest in the Trojan War following George Chapman's translation of the first seven books of Homer's *Iliad*, published in 1598. The Trojan story, however, was also known in the various versions made by the Athenian tragedians, the Roman poets, and medieval redactors. Perhaps Shakespeare's treatment seems puzzling because it doesn't show the story as suffused with epic grandeur, a quality modern schooling has led us to expect in works based on the Homeric classics. Shakespeare is out to burlesque the supposed heroes instead of presenting them as committed to a noble cause. The Trojans fight on to keep Helen although they recognize she is not worth the war, and the Greek commanders are not worthy of the subservience they think they deserve. The lovers, Troilus and Cressida, are manipulated into bed by Pandarus, Cressida's uncle, who seems to think her being a mistress of Prince Troilus would provide protection, since her father had deserted to the Greek camp. When Cressida has to join her father in the Greek camp, their lovers' vows cannot weather the separation. The situation could have been made pathetic, but Shakespeare steers clear of that possibility.

The characterizations of the principal roles are also given a satiric twist. Achilles is not sulking in his tent because Agamemnon wounded his pride; he stays out of action because of a vow he made to Hecuba, the Trojan queen, and oddly enough, because he wants to marry a Trojan princess. However, he seems to prefer lolling in a day bed with his friend, Patroclus. And when he does fight, instead of doing it fairly, he has his thugs surround and cut down the unarmed Hector. Ajax is represented as a brainless muscle man, illiterate, and easily misled by the flattery of Ulysses and Nestor. Finally there is Thersites, the satiric commentator on the action, an off-duty clown and coward whose best bits are in mocking the great ones with funny, fantastic, and nasty insults.

Nevertheless, there are some very insightful comments and moments in the play. If we suppose *Troilus and Cressida* was intended to be epic stuff, we are bound to be perplexed. If, however, we put ourselves in the mood for satire, which is serious at heart, we will find that the play includes some very insightful comments. Several examples are in Hector's argument for not continuing the war: "'Tis mad idolatry/ To make the service greater than the god." "Thus to persist / In doing wrong extenuates not wrong, / But makes it much more heavy." The fundamental note of satiric seriousness is sounded not so much in dialogue as in the irony of the situation. The audience knows that Troy will fall, while the Trojans blindly strut to their confusion.

There is so much in it like the sort of thing Marston was writing for the Children of Paul's, that some scholars suggest it may have been written for a private performance at one of the Inns of Court. Others maintain that the Ajax role was intended as a caricature of Ben Jonson and the Thersites role as a caricature of Marston,[195] as in the sequence of knock-about farce where the stupid giant Ajax beats up on the waspish Thersites [2.1].

In his younger days Ben Jonson was a violent man and something of a malcontent. When he served briefly in the army in Flanders. he challenged one of the enemy to single combat, killed and stripped him. In his acting days he killed Gabriel Spencer, a fellow actor. At the height of their rivalry he beat Marston and "took his pistol from him." [196] Marston and Jonson got on well enough once they decided who was the alpha dog in the pack. I don't suppose urbanity was ever Jonson's style. There is an anecdote illustrating Jonson as a pedantic plodder and Shakespeare as his quick-witted rival. It is probably not a true story, although recorded by a clergyman, Thomas Fuller.

> Many were the wit-combats betwixt [Shakespeare] and Ben Jonson, which two I behold like a Spanish great Galleon and an English man of War; Master Jonson (like the former) was built far higher in learning; solid, but slow in his performances. Shakespeare, with the English man of War, lesser in bulk, but lighter in sailing, could turn with all tides, tack about and take advantage of all winds, by the quickness of his wit and invention. [197]

The anecdote is relished because it is so like the story of David and Goliath, or of Harry the Fifth and the French, or Shakespeare's scene of Thersites and Ajax.

At the same time Marston was plotting plays and also studying law, he must have known Sir John Salusbury, a fellow member of the Middle Temple. He was married to Ursula Stanley, the illegitimate, but recognized, daughter of Henry Stanley, the 4th Earl of Derby, a family with powerful connections. After several crown appointments, including service as Deputy Lieutenant of Denbighshire, Salusbury was knighted by Queen Elizabeth in 1601. In celebration of that honor, Robert Chester, a sort of household laureate to the Salusbury family, published *Love's Martyr*, a large collection of verse he and others had written at various times. No doubt to dress the volume in the latest fashion, he included selections from some well-known poets such as John Marston, Ben Jonson, and George Chapman. [198] They either knew Sir John personally or were on the lookout for patrons and would have welcomed the chance to salute the new knight. A poem by Shakespeare was also included, but his contribution doesn't seem appropriate. The poem was the mysterious and lovely lyric, *The Phoenix and the Turtle*. As far as we know, this is the only poem Shakespeare ever wrote for inclusion in another man's book. Robert Chester had every reason to want it included. At the time Shakespeare was better known than the younger Marston, Jonson, and

Chapman, who were just becoming celebrities. One of the central puzzles of *The Phoenix and the Turtle* is that it seems to have nothing in it congratulatory to Sir John Salusbury. Simple as the words are, their final significance is, to say the least, elusive. The poem seems to be a celebration of love and constancy (the turtle dove) and truth and beauty (the phoenix) and a lament for the death of these rare virtues in "one mutual flame." As Chester's volume is largely made up of work he wrote over a number of years, it could well be that Shakespeare's poem was also written and presented at an earlier time, perhaps on the occasion of some marriage or funeral in the Salusbury family. Shakespeare would have known them through his connection with the Stanley family, either through Ferdinando Stanley, Lord Strange, or through Ferdinando's father, Henry Stanley, the 4th Earl of Derby and the father-in-law of John Salusbury. Chester may have had a copy of the poem, and saw no reason to keep it out of print.[199]

Productions by the Children of Paul's that began in 1599 only lasted for seven years. It seems their auditorium was too small for the enterprise to be profitable. Further, after 1600 a new company, the Blackfriars Boys became more popular with the wealthier residents and visitors to the city.[200] Marston began writing for them almost as soon as they were organized. He eventually acquired a sixth share in the company.

When Henry Evans organized his children's company to play at the Blackfriars, he called them the Children of the Chapel to suggest that they were choristers of the royal chapel. Since a children's company had played in the Blackfriars in the 1580's, he did not run into the same opposition James Burbage had when he leased the great chamber in the Blackfriars to convert it to a public theatre for the Lord Chamberlain's Men. Cuthbert Burbage, who inherited his father's lease for the Blackfriars playhouse, was left with the problem of finding someone who could use it. He struck a deal with Evans, who took a twenty-one-year lease for his Children's Company. Apparently both Evans and Burbage believed the control authorities had over public playing did not extend to performances held in a private hall. Thus, they counted on performances by the children's company to be less disruptive. The boys only played once a week and to comparatively smaller audiences. Higher admission fees assured that only the elite would attend and the managers could still pull a profit.

John Marston's most famous play for the new Children's company was *The Malcontent*.[201] "Malcontents" were people who felt cheated of their rightful place or discontented with their station in life. The term was a kind of buzzword, often used frivolously. When used seriously it signified a person who takes on the task of setting things right, like Hamlet, or a person driven by ambition and envy to destroy anyone who blocks their road to power from impotence, Richard III for example. Whether favored or feared, the true malcontent is a dangerous person.

Marston's *Malcontent* is a revenge play with a new twist. The traditional revenge play would be entirely tragic. It would include kings and queens and others of high station, their speeches decorated with highfalutin language and Latin tags to give it a classical aura, a play about secret crimes, sex, madness, murder, usurpation, treachery, war, and tyranny, ending with the sudden death of all important persons. Marston's new twist was to make *The Malcontent* end in reconciliation. The usurper repents and restores the throne to the rightful duke, who is reunited with his wife. It is a tragicomedy, not a tragedy and not entirely a comedy. Marston was following a trend for this mixture of dramatic genres that first appeared in the works of the 16th-century Italian playwrights Tasso and Guarini, and became very popular in the English theatre in the early 17th century. Marston knew what he was doing; when the play was registered for printing, it was named, "Tragicomoedia."[202]

Marston's plot goes like this: Giovanni, the rightful Duke of Genoa, when driven from Genoa goes into disguise as Malevole, a satiric court jester. He is accepted in the court of the usurper, Duke Pietro. There he lurks about the palace, commenting on the persons and events which well illustrate life in a corrupt court. His sardonic and ironic insults please the Duke's twisted sense of humor. Malevole reminds us of Hamlet, powerless at the moment, but secretly working to recover his dukedom. His first move is to reveal to the Duke that his Duchess is bedding down with the chief minister, Mendoza, an intrigue reminiscent of Shakespeare's *Othello*.

As the play develops, the court looks like a mud pit of sexual and political jockeying. Almost every character, of whom there are many, is some sort of malcontent, but the one who fits the Richard III type is Mendoza. He hires killers to get rid of the Duke, plans to kill the assassin, to marry the Duchess, and then kill her. She happens to be heiress to the Duke of Florence and on her death Mendoza would become the heir of Florence. Then to strengthen his claim to Genoa, he plans to marry Malevole's wife, the former Duchess of Genoa, who has all this while been in prison. Malevole, the rightful Duke, and Pietro, the usurper, discover these schemes in a surprising reversal—each had been hired to kill the other! Pietro repents and unites with Malevole to effect the happy ending.

Shakespeare's next play after *Troilus* was *Othello, the Moor of Venice*. Part of the background of *Othello* arises from the relationship of England and Morocco. Englishmen had been trading there, in fact, since the middle of the 16th century. From that country one could obtain gold, "copper of the reddist and best for artillery than is found anywhere, sugar, dates, gum Arabic for clothiers, amber, wax, skins dressed for wearing and horses better than in Spain."[203] Morocco, or Barbary, was important for another reason. It provided a safe base from which to harry Spanish shipping. "A Barbary pirate was usually an Englishman who … was engaged in singeing the beard of the Spaniard."[204]

To further their mutual interests, an Ambassador from Barbary and his retinue took up residence in London during the winter of 1601–1602. Of course the Moors' exotic costume and outlandish manners were the center of attention wherever they went, and a play about a Moor in Venice was bound to be of interest.[205]

Shakespeare had opportunities to observe the Moorish retinue on the streets of London. They might have visited The Globe, one of the attractions of the city, or they may have seen the Chamberlain's Men performing at court, since it was customary for the company to be called to entertain distinguished visitors. However, the portrait of Othello does not come out of the exotic dress of a Moor. Shakespeare knew the actor's skill of putting himself in the shoes of a stranger. What would it be like to be in a foreign country, where everyone else is exotic, but you are the center of gaping attention? Think of a feathered Indian in London. Take it a step further and think of a Moor in Venice, a city like London, but notorious for subtle vice and treachery. It was a city on the frontier from which the Ottoman Turks threatened Christian Europe and its traffic for oriental luxury.

As was usually the case with Shakespeare, he dramatized a story from another piece of writing. *Othello* comes from a collection of Italian *novelle*, Giraldi Cinthio's *Hecatommithi*. The story is about a Moorish Captain who is married to a Venetian Lady, Desdemona. An Ensign tells the Moor that his wife is having an affair with a corporal. The wife is killed, the Ensign accuses the Moor of murder. He is tortured but cannot be made to confess and thus is exiled.[206]

The Italian story is stretched out over many days and incidents, but almost nothing in it suggests the emotional turmoil that Shakespeare was able to make out of Cinthio's dry *novella*. The many more characters and incidents in *Othello* are squeezed into a few days. However, the great intensity of the drama comes from the way Othello's soul is affected by the insinuations that Desdemona is false, made by the malcontent Iago. Slowly he is shaken to the depths of his being, helpless to recover his balance; filled with murderous rage, he finally collapses into incoherent babble. He recovers control, then calmly and deliberately, with agonizing remembrance of how he loved her, kills Desdemona. In the final catastrophe, he learns that the accusation was false and dies by his own hand.

Some readers find that Othello is too easily made jealous. Perhaps they are misled by the maxim that the character of the hero in a tragedy has to be flawed, so ways are found to blame Othello for the misery that overwhelms him. That assumption about tragic heroes, popular as it is, turns attention from the plot and foregrounds the character of the hero to the exclusion of the circumstances that surround him. Often overlooked are the many details worked into the drama that would make Othello wary and bit by bit by bit complete the web of circumstance that ensnares him. It isn't all Iago's doing. It could be said that there are no innocent incidents in the whole drama. Everything works toward the destructive end. The design of the play is masterful.

The Othello role is a long, unrelenting, and difficult one. According to a contemporary backstage anecdote, Richard Burbage was heard to say after performing Hamlet, "I can do anything!" So Shakespeare went home, wrote *Othello*, gave the script to Burbage saying, "Bet you can't do that!"[207]

Iago is presented as a malcontent in the Richard III tradition. He feels cheated because Othello did not appoint him his lieutenant. Iago hates the black Othello, hates the man who was appointed lieutenant, and his twisted jealousy of the love between Othello and Desdemona drives him to fashion a way to get back at them all. Perhaps what is most intriguing is the absolute matter-of-fact way Iago goes about it. There is no show of emotion. While he does allow himself to chortle now and then, and sometimes there is a note of triumph in his voice, it is only when alone. He is as dry as the story in Cinthio's collection that Shakespeare used to craft his drama. Like Richard III, Iago tells the audience what he is up to, and we are forced into watching him succeed.

On March 9, 1603 the playhouses of London were shut down. Queen Elizabeth was dying in her palace at Richmond. She was nearly seventy years old and had reigned for forty-five years. Throughout her reign the question of who would be her successor was a matter of great anxiety. Would the hostilities with the Catholic powers continue? Would penalties on Catholic practice remain in effect or would the successor initiate more tolerant policies? The Privy Counselors were fearful that in the crisis of the Queen's death, the passing of power would be disrupted by hotheads who would object to whoever was named the successor. When the old Queen died on March 24, a month-long period of mourning was observed. Even after that, the theatres remained closed because of another outbreak of the plague.[208]

It has never been clear whether the Queen actually named her successor before passing on, although James VI, the King of Scots and a great-grandson of Henry VIII, was proclaimed James I of England and was accepted without any immediate repercussions. Lord Hunsdon, the patron of Shakespeare's company, although officially no longer the late queen's Lord Chamberlain, managed to get his younger brother, Sir Robert Carey, out of Richmond Palace immediately after Elizabeth's death and on the road to Scotland to be the first to salute James as King of England.

There were, of course, many office-seekers for the royal offices who hastened north to greet the King as he leisurely made his way toward London. In addition to the new king's largess, his queen would also have her own household, with attendant offices as would their son, Prince Henry. Their younger son, Charles, a frail three-year-old, was placed in the care of Lady Carey, the wife of Sir Robert, who got little else for his break-neck ride to Scotland. To others, titles, lands, pensions, and honors were given with a more lavish hand. The King ordered the release of Southampton from the Tower, eventually restored his Earldom, made him a Gentleman of the Privy Chamber, and a Knight of the Garter. The young Earl of Pembroke, another of those out of favor with Elizabeth, was cheered by the sun of the new regime. He too was made one of the Privy Chamber and a Knight of the Garter. At the coronation he kissed the king on the cheek instead of the hand, for which he was given a playful cuff on the cheek. James liked to have handsome young men about him. Very shortly after succeeding to the throne, James issued a royal patent to Shakespeare's company licensing them as his servants, "freely to use and exercise the art and faculty of playing." It may seem odd that the King would concern himself with giving an acting company the prestige and title of "His Majesty's Servants," when so much needed attention in the early days of his reign. Perhaps this signal mark of favor was prompted by Pembroke or, possibly, Southampton.[209]

Shakespeare and his fellows were not enjoying prosperous times. The return of the plague to London in the spring of 1603 closed the theatres and kept them closed until the following spring. The court avoided the city, as did anyone with an estate in the country or who had a friend there. Only the nobility were allowed to attend the coronation on July 25th in Westminster, and the royal entry through London from the Tower to Westminster, usually held in conjunction with a coronation, did not occur until March of 1604.

His Majesty's Players were on the road at this time. Records show them at Bath, Shrewsbury, Coventry, Ipswich, Maldon, and Oxford. In December they were at Mortlake in Surrey, near the home of their colleague, Augustine Phillips, away from the infected city, but close enough to make a quick return to London as soon as playing was allowed. From there they were summoned to Wilton, seat of the Earl of Pembroke, for a special performance before the king. A family tradition holds that Lady Pembroke wrote to her son, "telling him to bring James I from Salisbury to see *As You Like It*; 'we have the man Shakespeare with us.'"[210]

When the King celebrated his first Christmas revels in England, from December 26th to February 19th, his players gave seven performances at Hampton Court Palace and one at Whitehall. There is no record of which plays were presented, but eight performances at court are more than Elizabeth ever called for. The enthusiasm of the royal family for the King's Players may have been in part because the repertory was all new to them, as was the English style of theatre. Then too the king or one of his advisors was aware that as long as the plague kept the public theatres in London closed, the usual reward for a performance at court would help keep the company together through hard times. At the conclusion of the Hampton Court revels and by a warrant from the council, an award of thirty pounds over and above the usual payments for performances was signed over to Richard Burbage for "the maintenance and relief of himself and the rest of the company."[211] The London theatres were closed except for a brief period after Easter 1603, but closed a month later when the plague returned to the city.

The revels of 1604–1605 were kept at Whitehall. His Majesty's Players ran through a repertory of ten plays from All Saints Day to Shrove Tuesday: Shakespeare's *The Moor of Venice*, *The Merry Wives of Windsor*, *Measure for Measure*, *The Play of Errors*, *Love's Labour's Lost*, *Henry V*, and *The Merchant of Venice*, which was repeated by order of the King. In addition, there were two by Ben Jonson, *Every Man Out of his Humour*, *Every Man In his Humour*, and one anonymous and lost play called, *The Tragedy of the Spanish Maze*. But they were not the only company to perform. The Queen's Men, the new name for the old Lord Admiral's Men, presented one play, the Prince's Men eight, and the Children of the Queen's Revels, the new name for the Children of the Chapel, gave one performance.[212] The royal family had become theatre enthusiasts. The King, who was not always at court performances, may have preferred hunting, but his family liked all kinds of entertainment. For Twelfth Night in 1604, *The Masque of Blackness* was sponsored at great expense by the Queen and devised in contentious collaboration between the poet Ben Jonson, who wrote the dialogues and songs, and the architect Inigo Jones, who designed the elaborate scenic effects. The sensation of the production was the Queen's appearance with her Ladies as daughters of Niger dancing in black makeup. Dudley Carlton wrote to his friend, John Chamberlain:

> The presentation of the mask at the first drawing of the traverse, was
> very fair and their apparel rich, but too light and courtesan-like. Their
> black faces and hands, which were painted and bare up to the elbows,
> was a very loathsome sight and I am sorry strangers should see our court
> so strangely disguised.[213]

Conventionally dancers in a mask were dressed in outlandish and bizarre costumes; Queen Anne seems to have gone a step farther. It is possible that she came by the idea when she saw a performance of *Othello* in black face, the first performance of the court season three months earlier.

By the King's patent, the ten principal sharers of the former Lord Chamberlain's Company became servants of his Majesty with the rank of Grooms of the Chamber. This gave them prestige if not much in the way of perquisites. They were issued an allotment of red cloth for the royal livery they wore on ceremonial occasions as part of the large effects that troop with majesty. And so they appeared for the ceremonial opening of Parliament in March 1604. This doubled for the traditional coronation procession from the Tower to Westminster that was canceled at the actual coronation because of the plague. In August the King's Men attended the Constable of Castile and his entourage, who came to London to negotiate peace between England and Spain. This was a first step in King James' foreign policy designed to live up to his personal motto, *Beati Pacifici,* blessed are the peacemakers.

It is hard to know whether the King himself took a particular interest in the affairs of his players or regarded keeping them simply as one of the obligations of a monarch. However, as "Common Players" the King's Men depended on public performances when the theatres would be allowed to open.

In the early 18th century it was reported that Sir William D'Avenant, a godson of Shakespeare had "an amiable letter" that King James was pleased to write with his own hand to Master Shakespeare.[214] The amiable letter itself was never printed and has since disappeared, so we can't very well guess when the King had been prompted to write. It may have been after seeing *Measure for Measure* during the Christmas revels of 1604–1605.

The argument has been made that *Measure for Measure* reflects many of the characteristic notions and ideas King James expressed in his book *Basilicon Doron,* that is, "The King's Gift," a treatise on government written for his son, Prince Henry. It became a best-seller as curiosity about the new monarch developed.[215] Although Shakespeare may have had the royal ear in mind when he managed to work some royal opinions into the fabric of his play, perhaps it would be more helpful for us to notice that *Measure for Measure* takes its title from the Gospel text "Judge not, that you be not judged. For with the judgment you pronounce you will be judged, and the measure you give will be the measure you get" [Matthew 7:1–3]. Without giving much attention to that text, commentators often describe the play as a satiric and cynical picture of official hypocrisy and corruption. It used to be categorized as a "problem play," a presentation of a social problem to promote a discussion rather than a resolution. *Measure for Measure* remains comedic however, especially when we note the fantasy of its plotting.

Here is the situation. The ruling Duke leaves the city in the charge of a young deputy. The deputy takes himself and his duties much too seriously and he intends to enforce neglected ordinances against vice. He closes bawdy houses and tries to punish fornication and bastardy with a death sentence. A young man who violated the law is sentenced to death. His sister goes to the strict deputy to plead for the life of her brother, and the girl's eloquence and beauty has an unexpected effect on the deputy. He calls her for a second interview and proposes a wicked switch: if she will satisfy his lust, he will pardon her brother. But that isn't all. The girl was a novice preparing to enter a nunnery when she undertook to plead for her brother, and this aspect of her situation makes the deputy's proposal more shocking. It makes her innocence and naïveté more appealing, and even the deputy seems surprised at the violence of his feelings.

Told in this unvarnished way, there is little to laugh about, but it is obvious that the situation is fantastic. Not only is the extreme severity of the law a sort of fairy tale riddle, but the duke who appointed the young deputy has gone into disguise and has remained in the city to watch what would happen. We are aware that any moment he can come forward and reverse the movement toward the scaffold.

As it becomes clear that the deputy has no intention of fulfilling his part of the bargain, the play turns in the direction of farce as the disguised duke tries to control the action, pulling one hare-brained scheme after another out of his hat. Things don't always work as he expects, but he happens to know that the deputy had rejected a girl to whom he had been formally engaged. Knowing this the duke sets up a bed-trick, substituting the betrothed for the novice the deputy planned to seduce. The bed-trick opens the deputy to the charge of fornication. In addition, the disguised duke substitutes the head of a murderer for the head of the boy the deputy condemned to death for fornication. Thus, the deputy is trapped when the measure he gave to others becomes the measure by which he is judged. There are problems with *Measure for Measure*. Scenes of a bawdy house being shut down, the device of the bed-trick, and the substitution of severed heads, provide a strain of comedy displeasing to the squeamish.

Shakespeare's *All's Well That Ends Well* and *Measure for Measure* are comparable in many ways. In fact one critic wrote, "*Measure for Measure* and *All's Well* are obvious twins."[216] Again Shakespeare uses the device of the bed-trick to get a peevish youth to bed his bride. The leading young men in both plays would be unforgivably self-centered if they were not so young. Both plays are based on old and traditional stories, but the entertaining quality of a fairy tale and the pleasure of a well-planned play are not much appreciated by readers. Shakespeare's "problem plays" go over much better with audiences.[217]

In *All's Well*, Helena, the heroine, miraculously cures the King of France who rewards her by marrying her to one of his wards, Count Bertram, who despises Helena for being beneath him in station. He takes off for the wars in Italy. She follows him in disguise and tricks him into consummating the marriage. Count Bertram indeed is a very shallow fellow. Even his mother the Countess calls him a "rash and unbridled boy." But there are things to be said in his favor that come through by the way Shakespeare dramatizes the story. When his father died, Bertram became a ward of the King; he had the chance for a courtier's life and a chance to make a name for himself. As a youth he had been raised in a household that included Helena, a poor physician's daughter. He saw her as a servant. Leaving for the wars in Italy was indeed a way to shirk his responsibility to his family and king. He is also shown under the influence of a braggart soldier named Parolles, whose extravagant speeches about the honor of a soldier's life mislead the young count.

In both *All's Well* and *Measure*, Shakespeare works out a complicated final scene where deceptions and disguises are revealed. The erring young men are put in fear of their lives and then to public humiliation in front of the assembled characters. Finally when the controlling figure, the king or the duke, accepts their repentance, they are received again as worthy to marry the women who love them. Given the more realistic dramatic expectations of modern audiences as well as readers, these wrap-up scenes seem hopelessly contrived; all is unraveled so quickly we feel bamboozled into accepting them.

Probably from the time James VI of Scotland could hope of one day becoming James I of England, he dreamed of uniting the two kingdoms. From his first meetings with Parliament he tried to get approval of a plan to unite England and Scotland. Indeed, England and Scotland were often in open conflict, and the miseries that followed their border wars were strong arguments for unification and also unfortunately for mistrust. It is hardly possible that Shakespeare was unaware of this royal agenda, for the inevitable conflicts of a divided realm form the political background of his next play, *King Lear*. Although it was probably written earlier, in 1606 it was played before "the King's Majesty at Whitehall upon St. Stephen's Night in Christmas Holidays," as reads the title page of the printed copy.

The tragedy arises when Lear splits his kingdom in half, to be ruled by his rival daughters, the wives of the dukes of Albany and Cornwall. If that is in the background, in the foreground, as in all serious dramas, are the human relationships of fathers and children, husbands and wives, masters and servants. The play begins like a fairy tale with a childish riddle. King Lear is about to divide his kingdom among his three daughters. He asks them which one loves him most, hinting that the one who gives the most pleasing answer will get the most. His two eldest daughters respond with the expected flattery, but the youngest, preferring deeds to protestations, tells him simply that she loves him according to her bond. Lear is hurt and disowns this child. In the bitter consequences that flow from his misunderstanding, he learns, slowly but certainly, the difference between the cunning and the false and between the artful and the true. He learns that love cannot be bought, and a fact unbearably sweet, that love is something given, not something earned.

As the daughters who grasped at estates by flattering their old father turn on him, the play brings us face to face with disturbing facts. Those who bargain for love, or life, become the victims of an awakened lust that cannot be stopped in its ruthless and destructive pursuit of selfish ends. The hunger for power and possessions turns society into a jungle. Humanity preys upon itself.

In pursuit of his theme Shakespeare creates a host of characters ranging over many human relationships and delineates them in strong and incredible contrasts. The men and women are clearly divided between those who see their relationships as opportunities either to exploit or to express love and service. Between such natures there is a radical conflict. They cannot agree on what to call wisdom and folly, treason and loyalty, reason and madness, honesty and deceit. To opposite characters the words carry opposite meanings. The foundations are shaken. Perhaps this is best illustrated in scenes where a wise fool, a crazed king, and a madman try to make sense of a mad world, and in a scene where the king in rags tries to comfort a blind man betrayed by his own son.

But the tragedy is both disturbing and affecting. It contains the appalling scene of a father being tortured and blinded through the treachery of his son—surely the most terrible scene in Shakespeare—where the bond of filial piety is savagely violated. But the play contains as well the beautiful scene where Lear is reunited with the daughter he disowned, and where her bond is shown to have held through the dark night of hatred and rejection. To see *Lear* in a theatre or to read it is to sense there is more in it than we can embrace all at once. It is like a complicated piece of music, hinting at but not quite expressing a distant harmonic resolution. Something has happened that has to be explored further. Many of Shakespeare's plays possess that inexplicable quality, but none, I think, in quite the degree that *Lear* does.

Shakespeare's *Timon of Athens*, written about the same time as *Lear*, has, I think, something of that same quality, although it has not fared well with commentators. One critic, who shall be nameless, called *Timon*, "the after-birth of *King Lear*." This nutshell comment includes at least two points, that *Timon* and *Lear* come out of the same matrix, and that *Timon* is a repulsive and chaotic play. The story of Timon certainly has similarities to the story of Lear. Timon is a fabulously wealthy man who carelessly gives away his fortune, supposing he can always rely on the gratitude of those who gained by his lavish give-away program. After he has squandered everything, his creditors gang up on him, and his fair weather friends deny his appeals for aid. There follows a terrific reversal: Timon shifts from riotous benevolence to rooted malevolence. From then on his speeches seethe with some of the most vitriolic tirades ever devised by a misanthropic imagination. They are like King Lear at his most bitter, only more extensive and exciting. He curses Athens and all of mankind, avoids human contact, and takes up a solitary life in the woods.

For all the similarities, *Timon* is more than a variation on themes from Lear. Timon's former steward is the one person who tries to relieve him. But unlike Lear who can finally accept and return the love of his faithful daughter, Timon, though shaken by the faithfulness of his steward, sends him away, resolved to die alone. As to the point that *Timon of Athens* is repulsive and chaotic, even those who like the play will admit that Timon's bitter speeches are too much. Shakespeare doesn't seem able to stop, and there may be too many illustrations of the same point, but there is something to be said for excess, and a tirade cut short is no longer a tirade.

The additional criticism that the play seems chaotic owes something to the simple but innovative form in which it is written. In a naïve and straightforward manner, the play divides into two parts. Timon is rich, the center of a social whirl, then an alienated bankrupt, but the one part does not lead inevitably to the second. Put another way, the second part does not resolve what is amiss in the first part. It is a radically different play from *Lear*. To be fair, it would be better to put *Lear* aside and assume the playwright was after something else. Let us consider, for example, that Shakespeare's aim was to expose the abuse and abusiveness of money, something that calls for a different dramatic form, one more abstract and less personal than one about human relationships. Some commentators, noticing the energy and preciseness of the writing and the simple effectiveness of the plotting, still sense that the play is formless because the printed script shows signs of being an unfinished or an unpolished draft. We have an apparently unbridgeable division of opinion both about Timon the character and *Timon* the play.[218]

It is intriguing, however, to notice the moment that comes near the end of the play, when the senators of Athens seek Timon out in the woods to urge him to return to the city. Timon says:

> Why, I was writing of my epitaph;
> It will be seen to-morrow. My long sickness
> Of health and living now begins to mend,
> And nothing brings me all things.

(5.1.185–188)

In that brief moment of clarity there is a glimmer of recognition that he had it all wrong. Those words are bleak. They come from an alien, a stranger, an oracle with a message for meditation.

⁊

In 1604, the King's Men got hold of a copy of Marston's *Malcontent*, originally written for the Children of the Queen's Revels, that is, the former Blackfriars Boys. With the help of John Webster, and possibly of Marston himself, alterations were made in the script. Since performances in the children's indoor playhouse featured musical interludes, and the King's Men, except for noisy drums and trumpets, couldn't use music effectively in their outdoor amphitheater, additional dialogue was provided to make up for the time given to music between the acts in the Blackfriars. About 450 lines were added or about a half hour of playing time. This included an "Induction" in which the actors pretended to be part of the audience. One lively exchange goes like this:

Sly [pretending to be from the country]. I would know how you came by this play?

Condell [speaking for the company]. Faith, sir, the book was lost, and because 'twas pity so good a play should be lost, we found it and play it.

Sly. I wonder you would play it, another company having an interest in it?

Condell. Why not Malevole in folio with us, as Jeronimo in decimo-sexto with them?

They taught us a name for our play. We call it *One for another*....

Sinklo [pretending to be another countryman, speaking of Burbage]. Doth he play the Malcontent?

Condel. Yes, sir.

Sinklo. I durst lay four of mine ears, the play is not so well acted as it hath been.

(Induction 70–77, 83–86)

The joke about the book—their word for a script—being lost and found could only be taken seriously by countrymen. You don't filch a play from the Queen's Revels without some sort of agreement, probably with Marston himself. The "one for another" comment suggests that the children's performance of *Jeronimo* (another name for the *Spanish Tragedy*) is another piece of whimsy, since by then the old play was common property that seems to have been a regular source of ridicule.

When George Chapman, Ben Jonson, and John Marston collaborated in writing *Eastward Ho*, another play for the Children of the Queen's Revels, published in 1605, an apprentice who wasted time at the theatre sounded off with the opening lines from *The Spanish Tragedy*:

When this eternal substance of my soul
Did live imprisoned in my wanton flesh ...
I was a courtier in the Spanish court.[219]

The production of *Eastward Ho* created some problems for the playwrights. Some lines in the play implied criticism of King James for favoring so many of his fellow Scots in the court, for selling knighthoods, and for the plan to unify Scotland and England. A Scottish noble, Sir James Murray, took offense at the play and complained to the king. The playwrights were arrested and thrown in jail. Marston left town, but Jonson and Chapman were threatened with having their ears and noses cut off. In a short time, however, the offenders were released without the threatened mutilations being carried out.[220] There is more to tell about the Revels Company taking risks in offending courtiers that will be reviewed in the next Chapter.

As a regular member of the company, it is probable that Shakespeare took a role in the adaptation of Marston's *Malcontent* staged by the King's Men, but there is no way of knowing which role he took. Unfortunately Shakespeare was not one of the five actors who performed in the "Induction" written for their production. If he had been, perhaps we would have a better idea of the kind of roles he might have wanted to play. We can tell from the Induction, for instance, that Will Sly and John Sinklo took the roles of men from the country, while Henry Condell was given a role as a spokesman for the company with an ironic edge to his straightforward responses.

Early in the morning of November 5,1605, a mysterious stranger and thirty-six barrels of gunpowder were discovered in a room beneath the House of Lords in Westminster. If someone had detonated the powder when the King, Queen, Prince, and lords were gathered for an opening of Parliament, all would have died in one monstrous explosion. One discovery led to another until it was revealed that a conspiracy of a few Catholic gentlemen had planned this outrageous violence as preliminary to setting up a new regime. They seemed to think they could use the nine-year-old Princess Elizabeth as a figurehead, although they had not lined up a regent and were convinced there would be aid from Spain, although a treaty of peace between Spain and England had been concluded only a few months before.

What could have provoked them to set off on such a mad escapade? A partial answer to the mystery has something to do with the hope the English Catholics once had for better times under James I. During the years following the attack by the Spanish armada, Elizabeth's ministers imposed more and more stringent fines against recusants who refused to attend Protestant services, and harsh penalties were imposed for harboring a priest or for hearing mass in a private chapel. When James was the presumptive heir, he cannily avoided saying anything that might alienate his future Catholic subjects, who saw his ambiguous silence as a sign that he might be more tolerant. For one thing, Queen Anne had converted to Catholicism. While she attended Protestant services, at the coronation she refused to take Communion with her husband. And when James was first installed he allowed a one-year suspension of the fines levied on recusants. A new day seemed to be dawning. But as soon as the royal treasury needed cash, the fines were reinstated. From his pronouncements in Parliament and at the Hampton Court Conference, which laid the groundwork for the King James translation of the Bible, the king finally made it clear that the laws would not be changed. The Gunpowder Plot was the conspirators' reaction. They were real life malcontents. As recusants they were tired of the fines and restrictions. The priests who secretly ministered to the recusant community may have preached patience and that things would only be made worse by even a whisper of recalcitrance. The conspirators had no time for such talk and went forward gathering horses, weapons, and gunpowder.

In the end they were hunted down. Although some escaped to the continent, others were killed in the chase or captured and tortured for further information. The remaining conspirators were executed in the ghastly process reserved for traitors: hanged on a scaffold, cut down while yet alive, their guts ripped out, emasculated, and their bodies finally cut into four pieces.

The English still commemorate the November 5th discovery by burning Guy Fawkes in effigy. Although Fawkes was not the chief architect of the conspiracy, he became so in the popular mind, for he was the mysterious stranger discovered with the powder kegs under the House of Lords.[221]

It was difficult for the government to believe that the few men who planned the treasonable gunpowder plot devised their astonishing scheme without the encouragement and direction of others. It seemed obvious that Jesuits working underground were to blame and must be caught in the same net. The suspects were all devoted Catholics; surely they had said something to their spiritual advisors? And if priests were obligated not to reveal what they heard in a confessional, that gave the Attorney General an opening to infer all sorts of dark secrets. And he had another card to play. As it happened, the Superior of the Jesuits in England was Father Henry Garnet. He was found to be the author of "A Treatise on Equivocation," a discussion of ways to avoid betraying secrets by answering questions with ambiguous and equivocal statements. After Father Garnet was captured and put on trial, Sir Edward Coke, the Attorney General, worked very hard to insinuate that Garnet, the great equivocator, was in back of the conspirators or aided them by not reporting what he knew. Garnet was convicted and executed as a traitor.

The discovery of the attempt to blow up the government was deeply disturbing and threatening. It created a mood in some ways analogous to the one immediately after the destruction of the World Trade Center in New York. The sense of terror from a mysterious evil is reflected in Shakespeare's *Macbeth*, his most concentrated and haunting tragedy.

It is worth noticing how the topic of equivocation pervades the play. In the context of the trial of Father Garnet, it is easy to conclude that making equivocal statements is the same as telling lies. But the matter is not that simple; equivocation takes many forms. In fact, it could be said that William Shakespeare was a master of equivocation. Riddles, puns, double meanings, ironic meanings and ironic situations are the very lifeblood of his drama. The action in *Macbeth* arises from the oracles of witches and from ambiguous images conjured by sorcery.

Early in the tragedy, after saving King Duncan of Scotland from rebels supported by foreign invaders, Macbeth and his fellow captain Banquo encounter three ambiguous figures who give them prophetic greetings. We can't quite tell what they are—men, women, witches, emanations? Their salutations imply that Macbeth will be Thane of Cawdor, then King of Scotland and that his fellow captain Banquo will be the father of many kings. The prophecies turn out to be true.

Anticipating that, Macbeth and his wife take steps to make sure that they do. They secretly murder King Duncan and the grooms of his chamber. Although they are accepted as the new King and Queen, the nobles of Scotland soon suspect foul play, and Macbeth finds himself using all the tricks of a tyrant to secure his throne. He hires thugs to kill Banquo, because he knows too much. And he uses spies and informers to keep eyes out for any sign of disaffection, desperately trying to hide the truth from himself and his subjects. Since no one dares trust anyone else, not knowing who is in the pay of the tyrant, in scene after scene Shakespeare shows how the minor characters must talk guardedly, using equivocation to avoid the truth. For example:

> *Rosse.* Here comes the good Macduff.
> How goes the world, Sir, now?

> *Macduff.* Why, see you not?
> *Rosse.* Is't known, who did this more than bloody deed?
> *Macduff.* Those that Macbeth hath slain. *[that is, the grooms]*
> *Rosse.* Alas, the day! What good could they pretend?
> *Macduff.* They were suborn'd
> Malcolm and Donalbain, the King's two sons,
> Are stol'n away and fled; which puts upon them
> Suspicion of the deed.

> (2.4.20–27)

Suspicion of Macbeth is expressed by stating the official line in the dry tones of irony, by equivocation. No more straight talk. Even the Macbeths are cut off from each other. She eventually is overwhelmed by guilt and fear; he feels he must wade on in crime, but avoids telling her what he is doing.

As rebellious forces gather, Macbeth goes to sorcerers for a new set of prophecies. In a scene modeled on the story of King Saul and the Witch of Endor, Macbeth finds the witches and demands to be shown the future [4.1]. They conjure up mysterious apparitions who show and tell him what he wants to know: to beware Macduff; that none of woman born shall harm him; that he cannot be vanquished till Birnam wood come to Dunsinane. Just as the opening prophecies of the witches led him to the murder of Duncan and Banquo, Macbeth acts on his own understanding of these ambiguous apparitions. When he learns that Macduff has gone to England to get Malcolm, the son of Duncan, to claim the Scottish throne, he sends a death squad to destroy Macduff's family. Macbeth then strongly fortifies his castle at Dunsinane, which is captured by an army camouflaged by branches from Birnam forest. He begins to see how he misread the apparitions.

In Dunsinane castle Macbeth is cornered by Macduff who tells him, "Macduff was from his mother's womb / Untimely ripp'd" [5.8.15–16]. Macbeth recognizes the equivocation of the phrase, "none of woman born."

> Accursed be that tongue that tells me so, …
> And be these juggling fiends no more believ'd,
> That palter with us in a double sense,
> That keep the word of promise to our ear,
> And break it to our hope.

> (5.8.17–22)

Returning to the scene of sorcery, the last illusion Macbeth sees is in response to his question, "Shall Banquo's issue ever / Reign in this kingdom?" Out of the witches' cauldron appears a line of kings stretching out to the crack of doom. There is something ambiguous about that royal parade, perhaps not to King James who claimed descent from Banquo. Others may be tempted to ask, how did Banquo's line become kings of Scotland? Macbeth did not sit on the throne without murder; nor did Malcolm without invasion and rebellion, the same situation of rebellion and invasion with which the play opened.[222]

There are however other moments in the play that could be read as directed to the special interests of King James.[223] The tragedy was probably first performed during the summer of 1606, when King Christian of Denmark visited England for a visit with his sister, Queen Anne. The two kings spent a lot of time hunting and tilting, but performances by the King's Men were featured in three evenings. For ordinary folk the high point of the visit would have been the elaborate procession through London to welcome the royal visitor. At a pageant erected at Cheapside, John Marston wrote a speech for a figure representing "Concordia" in praise of Peace and Unity, thus alluding to King James' program for peace with Spain and for unity with Scotland. Marston wrote in Latin, a language both kings could understand, although probably not many in the crowd that lined the street. The King's Men as Grooms of the Chamber were called out in their red liveries to be part of the large procession, and it seems likely that Shakespeare heard "Concordia's" speech, for some lines in *Macbeth* allude to it. On hearing Macduff's plea to lead an uprising to supplant Macbeth, Malcolm tests Macduff by claiming that he would be a worse tyrant than Macbeth:

> I should
> Pour the sweet milk of concord into Hell,
> Uproar the universal peace, confound
> All unity on earth.
>
> (4.3.97–100)

For the moment Malcolm slanders himself, equivocating to test his visitor.

While it is true that much of the play reflects the particular interests of King James such as witchcraft and demonology, the setting in Scotland, the gunpowder treason, and the fear of Jesuit plotting indicate the play is not simply a grab bag of opinions and situations set up to please the king. There is, as always in a play by Shakespeare, a voice from the other side. The witches are spiteful creatures, outside of the political and social order. To them a battle is both lost and won. They have no stake in the outcome; fair is foul and foul is fair. They are punished, tortured, burnt as were the gunpowder conspirators, made vicious and evil for not being allowed to be themselves.

CHAPTER 7

MUCEDORUS
1606–1613

Wife. Hold up thy head *Rafe*, show the gentlemen what
    thou canst do, speak a huffing part, I warrant you the
    gentlemen will accept of it.
Citizen. Do *Rafe*, do.
Rafe. By heaven me thinks it were an easy leap
    To pluck bright honor from the pale-fac'd moon,
    Or dive into the bottom of the sea,
    Where never fathom line touch't any ground,
    And pluck bright honor from the lake of hell.
Citizen. How say you gentlemen, it is not as I told you?
Wife. Nay, gentlemen, he hath played before, my husband
    says, *Mucedorus* before the wardens of our company.
               (*The Knight of the Burning Pestle,* Induction)

DURING the first ten years of the reign of James I, that is 1603-1613, public performances in London were severely interrupted by nearly annual visitations of the plague.[224] Locked out of The Globe in plague time, particularly from May to November, the King's Men had to rely on touring, private, and court performances to keep themselves together and their repertoire fresh. This, of course, restricted the number of new plays they would need to produce. As a rule, Shakespeare had provided his company with two new plays a year up until 1603; after that his average was down to one a year.

There are some commentators who suggest that his work after 1603 was no longer up to his usual standard and that his best work had already been done. But I think he was now doing some of his most fascinating and affecting dramas.

With more time to devise and rehearse, he tried new and more complicated forms of drama that could even be called experiments. Certainly he pushed beyond the usual limits of theatrical practice in his time, as successful dramatists like Sophocles, Euripides, and Ibsen had done when they wanted to go beyond past achievements and move on to something new.

Shakespeare was never one to repeat himself. He often returned to similar themes and stories, but he always handled them with an imaginative and inventive twist. He returned, for instance, to matters of Roman history he had used in *Titus Andronicus, The Rape of Lucrece* and *Julius Caesar* when he wrote *Antony and Cleopatra* and *Coriolanus*. The difference is that in those two later plays the story unfolds through numerous scenes and characters spread out like an historic tapestry instead of being concentrated in the manner of tragedy. In both there are moments when powerful and unexpected emotions sweep over the stage, but for the most part the pace is almost leisurely.

Modern readers of *Antony and Cleopatra* often overlook its simplicity and think of cinematic and operatic grandeur in an attempt to call up Rome and Egypt in the pompous style of Hollywood or of Verdi's *Aida*. This path to windy spectacle is not the way Shakespeare imagines the story. He is much more solid and down to earth. For all the rich historic detail deftly sketched from reports of off-stage events, the action is staged in private places. Messengers, even ambassadors, are heard in privacy, not in audience halls. Negotiations are concluded in Rome by secret agreement and celebrated by drinking bouts. The play might be called "Private Lives, or The Inside Story of Antony and Cleopatra." Cleopatra is usually accompanied on stage by Charmian and Iras, who are presented more as play fellows than as ladies-in-waiting. Antony puts on his armor in the boudoir after one more gaudy night. We can imagine Cleopatra in the regalia of sovereignty only in the final scene, and even then the dialogue suggests she is dressing for marriage with Antony.[225]

At the center of the play is an adulterous affair. Shakespeare goes as far as he ever has in showing the heat of a stormy, sensual, and consuming passion. Both lovers are tied not only by lust, but also by complicated political considerations. To the Romans, Antony is a doting fool, an old ruffian cooling his lust with a gypsy, a view that Octavius Caesar exploits as he moves toward seizing absolute power. Cleopatra must hold on to Antony to have some voice in the affairs of Rome but all the while she suspects that he might compromise her position by striking a deal with those opposed to Egyptian influence. Antony, to keep his part in the triumvirate of power set up after the death of Julius Caesar, must control the eastern part of the empire, which means he must control Cleopatra. Yet he suspects that she might betray him to Octavius to secure her place as Egypt's queen. These calculations, though indirectly spoken, are what lie behind their tormented and torrential quarrels.

The political side of *Antony and Cleopatra* is somewhat obscured by the superb characterization of Cleopatra. She is a woman of "infinite variety," imperious, playful, devious, funny, and one step ahead of all the men in her life—not unlike the image biographers give us of Queen Elizabeth. Cleopatra so dazzles us that we hardly notice the net tightening about her. Her opposite is Octavius. He is sober, cold, efficient, and dull, determined to become the next Caesar. Antony comes across as the man in the middle, with something of Cleopatra's attractiveness and, unfortunately in contrast to Octavius, too impressed with his past achievements and impeded by an unrealistic political sense. This subtle and convincing interplay of characters adds luster to Cleopatra and also, I think, distracts us from noting the political realities Shakespeare developed in his treatment of the story.

Coriolanus, written about the same time as *Antony and Cleopatra*, again develops the story of a man caught in a political struggle too complex for him to understand.[226] The protagonist, Caius Marcius, is a Roman aristocrat presented as courageous, skillful, and deadly, an ideal member of the warrior class. Early in the play, as a one-man army he captures the enemy town of Corioli. When the gates open and the enemy soldiers sally forth, the common soldiers of Rome break and run. Caius Marcius rashly storms through the open gates. When the common soldiers refuse to follow, he gets trapped inside as the gates are closed. Alone, he fights so ferociously and kills so many that the town surrenders. To celebrate this amazing feat, the Roman general and fellow soldiers by acclamation honor him with the surname Coriolanus.

The story then turns from the field of battle to the forum of civil life. The Senate nominates Coriolanus for the post of consul, the highest ranking political office in ancient Rome and often with military generalship. There is no question that Coriolanus is qualified for that post, except for his irascible and uncompromising manner. The problem is that the appointment is not simply a senatorial one. The candidate must ask the people to approve the nomination, seemingly a rubberstamp, *pro forma* procedure. But Coriolanus hates the whole idea. He has no respect for the people and finds it insulting to beg anything from them. He has experienced their cowardice in battle, and as far as he can see, they deserve no voice in public affairs.

The matter is exacerbated by an innovation in the governmental structure of the Roman republic. Tribunes have been recently created to represent the interests of the people. The tribunes are of course anxious to assert their new powers and insist that Coriolanus must beg the suffrage of the people. He reluctantly appeals for votes while making it clear he thinks he deserves automatic approval. The tribunes pounce on his churlish compliance and manipulate the crowd to demand that Coriolanus be banished from the city.

At this point, the great climax and turning point of the drama, Coriolanus proudly turns his back on the city with the defiant cry, "I banish you!" Then he does what made his name a byword: he deserts Rome and offers his services to Corioli, the enemy city, and leads their army in an attack on Rome. Shakespeare's insight is that Coriolanus has no inkling of the consequences of turning his back on his friends and family. He acts as if he were "author of himself." Anger and pride have consumed his reason. The pleas for mercy and forbearance from his former companions-in-arms, his friends, even the mute gestures of his wife and son are dismissed without a sign of remorse. Only a long harangue from his mother moves him finally to relent. As an exile from Rome he returns to Corioli where he is assassinated for betraying the interests of the enemy town.

If during 1607 the London theatre was relatively inactive because of plague visitations, Shakespeare's off-stage life could not have been dull. On June 5, 1607 Shakespeare's daughter Susanna was married to John Hall, a physician and the son of William Hall, formerly of Carlton, Bedfordshire, later of Acton, Middlesex. John was sent to Cambridge where he took the Master of Arts degree in 1597. He probably studied medicine abroad and eventually settled in Stratford to begin medical practice in the area. At that time the town had barber-surgeons and apothecaries but no physician. Hence there was a need in the district, particularly among the well-to-do, to consult a physician to diagnose diseases and to prescribe medicines and treatments. Hall was certainly a gentleman of some means who shortly after his marriage inherited the bulk of his father's estate.[227] Shakespeare did well by his daughter and pledged 105 acres of land as part of the marriage settlement.

John Hall was a diligent practitioner, keeping careful notes of his cases in Latin. He compiled a selection of these notes, which were published in an English translation in 1657, twelve years after his death. The book was published three times, and the last edition was reprinted twice. Whatever value it once had as a medical text, or today as a window on 17th-century medical practice, biographers of William Shakespeare are disappointed because Hall selected none of his notes on his father-in-law for publication.[228]

At the time of their marriage, Susanna was twenty-four years old and John was thirty-two. Elizabeth, their only child and Shakespeare's first grandchild, was christened February 21, 1608. It is probable that the new family lived in the impressive and delightful Elizabethan house now open to the public near the Stratford Church and known as Hall's Croft. After Shakespeare's death, if not before, the Halls moved to New Place, Shakespeare's mansion near the Guild Chapel.[229]

Another family matter came up in 1607. In July, Edward, a base-born son of Edmund Shakespeare, player and William's much younger brother, was baptized at St. Leonard's Shoreditch. Two months later the child was buried at St. Giles, Cripplegate. It could be inferred that Edmund was connected with The Curtain Theatre in Shoreditch where Queen Anne's company performed, and later was living in the parish of St. Giles, Cripplegate, and connected with The Fortune Theatre where Prince Henry's company performed. At the very end of the year, December 31, Edmund Shakespeare himself was buried in St. Saviour's Church, now Southwark Cathedral, not far from The Globe Theatre. There was a forenoon knell of the great bell of the church, possibly twenty-seven times for the age of the deceased. Who else but brother William would have made these arrangements? The only traces found of Edmund Shakespeare are in church registers. The fragmentary theatrical records of the time say nothing further. To speak well of him for whom the bell tolled, Edmund might have been on his way to fame as an actor. If William had died at age 27, we might not even have known his name except by the records in the Stratford church.[230]

As far as we know William Shakespeare had no base-born children, although gossip about him tickled some ears in the latter part of the 17th century. John Aubrey's notes and jokes on some well-known characters included this story about Sir William Davenant the famous playwright and theatre manager in the time of Charles II:

Sir William Davenant … was born about the end of February, 1606, in the city of Oxford at the Crown tavern. His father was John Davenant, a vintner there, a very grave and discrete citizen. His mother was a very beautiful woman, and of a very good wit, and of conversation extremely agreeable.

Mr. William Shakespeare was wont to go into Warwickshire once a year, and did commonly in his journey lie at this house in Oxford, where he was exceedingly respected. I have heard Parson Robert [the eldest son of the Davenants] say that Mr. W. Shakespeare has given him a hundred kisses. Now Sir William would sometimes, when he was pleasant over a glass of wine with his most intimate friends … say, that it seemed to him that he writ with the very spirit that Shakespeare [did], and seemed contented enough to be thought his son … in which way his mother had a very light report.[231]

There were other writers who recorded the story. Some added the detail that Sir William Davenant was Shakespeare's godchild and embellished the story by adopting an old joke. The boy is running through Oxford, and a man of the cloth stops to ask him why he is in such haste. The boy replies, "My godfather is come to town and I am going to ask his blessing." The boy is then admonished, "Be careful child, do not take the Lord's name in vain."[232] What Davenant was contented to have suggested over a glass of wine in the scandalous times of King Charles II may have had little to do with what actually happened in an Oxford tavern sixty years earlier. Shakespeare certainly was a friend of the Davenant family, as the story of his giving William's older brother Robert a hundred kisses suggests. And Shakespeare may have been godfather to William Davenant.

The Davenants were a Huguenot family and not the only one with which Shakespeare had more than a passing acquaintance.[233] Having spent most of his working days away from his Stratford household, Shakespeare shifted his rented lodgings in London often enough to make it difficult for us to trace his steps. Some records show that his moving about also made difficulties for tax collectors. Perhaps that evasive trait was inherited from his father. In any case, Shakespeare once lived with the Huguenot family of Christopher Mountjoy, his wife and daughter, both named Marie. At that time Madame asked Shakespeare to help her persuade the Mountjoy's apprentice, Stephen Belott, to agree to marry their daughter Marie. The marriage was agreed to, but in 1612, eight years after they were married, Stephen brought an action against Christopher Mountjoy, claiming his father-in-law was delinquent in paying the agreed upon dowry. Shakespeare made a deposition answering queries about the specifics of the agreement. It was so long ago that he couldn't recall much and was able to offer nothing to help decide the case.

In the year following the death of Edmund Shakespeare, William's mother Mary was buried in Stratford on September 6, 1608. She was living in her home on Henley Street with her daughter Joan, wife of William Hart, and her Hart grandchildren. She was about seventy years old. Only four of her eight children survived, and she had been a widow for seven years. We know little about the details of her life, but there is a record of her being a witness for John Sadler when he was sued by a surgeon named Robert Reade; she was one to stick by an old family friend.[234] When John Shakespeare was off on his journeys pursuing the wool trade through the midlands or in London, Mary probably kept an eye on the workers in the Stratford glove and wool shops.

On March 11, 1608 the children's company playing in the Blackfriars got into serious trouble. They had a reputation for "railing" plays and for taking satiric jabs at various public policies and persons as in the case of *Eastward Ho* mentioned earlier. Reports of two plays so infuriated the King that he finally demanded their suppression and sent a messenger to deliver this royal command to the Privy Council.

> His Grace has vowed they should never play more, but should first beg their bread and he would have his vow performed, and therefore my lord chamberlain by himself or your lordships at the table should take order to dissolve them, and to punish the maker besides.[235]

The patent of the company was revoked, and the company dispersed. John Marston may well have been the "maker," or one of the makers, the King wanted punished. He was committed to Newgate Prison on June 8, 1608 for a short period. Exactly why is unknown, so it may have had nothing to do with the brouhaha about the Blackfriars company. In any case, Marston gave up play writing. The following September he was ordained a deacon and in December 1609 entered the priesthood.

Another consequence of the royal rage is of some importance to the story of Shakespeare's career. Since there was no point in paying rent for a hall with no company to perform in it, Henry Evans, one of the managers of the children's company, surrendered his lease of the playhouse to the owner, Cuthbert Burbage who saw a chance for the King's Men to use the hall. It could be an ideal arrangement to use the indoor Blackfriars as their winter house and to use the outdoor Globe arena as their summer house.

Twelve years earlier the residents of the Blackfriars district had objected strenuously to having the company, then the Lord Chamberlain's Men, operating in their upscale neighborhood. They persuaded the Privy Council to forbid the use of the hall by common players. But things seem to have changed. The private performances of the children's company that followed may have accustomed the neighbors to that kind of intrusion. And considering that the Blackfriars Playhouse could only hold a small, select audience, a somewhat different audience from those who crowded into The Globe, no objections were raised as far as we know. By then the Lord Chamberlain's Men had become His Majesty's Players, and the company had a much brighter image, both because of the King's well known and persistent patronage and because of the excellence of their repertoire and performances.

To insure the success of the scheme, Cuthbert Burbage did an unusual thing. He decided to divide ownership of the playhouse into shares to be held by certain key members of the playing company who were also part owners of The Globe: Richard Burbage, John Hemings, William Shakespeare, William Sly, and Henry Condell. This made it advantageous for the actors to use the Blackfriars, for as part owners they needed income at the door to meet the expenses of maintenance. They would then also gain the usual rental fees for the playhouse. Two others who were not actors, Cuthbert Burbage and Thomas Evans, were also made sharers as financial backers. The plague returned in the summer of 1608, which meant that the King's Men were not able to use the Blackfriars until late in 1609.[236]

Something should be said about the architecture of the Blackfriars Theatre as it was converted by James Burbage. He was a joiner by trade, not simply one who could work timber to make partitions, paneling, staircases, and scaffolds, but also one who could design the timber framing for a building. He may well have been an architect before that specialty became separated from other building trades.[237]

James Burbage was an actor by profession and once a leading member of the Earl of Leicester's Men. His younger son Richard inherited that talent and was the leading creator of the great Shakespearean roles. The elder Burbage's lifelong familiarity with the practice of performing would have been invaluable when in 1575 he came to build "The Theatre" in the fields north of London. His sons claimed, "he was the first builder of playhouses."[238] His theatre was indeed the first in England that was not a converted inn yard or hall, but a building designed and built as a playhouse. It became a model for the later amphitheaters built in London, such as The Curtain, The Rose, The Swan, The Globe, The Hope, and The Fortune. Twenty years later in 1596, he undertook the redesign of rooms in the Blackfriars for use as a playhouse, which became the precursor of the modern indoor theater. The basic feature of a Burbage theatre was to surround an open platform-stage with a seated and standing audience. Later experiments in stage scenery, lighting, and various audience configurations have confused a plan that simply gathers an audience in close contact with the stage and puts the focus of attention on the actors. The recent and careful re-constructions of the outdoor Globe in London (1996) and of the indoor Blackfriars in Staunton, Virginia (2001) reveal the practicality of those playing spaces, especially for the performance of spoken drama. We call such buildings Elizabethan or Shakespearean theaters, so it is easy to forget about James Burbage, the architect who developed their basic design.

Soon after *Antony and Cleopatra* and *Coriolanus*, Shakespeare continued his exploration of unusual dramatic forms in writing *Pericles, Prince of Tyre*. The play seems so old-fashioned and unsophisticated that many critics have remarked that Shakespeare's masterful style is missing until the third act. The evidence now points to scenes that were written by George Wilkins, a co-author of the play.[239] Wilkins was a playwright best known for *The Miseries of Enforced Marriage* (1607). He wrote a novel based on the Pericles play titled, *The Painful Adventures of Pericles, Prince of Tyre* (1608), rather good evidence of the popularity of the play, which was published the same year.

Pericles is based on the romance of Apollonius of Tyre, a popular romance inherited from the Middle Ages. Earlier, Shakespeare adapted a story line of the romance to serve as frame for *The Comedy of Errors*. Now he uses the story in full. As he tells the tale, Pericles sets out for Antioch to solve a riddle and win the princess. He then learns that her father, Antiochus the Great, is using her incestuously. Suspecting the king will kill him to keep the loathsome secret, Pericles flees to Tarsus where he arrives to find famine in the city. He supplies grain from the hold of his ship, but sets sail again, fearing the king of Antioch is still in pursuit. However, a storm destroys his ship, and he lands alone on the shores of Pentapolis. Using the rusty armor accidentally found by fishermen and which once belonged to his father, he wins a tournament and eventually the hand of the beautiful princess, Thaisa. Learning that Antiochus is dead, he sails home to Tyre. He suffers another storm and the loss of his wife Thaisa who dies giving birth to their daughter, Marina. Thaisa's body is placed in a coffin and dropped overboard. Pericles stops by Tarsus and leaves the new-born Marina in the care of the king and queen who remember with gratitude how Pericles delivered their city from famine.

Now, we are only half way through the play, and so I will summarize more drastically. Thaisa's coffin washes ashore at Ephesus where she is revived and placed in Diana's Temple. Years later Marina is captured by pirates and sold to a brothel in Mytilene; Pericles is told she is dead. His ship stops at Mytilene. He is in a deep depression apparently bordering on insanity. Marina, who has talked her way out of service in the brothel, comes to the ship to sing the madman back to sanity. In a great recognition scene, Pericles and Marina are reunited. The goddess Diana appears and orders Pericles to go to her temple in Ephesus where he is reunited with Thaisa; each thought the other had died.

This summary of such an eventful play suggests that it is hardly one that could be shaped into a unified dramatic action. In reading the play, one wild turn after another does tire one's patience. But this seldom happens when the play is performed, thanks to the strong emotional appeal concealed in a story of separation and miraculous reunion. It is nevertheless possible that an audience trained to expect the tempo of comedy, the gathering storm of tragedy, or the realism of modern drama, will not be charmed by this mixture of modes, motifs, and myths.

Shakespeare's audience responded differently. If book sales are any indication of a play's popularity and its continued appeal, *Pericles* was among Shakespeare's most popular plays; it was printed six times. Only *Richard III* and *Henry IV, Part I* have a similar record. There was one disapproving voice. In his *Ode to Himself*, Ben Jonson complains that people are flocking to some moldy tale, like *Pericles*, while neglecting his own more serious work.[240] They were still flocking in 1631 when Jonson fired that shot, over twenty years after *Pericles* was first produced.

The popularity of *Pericles* was overmatched by another "moldy" tale dramatized as "*A Most Pleasant Comedy of Mucedorus the King's son of Valencia and Amadine the King's daughter of Arragon.*" So runs the title page of the first edition (1598). By 1668 it had passed through seventeen printings, more than any other play of the 17th century. Its nearest competitor would be *The Spanish Tragedy* with twelve printings. The title of page of *Mucedorus* adds, "Newly set forth, as it hath been sundry times played in the honorable City of London." It was certainly not a new play in 1598; it is much more like comedies being written in the early 1590's. Further, Shakespeare's *Two Gentlemen of Verona* is like it in many ways. The title page gives no hint of who wrote it or which company first produced it.[241] Perhaps the title page omits that information because by then *Mucedorus* was being produced by a variety of acting companies and amateur groups. The play would run about a mere hour and a half making it manageable by amateurs. In addition, on the back of the title page is a chart showing how fifteen roles can be played by eight actors. Only amateur players would need guidance on how to double cast a script. The quotation from *The Knight of the Burning Pestle* at the head of this Chapter makes fun of an apprentice who once played the title role of Mucedorus and who auditions by using a Hotspur speech from *Henry IV, Part I*—the other Shakespearean play of perennial popularity.

Mucedorus touches on the career of William Shakespeare in several ways. First, the title page of the 1610 edition adds this information, "Amplified with new additions, as it was acted before the King's Majesty at Whitehall on Shrove-Sunday night. By his Highness Servants usually playing at The Globe." The "new additions" are very slight—a prologue, three short scenes, and some revisions of the epilogue, and part of the final scene. It is easy to imagine that Shakespeare did some rewriting for the performance at Whitehall, although the changes are minimal and can't be said to improve the original. Whether he made the additions or not, he had to be more keenly aware of the phenomenal popularity of *Mucedorus,* and this may have nudged him to go further into the field of romance and so to begin work on *Pericles.*

The point will be clearer if we review the story of *Mucedorus.* The Prince of Valencia, disguised as a shepherd, travels incognito to see for himself the reported beauty of Amadine, the princess of Arragon. In the forest he sees Amadine and a courtier being pursued by a bear. The courtier flees like a coward, and the abandoned princess is saved by Mucedorus who cuts off the head of the bear. On seeing Amadine he takes her for a goddess. Amadine falls in love with the "shepherd," and her father accepts him in the royal court. The courtier who fled from the bear envies the favors given the "shepherd" and plots to have him killed. In self-defense the "shepherd" kills his attacker. He is about to be executed for murder when the princess tells the king how he saved her from the bear. So instead of being executed, the "shepherd" is banished, but not before Amadine makes plans to run off and meet him in the forest.

On going to the forest she comes across a wild man, a cannibal armed with a monstrous club. He is about to devour her when, on closer inspection, her beauty enthralls him and he takes her off to his cave to be his queen. In the meantime a search party enters the forest looking for the lost princess and the shepherd. Alarmed by this activity, Mucedorus decides to go home, but the thought of beautiful Amadine changes his mind. He stops being a shepherd and re-disguises himself, this time as a hermit. Then he finds the princess and the wild man. When she tells the "hermit" of her love for the "shepherd," the prince puts the wild man off his guard and kills him. Finally the "hermit" reveals he was the "shepherd" and is really the Prince of Valencia. When the king is reunited with his daughter, the way is now clear for the heirs of Valencia and Arragon to be married. The King of Valencia, who thought his son was gone forever, comes to Arragon and gives his consent.

The situations and characters in *Mucedorus* are echoed and repeated in many an old romance of wandering knights, distressed damsels, banished lovers, and forest monsters. Such conventions—the stock in trade of romance writers—are satisfying in the same way Westerns and spy novels are, by playing variations on familiar themes. Shakespeare was very good at taking such corny stuff and making it fresh. *Pericles* is a more notable example, but it was not his first play to raid the storehouse of myths, marvels, and miracles. The motif of a disguised character traveling in a strange land appears in nearly all his comedies. There is also the frequently repeated situation where a parent or lover is miraculously reunited with a dear one they assumed to be dead. And usually there is some hint of divine intervention in the wrap-up scenes.

After the success of *Pericles,* Shakespeare fully indulged his personal style of romantic comedy by writing *Cymbeline, The Winter's Tale,* and *The Tempest.* Like *Mucedorus,* all these plays introduce scenes in the pastoral mode, where shepherds and other country folk mingle with disguised royalty. The opposite and more realistic style of comedy was being written by his rival Ben Jonson. In his "Induction" to *Bartholomew Fair*, Jonson fired another spit ball at Shakespeare, writing that he himself was not one of those who "beget tales, tempests, and such-like drolleries." Those who accept Jonson's view of what comedy should be forget to notice that Shakespearean comedy won the day long ago.

Cymbeline partly concerns an early British king confronting an invasion by a Roman legion in the time of Augustus, although there is nothing in it to echo any of Shakespeare's "Roman" plays. That part of the play is an historic fantasia designed as a frame for other excitements. The drama begins with a version of the "wager story," best known as it appears in Boccaccio's *Decameron* (Day 2, Novel 9). It is about a husband who accepts a wager that his wife cannot be seduced. The man who proposed the wager attempts to seduce the wife and is repulsed. But to win the wager he fools the husband into believing his efforts at seduction succeeded. The enraged husband engages someone to murder his wife. However, she goes into disguise as a man and after several adventures is able to meet and disabuse her husband. The wife in *Cymbeline* is Imogen, daughter of the king. Her husband is a commoner who was banished by the king. The wager story is enacted while they are separated. The story could easily have been dramatized pretty much as is, but Shakespeare was more ambitious. He mixed it with material we know as the story of Snow White. The girl, persecuted by a wicked stepmother, takes refuge in the forest with seven dwarves. The stepmother finds the girl, poisons her, and she seems to die, but is revived by Prince Charming. Shakespeare's Imogen is the Snow White figure. Disguised as a man she goes to Wales to find her husband and runs into some mountaineers who care for her as the dwarves do for Snow White. Two of them turn out to be British princes kidnapped by a banished soldier and raised in a mountain cave. They are actually long-lost brothers of Imogen. Later they turn the tide of battle against the invading Roman legion. Princes raised in mountain caves far from court always show their royal lineage when crunch time comes, at least in chivalric romances.

There is much more in *Cymbeline* that cannot be summarized without creating unnecessary confusion. Indicating the sources of the threads woven into *Cymbeline* does no more than reveal the complexity of the tapestry. It is more useful to pursue another line of discussion. How are these story lines, picked from the grab bag of pseudo-history, novella, fairy tale, and chivalric romance related? There is the central figure of Imogen whose unshakable loyalty to her husband adds weight to nearly every scene and situation. There is, however, another aspect beside the central character that gives unity to the play. It lies in Shakespeare's brilliant use of the device of dramatic irony. In scenes and situations, one after another, all the characters cannot be aware, as the audience is, of what is really going on. Shakespeare manages to keep the device of audience knowing entirely in the audience's hands until the very last, long, scene. Then in a virtuoso display of theatrical fireworks, preceded by a thunderous set of oracles by Jupiter himself, mounted on an eagle, the accumulated misunderstandings are opened one by one.

Perhaps in *Cymbeline* Shakespeare was being too clever by half in showing his masterly control of mood and pace as well as his technical skill in linking quite disparate matters together. By contrast his next play, *The Winter's Tale*, is more powerful, and more plain and direct. The story, taken from a romance by Robert Greene, is about a King of Sicilia possessed by the demon of jealousy. Suspecting his Queen of unfaithfulness, he orders his baby daughter to be exposed as a bastard. In a climactic scene where he refuses to believe an oracle from Apollo declaring his wife to be clear of his suspicions, his wife and son die. He immediately collapses in an agony of remorse. The first and tragic part of the play has become increasingly tense and terrible.

The claustrophobic atmosphere is snapped by a thunderstorm, and rapid new developments follow. The baby daughter is abandoned on the coast of Bohemia by a lord who is attacked by a bear. The ship is destroyed by the storm. The baby is found and adopted by a shepherd. To set things into motion again, Father Time, complete with wings and hour-glass, enters to announce that sixteen years have passed.

The once abandoned princess, now the adopted daughter of a shepherd, presides at a sheep-shearing festival. She has, of course, the beauty and grace natural to a princess and has attracted the devotion of the Prince of Bohemia. The prince's father learns of his infatuation and threatens the young couple. They escape to Sicilia, and the lost princess is returned to her homeland. The penitent King of Sicilia is able to recognize his daughter by tokens found by the shepherd. They go to a chapel to see a statue of the late Queen of Sicilia. Then in an absolutely thrilling and solemn *coup de théâtre*, the statue returns to life. The family ruined by jealousy is reunited in the chapel.

Marina in *Pericles*, Imogen in *Cymbeline*, and Perdita in *The Winter's Tale*, are virginal princesses separated or alienated from their heritage. The ones closest to them believe they have died. When they eventually return to life, as it were, they are miraculously reunited with their fathers and married to a worthy suitor. Possibly this story line came to play in Shakespeare's imagination by a renewed awareness of his daughter, Susanna, the circumstances of her marriage and the birth of his granddaughter, Elizabeth Hall.

The Tempest has a similar figure, a girl named Miranda, separated from her heritage and sharing exile with her father, Prospero. He is a great magician who once was Duke of Milan, but whose place was usurped by his brother. Prospero and Miranda were set adrift in a leaky boat. But they landed on a desert island, inhabited by spirits under the control of a magician who, by using his secret and dangerous art, is able to command elemental forces. The spirits raise a fierce tempest, which drives a ship so near the rocky shore that the passengers panic and jump overboard. They are the enemies who exposed Duke Prospero and are made to suffer as he and Miranda suffered when banished and set adrift. The Duke's enemies, seemingly having lost their ship and having been tossed onto the island, are now in the Duke's power. Then in a long narrative passage, Prospero tells us the whole story of how they all got there and why he wants to punish his enemies. After that long narrative exposition, *The Tempest* becomes a play of unusually concentrated storytelling.

In this regard it is quite different from the other romances of Shakespeare. It is very short, and the character groups, separated to various parts of the island, pursue different agendas. However, by analogy, distortion, repetition, and echo, they reflect different aspects Prospero's story, as for example, how he was wronged and how he is driven to get back at his enemies. With the aid of a tricky invisible spirit, Prospero wants to punish his brother who, with the aid of the King of Naples, banished him. After the shipwreck, the wicked brother tempts a younger brother of the same King of Naples to kill his brother the king and claim the Neapolitan crown. The initial wrong done to Prospero is about to be reenacted. "What is past is prologue." Caliban, a native of the island, enslaved by Prospero, meets two drunken escapees from the shipwreck, a butler and a court jester, and enlists their aid in a scheme to kill Prospero and rape Miranda. The Prince of Naples, searching for his father, finds and falls in love with Miranda. His devotion to her is parodied by Caliban's lust. The attempt of the false brother to have the King of Naples murdered is parodied by Caliban's attempt to get the drunkards to kill Prospero for him. The stories developed for each character group are closely interwoven, so that the action of one group reflects that of another.

Such interweaving can be seen in three displays of symbolic pageantry: the royal party from Naples is tempted to a sumptuous banquet which suddenly changes into a horror show; the young lovers' betrothal is celebrated by a dance of nymphs and shepherds, presented by phantoms of Iris and Juno; Caliban and his dissolute companions are distracted from their plan to murder Prospero by a clothesline of grand robes and are driven into a stinking swamp by vicious dogs. These shows created by Prospero's magic symbolize the moral status of the interwoven story lines.

Since it is so unusual in its dramaturgy and also nearly the last of Shakespeare's plays, *The Tempest* has tempted many to imagine that the pageantry of the play was intended to serve as a final demonstration of his own powerful art and as his farewell to the stage. The point where this tragicomedy turns toward a resolution is Prospero's line, "The rarer action is in virtue than in vengeance" [4.3.76]. Having brought his enemies to recognize and repent their crimes, he is able to resume the office of Duke and return to Milan.

Shakespeare was about to lay down his magic staff when the King's Men were called to extraordinary service. Plans developed for King James' daughter, Elizabeth, to be married to Prince Frederick of Heidelberg, the German Elector from the Palatinate. The wedding was to take place on Twelfth Night, 1613. However in October of 1612, Henry, the 18-year-old Prince of Wales suddenly became ill and died on November 6. This shattering blow to the royal family and to the many who were attracted to the personality of the Prince, initiated a time of deep mourning. Public performances in London were suspended.

The wedding of the Elizabeth and Frederick was put off for six weeks until St. Valentine's Day, 1613. That may have shortened the period of mourning, but Frederick, who had been in England since October, was eager to return to Germany. Postponing the marriage might have suggested that James was wary of an alliance with a leading prince of the Protestant cause. So there was a rush of activity to go forward with plans to celebrate with impressive magnificence. As it was, the couple was not able to leave for Germany until the 10th of April.

The most important national holiday of that time took place annually on the 24th of March, Accession Day, marking King James's coming to the throne. It was an occasion like the great feast days of the church when bells were rung, bonfires blazed, and special prayers and sermons were offered in nearly all the towns and parishes in the country. The custom originated in Queen Elizabeth's time and was especially enjoyed by common folks glad for the holiday and by grand folks who saw Elizabeth as their savior from Roman Catholicism.[242] Of the celebrations the most lavish were the tournaments arranged by courtiers and court officials. These mock combats were held in the tiltyard of Whitehall Palace. The main event was a contest involving pairs of mounted knights charging full tilt, aiming a lance to strike an opponent. Judges awarded points according to where the blow fell. If it hit home, the lance would break on the armor of the opponent. It made for a dashing display of agility and athletic prowess, not unlike modern polo. But the more distinctive feature was the display of elaborate, colorful, and costly costumes, and in the fancy equipment for horse, man, and the accompanying retinue. The participants took names from knights of Arthurian legend or chivalric romance, e.g., the Knight of the Swan, the Star, the Red Dragon and so forth. Some chose a more enigmatic name like Peregrine or Silvanus, thereby expressing their fortunes and fate. The tournament thus became highly dramatic. At their entrance, passing by the throne of honor, they presented an *impresa*, a small shield painted with a symbolic picture and a brief phrase or motto expressing some obscure conceit. A simple example can be found in Shakespeare's *Pericles*. Called "The Mean Knight," because of his rusty armor, Pericles enters the lists, presenting an *impresa* to the Princess described as "A wither'd branch, that's only green a top; the motto, *In hac spe vivo*" [2.2.42-43]. The Latin says, "In this hope I live." The *impresa* of participants in an Accession Day tournament would have been more abstruse, but they too were hoping for favor from the monarch by honoring and celebrating the accession.

For the practical staging of *Pericles*, Shakespeare greatly simplified the tournament ritual. Beside the actual contest, which took place off stage, he left out the tradition of a speech delivered by a page on presenting the *impresa*, which hinted at its meaning and its intended flattery. Out of the need for a clever *impresa*—emblematic picture and motto—and an equally clever speech of presentation, courtiers often relied on the outside help of poets and painters.

And so it was that the Earl of Rutland commissioned Shakespeare's services for the Accession Day tilt of 1613. Presumably after consulting with the Earl, Shakespeare wrote the speech to complement the shield and motto. The Earl's steward paid Shakespeare 44 shillings in gold. Richard Burbage, Shakespeare's colleague and an artist, was also called to work on the *impresa* and was paid "for painting and making it in gold." After the presentation the shield was hung according to custom in the Shield Gallery at Whitehall for all who were allowed in to see. This Earl of Rutland, Francis Manners, had just inherited the title from his older brother, Roger, the friend of Southampton, and was spending lavishly to let everyone know he was out to cut a figure in court circles.[243] Considering how themes from chivalric romance and Arthurian legend were pressed into the service of dramatizing a courtier's service and devotion to King and country in the Accession Day tournaments, the popularity of plays like *Mucedorus* and Shakespeare's *Pericles* can be understood as having had a similar appeal for those who enjoyed Sidney's *Arcadia* and Spenser's *Faerie Queen*.

In addition to the tournament, the wedding of Frederick and Elizabeth was celebrated with banquets, masques, fireworks, bear bating, bonfires and a mock sea battle. The Revels Office also scheduled an extraordinary number of plays both before and after the wedding. From January 1st up to May 20th, The Prince's Men, the Lady Elizabeth's Men, the Children of the Queen's Revels, and the Elector Palatine's Men gave some ten performances. But in the same period, The King's Men gave twenty-two; eight were by Shakespeare: *Much Ado About Nothing* (twice), *The Winter's Tale, Othello, Julius Caesar, The Tempest, Sir John Falstaff,* [*I Henry IV?* or *Merry Wives?*], and seven were by the collaborators Francis Beaumont and John Fletcher: *The Maid's Tragedy, A King and No King* (twice), *Philaster* (twice), *The Captain* (twice), and seven other plays by a variety of playwrights, including one that has since been lost, *Cardenio* written by Fletcher and Shakespeare in collaboration.[244] No other playing company in King James' time could have had such a stock of plays, nor could any other court in Europe have gone on such a theatrical binge. The bulk of the King's Men's repertoire consisted of the established plays by Shakespeare and the more recent ones by the team of Beaumont and Fletcher. What creates some interest is that *Cardenio* was written by Fletcher and Shakespeare. Although neither a manuscript nor a printed copy of the play has survived, the collaborators were named as the authors in a 1653 entry in the Stationer's Register, which recorded fees paid by a publisher for the exclusive right to print a book.[245]

By 1613 the 33-year-old John Fletcher had become in practice, if not formally, the successor to the 47-year-old Shakespeare as chief playwright of the King's Men. His best plays were written in collaboration first with Francis Beaumont and later with Philip Massinger. They are skillfully put together and much in the vein of the kind of tragicomedy Shakespeare was writing at the time. As the Stuart wedding celebrations were being planned, Shakespeare worked on two other plays and like *Cardenio* written in collaboration with John Fletcher, *The Two Noble Kinsmen* and *King Henry VIII or All is True.*

The Two Noble Kinsmen features a Morris dance taken—lifted might be a better word—from Beaumont's *"Masque of the Inner Temple and Gray's Inn,"* presented as part of the celebrations of the royal wedding in February 1613. The Morris served as the second "Anti-masque," a grotesque dance to set off the splendor of the dances performed by the gentlemen in the Masque proper. It is entirely likely that the best dancers of the King's Men performed the "Anti-masque" and were able to transfer it with minor adjustments into *The Two Noble Kinsmen.* This sort of transfer from masque to play may have been done in *The Winter's Tale* when a group of three dancers, disguised as Satyrs, are introduced as having "danced before the king" [4.4.337-338].[246]

Collaborative play writing meant the same thing in Shakespeare's day as it does today. It is a cooperative effort on the part of two or more playwrights to compose a drama. Brian Vickers has explored in detail what is known about the plays on which Shakespeare collaborated with other writers, as well as the various methods used by scholars to identify who were the co-authors.[247] A playwright is only one of many expert and experienced people who cooperate in making a play. Writers working together can produce as coherent a play as can be done by one writing alone. The task of identifying the co-authors of a work in this period is somewhat simplified by the way co-authored works were usually planned. A scene by scene scenario, which is essentially the plot in outline, was prepared and the scenes were divided up so each author could work alone. When the play was finally put together, unless extensive rewriting was undertaken, the style and habits of each author would be preserved in his scenes and can now be used to identify which scenes were written by which co-author. Knowing the distinguishing marks of Fletcher and Shakespeare naturally contributes to our understanding of their writing styles. However, since comments on the dramaturgy and themes of the plays in a study such as this have to be brief, even a bit perfunctory, it would be better to discuss the co-authored plays without exploring the issues and details of co-authorship.

The Two Noble Kinsmen is based on a classic legend best known from "The Knight's Tale" in Chaucer's *Canterbury Tales*. It seems suited for a royal and stately audience, or for anyone curious about how the nobility behave on great occasions. Everything is grandly fitted out with spectacular and formal rituals, ceremonies, pageants, and processions, not unlike the pomp and circumstance of a royal tournament. Having the trappings of chivalric romance, however, does not so much lend the aura of high adventure as the autumnal colors of melancholy.

It tells the story of two young princes, wounded and captured in the war Theseus waged against Creon, the tyrant of Thebes. In captivity Palamon and Arcite are quite content with each other's company until they see walking in a garden the beautiful Emilia. Immediately they become rivals. When Arcite is released from prison, he is banished on pain of death. He goes to the forest but is tortured by the thought that his rival may occasionally catch sight of Emilia, and he therefore returns in disguise as a country fellow. Palamon is taken to a room in the prison and is now similarly tortured having been deprived of a chance to enjoy the sight of Emilia.

Meanwhile the jailer's daughter has fallen into a love sickness for Palamon and contrives his escape. In the forest Arcite wins the country games and is rewarded with a place in the service of Emilia. Finally Arcite and Palamon meet up and decide to end their rival claims by combat. They manage to equip themselves and are on the point of attack when interrupted by Theseus and an Athenian hunting party. The combat is then transferred to a formal jousting field where the loser will be executed and the other will marry Emilia. After elaborate ceremonies, invoking the aid of the gods—Mars by Palamon, Venus by Arcite, and Diana by Emilia—the gods respond with ambiguous signs emanating from their altars. As a subplot to all of this we see the jailer's daughter go mad for the love of Palamon. Presumably she is cured when her wooer comes to her disguised as Palamon. This subplot provides some release from the epic-like tensions of the main plot and is an odd comic parody of it. It is very artfully balanced between a disturbing pathos and the comic bumbling of the jailer, a doctor, and the girl's wooer. Like the main plot, the subplot keeps us in suspense. Try as we might, we are at a loss to imagine what might happen, but whichever way things may go, they can hardly go well. This suspenseful tension plays right through to the last moments of the last scene. At first, Arcite is the victor and wins the hand of Emilia, while

Palamon is condemned to death. As the execution is about to be carried out, we learn that Arcite has fallen from his horse and is himself on the point of death. He freely yields Emilia to his kinsman, dies and thus releases Palamon from the forfeit of his life.

A kind of release comes in the final speech of Theseus. He addresses the "heavenly charmers," the gods we petition for what we think we want:

> Let us be thankful
> For that which is, and with you leave dispute
> That are above our question.

(5.4.134–135)

Scholars, following a hunch rather than external evidence, believe that *Henry VIII* was another joint effort of Shakespeare and Fletcher, while the plot outline is presumed to be Shakespeare's. Although we have no record of whether *Henry VIII*, Shakespeare's last play, was performed at court, it seems crafted to take advantage of the excitement generated by the wedding of Princess Elizabeth. In *Henry VIII* Shakespeare wrote a series of histories or tragic histories tracing a succession of powerful persons—the Duke of Buckingham, Queen Katherine, Cardinal Wolsey, Anne Bullen, Bishop Cranmer—who make a scene or two and then disappear. The theme and a summary of the play are anticipated by the Prologue:

> Think ye see
> The very persons of our noble story
> As they were living: Think you see them great,
> And follow'd with the general throng, and sweat
> Of thousand friends; then, in a moment, see
> How soon this mightiness meets misery.

(Prologue 29–30)

Whatever else may be said of this odd ramble through history there is no doubt it is filled with wonderful roles for actors. The scene where the Queen confronts Cardinal and King in court brings the drama to an astonishing climax and provides the actors with their grandest moments. And whenever it was acted in the Blackfriars Chamber, there would have been an extra interest in the moment of the trial since the very hall where the trial occurred had been converted to a stage.

In *The Tempest* and *The Two Noble Kinsmen*, Shakespeare relied on pageantry and spectacular scenic effects to illustrate or symbolize crucial moments. *Henry VIII* exploits the same technique. The stage is very crowded in such moments, and the costume demands are extraordinary. Staging an uncut version of this three and a half hour play is a challenge to any company and probably displayed the King's Men at the height of their organizational, technical, and artistic powers.

There are records of one performance that suggests the company may have stretched itself too far. *Henry VIII* played at The Globe on June 29th, St. Peter's Day, 1613. During the afternoon performance the theatre caught fire and burned to the ground. Sir Henry Wotton described the accident in writing to his nephew in July:

> Now, King Henry making a masque at the Cardinal Wolsey's house, and certain chambers [cannons] being shot off at his entry, some of the paper, … wherewith one of them was stopped, did light on the thatch, … it kindled inwardly, and ran round like a train, consuming within less than an hour the whole house to the very grounds. This was the fatal period of that virtuous fabric, wherein yet nothing did perish but wood and straw, and a few forsaken cloaks; only one man had his breeches set on fire, that would perhaps have broiled him, if he had not by the benefit of a provident wit put it out with bottle ale.[248]

In earlier days flourishes of drums and trumpets were enough to announce the entrance of a king, now the working crew in the stage tower could fire cannon. The players' misfortune was printed up by ballad makers; one advised the players to rebuild with tiles instead of thatch:

> Be warned you stage-strutters all,
> Lest you again be catched,
> And such a burning do befall,

> As to them whose house was thatched;
> Forbear your whoring, breeding biles,
> And lay up that expense for tiles. [249]

The owner-sharers were able to open the rebuilt Globe almost exactly a year later, June 30, 1614. The roof was tiled instead of thatched and redesigned to cover more of the stage and pit and to eliminate the need for the supporting pillars on stage. One further innovation was an onion-dome turret, possibly to admit more light at the rear of the stage since the larger roof made a deeper shadow. By all accounts it was as gorgeous and grand as ever.[250]

"The fatal period to that virtuous fabric" also put a period to Shakespeare's theatrical career. As far as we can tell, Shakespeare who owned a 14th interest in The Globe did not contribute toward the rebuilding. Perhaps he sold his interest and so was no longer required to pay his share in the cost of the replacement. About the same time or somewhat earlier Shakespeare had sold his interest in the lease of the Blackfriars Theatre as well. Another indication of Shakespeare's movement toward retirement is that he had ceased acting, possibly as much as ten years earlier. The few cast lists of plays produced by the King's Men that survive do not include Shakespeare's name after 1603, when he appeared in Jonson's *Sejanus*. Acting is demanding work for a man approaching fifty, especially if he became bulky enough to lose the agility of youth. Not only the leading roles, but even doubling in a series of smaller roles would have been challenging. The almost daily switch from one play to another would set a difficult pace, however much satisfaction acting could bring to a younger man.

Shakespeare, however, was not entirely ready to give up his interest in the theatre and in London. In March 1613, he purchased a lodging and a plot of ground inside the Blackfriars precinct. The lodging was a top floor apartment of the gatehouse at the east entrance to the district. Probably he planned to use it as a residence when visiting the city. At £140 it was an expensive property, and so he must have felt he had to have it. One of its attractions was that it was near the Blackfriars Theatre and not far from the river where boatmen stood ready to carry patrons to the south bank and The Globe Theatre.[251] Shakespeare passed the property on to his daughter and son-in-law, Susanna and John Hall.

It could be that Shakespeare made the Gate House purchase as an investment, not really thinking of using it himself. It seems more likely to me that he would not find it easy to turn his back on the London theatre scene. Another consideration is that while Shakespeare had inherited and invested substantially in Stratford real estate, which demanded some attention there, London was nonetheless the center of financial and legal transactions. Thus, the landed gentry, then as now, could always find use for a London residence.

EPILOGUE
1613–1616

Now our sands are almost run,
More a little, and then dumb.

(Pericles 5.2.1–2)

CAPTIVATED by pictures in travel brochures of Stratford as a quaint and quiet country town, one might easily imagine that Shakespeare went to a peaceful retirement at New Place. Unfortunately that picture disappears once we take a closer look.

In 1612 William's brother Gilbert Shakespeare died. Gilbert was a haberdasher in London, but eventually returned to Stratford. In 1602 he acted as William's agent when he purchased a cottage in Chapel Lane across the street from New Place. It seems likely that he represented William on other occasions. Not much else is known about him. The other brother, Richard, about whom even less is known, died in February 1613. Of Shakespeare's siblings only his sister Joan remained. She was living at the old home on Henley Street with her three sons and husband, William Hart, a hatter who was to die a few days before Shakespeare himself in April 1616. Shakespeare's immediate family, all living in New Place, included his wife Anne, his daughter Susanna Hall, her husband John Hall, their daughter Elizabeth, and Shakespeare's unmarried daughter, Judith. Father's house had many mansions.

In July 1613 Susanna Hall brought an action of slander against John Lane, Jr. of Stratford in the Bishop's Consistory court in Worcester. The slander was that Mistress Hall had the running of the reins, that is, gonorrhea, and had been "naught" with Rafe Smith at John Palmer's. John Lane was summoned to answer the charge of slander and was excommunicated for not appearing. An authority on Elizabethan church courts, Dr. Brinkworth writes:

> In spite of its prevalence, sexual immorality was viewed very seriously. It was not counted among mere rustic peccadilloes or lightly regarded.... And the evidence everywhere makes it certain that by the great majority the church courts on this point at any rate were feared.... Everyone's private life was closely supervised: in those close-knit little communities few secrets could be hid and most desires known.[252]

Susanna was not one to allow a slobbering tongue to damage the reputation of her family, a family important enough to attract that kind of backbiting in Stratford.

A further indication of the seriousness in which this matter was taken is that the case went to the court of the bishop of the diocese, not to the court of the parish where the slander had been spread. The church court in Stratford, popularly known by the scornful as the "bawdy" court, ordinarily met annually, when the wardens drew up a list of delinquents whose behavior, such as fighting, sexual immorality, theft, or simply being some kind of nuisance to neighbors, might in any way disturb the good order of the community. Punishment for those cited was often commuted by a fine, but in more severe cases the penitent had to make a public confession before the congregation on a Sunday morning and stand in a white robe through the sermon.

The surviving records of the bawdy Court of Stratford are fragmentary, but they do reveal how closely private lives were watched. For example, Susanna Shakespeare, the year before her marriage to John Hall, was cited for not receiving the Easter communion, which she was then ordered to receive and certify at the next court. She did, and the case was dismissed. The name of Richard Shakespeare is cited once, July 1, 1608, but the charge was not written down. He confessed and was fined 12 pence to be given to the poor of the parish. Another unspecified citation, October 14, 1608, was for William and Joan Hart, Shakespeare's sister and her husband. There is no record of what happened in the case; perhaps they challenged the charge.[253]

A few years later something more substantial to trouble the family came to the attention of the churchwardens. Judith Shakespeare was nearly thirty years old; it was about time her father negotiated a suitable marriage for her, and this was done with apparent success. The betrothed was Thomas Quiney, a younger son of the late prominent and influential Stratford bailiff, Richard Quiney. Thomas was a vintner who leased a tavern on High Street.

There are things to be told about the Quiney family before we can get on with the story of Judith and Thomas,. They were active in Stratford affairs through several generations. Thomas Quiney's grandfather, Adrian Quiney, was chief alderman when John Shakespeare was Bailiff, and the following year Shakespeare was chief alderman and Quiney the bailiff. The family lived on High Street not far from John Shakespeare. Richard Quiney, the father of Thomas, had twice served as Bailiff of Stratford and traveled nearly annually to London on town business where he had several contacts with Shakespeare. The only surviving letter written to Shakespeare was from Richard Quiney, although it could not have been delivered since it was found unopened among Quiney's papers. That was in 1598 when as bailiff he was in London negotiating for a revised charter for Stratford and for tax relief, since the town had suffered from two disastrous fires. The letter asked Shakespeare, his "loving countryman," for a loan of £30 to pay the debts he had run up during his protracted stay in London. In his various efforts to support the interests of the town, Richard Quiney had provoked the hostility of the then Lord of Stratford Manor, Sir Edward Greville. One night Quiney was struck on the head while trying to quiet a rowdy gang. He seemed not to be seriously hurt, but he died within the month at the end of May 1602. It has been suggested that the blow was struck by one who knew his attack on Bailiff Quiney would not be disliked by the Lord of the Manor.

There are several indications that the Quiney family suggested to Shakespeare investments he could make in Stratford lands and tithes. That was plausibly aimed to cement an old alliance in town politics. A further connection is shown when in December 1611 Elizabeth Quiney, then the widow of Richard Quiney and the mother of Thomas, sold some property, and one of the witnesses at the signing of the deed was Judith Shakespeare.[254] Considering this history of continuing family ties, it is obvious that Shakespeare did not need to search beyond the neighborhood to light on an eligible bachelor. In 1611 Thomas Quiney was 22 and an established vintner. Judith was 26 and friendly enough with her future mother-in-law Elizabeth Quiney to witness her deed of sale. They married, but why not until February 1616? While it would take some time to work out a financial settlement on the couple, four years seems a long time. Perhaps Shakespeare was either too busy in London to pay attention to doings in Stratford or so focused on building his fortune that he shied away from thinking about an outlay for a dowry.

Another consideration is that there was a crisis in the town that jostled for attention. John Combe, the wealthiest man in town, tried to enclose the common farmlands in several neighboring villages. He could drive the farmers off and use the land to graze sheep. The enclosures would create great hardship for the farmers and for the town council who would have to deal with the poor and homeless. The aldermen unanimously opposed the plan. The tithes on these lands were leased out by the Stratford Corporation. Shakespeare had purchased a half share of the tithes in three neighboring areas for £440 in 1605. Ten years later he was close to recovering his investment, but enclosure could lessen the value of the leases if he were to sell them.

We have little to go on to surmise what Shakespeare thought about the enclosure question. He probably stood to lose because William Replingham, representing those for enclosure, called on Shakespeare in October, 1614 to persuade him he would not lose income. On the other side, the town clerk Thomas Greene kept a diary during the crisis, detailing his efforts on behalf of the council to block the enclosure. His diary entry for 17 November, in London, reads as follows:

> My cousin Shakespeare ... coming yesterday to town, I went to see him how he did. He told me that they assured him they meant to enclose no farther than gospel bush and so up straight ... to the gate in Clopton hedge ... and that they mean in April to survey the land and then give satisfaction.... He and Mr. Hall say they think there will be nothing done at all.[255]

Shakespeare had it wrong. A month later workmen began digging a ditch to plant enclosure hedges. Two aldermen began filling in the ditches and were routed by the diggers. The next move was a secret nighttime raid on the ditches by women who filled the ditches in again. Elizabeth Quiney could have been among them, for she let everyone know she was against enclosure. The women blocked the work for a while, but it wasn't until the autumn of 1618 that orders came from London forbidding the project. [256]

Now for a closer look at the marriage of Thomas Quiney and Judith Shakespeare. It took place in the parish church on February 10, 1616. The next month on March 15th, one Margaret Wheeler died in childbirth along with her child, and Thomas Quiney was named as the father. Surely this allowed some neighbors to wag their tongues about the high and mighty Quiney-Shakespeare alliance. On the 26th Quiney appeared in open court in the Parish Church presided over by the Vicar. The record reads

> Thomas Quiney: for incontinence with a certain Margaret Wheeler: …
> he appeared: admitted that he had had carnal copulation with Wheeler:
> submitted himself to the correction of the Judge: ordered public penance
> in a white sheet on three Sundays in the church of Stratford: thereafter he
> proffered 5 s[hillings] for the use of the poor of the parish and petitioned
> the penance to be remitted: ordered to acknowledge the fault in his own
> attire before the minister of Bishopton.[257]

Confessing in the chapel at Bishopton would be less embarrassing than before the congregation in Stratford. It looks like the marriage got off to a rocky start, although the couple had three sons, and Thomas Quiney eventually served as Constable and later Chamberlain to the Stratford Corporation. William Shakespeare would never see how things turned out. He made the final revisions in his will within a month after Thomas Quiney's confession.

Many writers assume that Shakespeare was shocked and went so far as to cut Thomas and Judith Quiney out of his will. I doubt he was shocked enough to do that, although reading his will anachronistically could lead to that conclusion. In that culture wills were usually written to pass the bulk of a family estate to one heir, usually the oldest son or daughter and not to parcel it out equally to all the children. Shakespeare's will passed the estate to Susanna and John Hall. It included real estate in the Stratford area, New Place, two tenements on Henley Street, and all other properties in Stratford, Old Stratford, Bishopton, Welcombe, the Blackfriars tenement, and "all other lands, tenements, hereditaments whatsoever." And the will insists that these properties then pass to Susanna's oldest child and her oldest and so on and on until the line runs out, and then to Judith and her oldest. But Shakespeare certainly did not cut out daughter Judith. She was given £150 for her marriage portion, provided Thomas Quiney settled an equal amount to her dower, a provision probably in accordance with agreements made before the marriage. In addition Judith was to have the income, but not the principal, from an additional £150. This would insure that Judith had an income and no one including her husband could dip into the principal. If Judith or any issue of her body were not living at the end of three years, the additional £150 would go partly to Elizabeth Hall and £50 of it divided equally to the children of Joan Hart, Shakespeare's sister. Joan was given £20 and all his clothes, and her three sons were each given £5. Joan could remain in the Henley Street house for a token rent of 12 pence.

There were several other token gifts to friends and family, the most notorious being his "second best bed" willed to his wife, Anne. The sensible way to read this item is to assume that the bed was the one she was used to in New Place, where she would continue to live in the household of her daughter, Susanna. The best bed would be the one in the guest chamber. £10 were left for the poor of Stratford. Money to purchase memorial rings were left to friends including his long-time colleagues in the King's Men: Richard Burbage, Henry Condell, and John Hemings. These sharer-owners of the company also had control of the scripts of his plays. In 1623,[258] seven years after Shakespeare's death, they were able to pass them on to the world when they published his comedies, histories, and tragedies in the large impressive folio format.

A recent study of Shakespeare's texts by Lukas Erne argues that the plays were usually acted in a shortened form to fit into the two-hour playing time allowed for performances. However, Shakespeare wrote the full texts and in some cases revised them with the expectation that when printed they would provide a fuller sense of their imaginative richness than a script as performed could make available to readers. This is a radical idea, bringing into question many speculations that have been made about the nature of the printed texts that have come down to us. It also challenges the view that Shakespeare was indifferent to his literary reputation, that he wrote for performance rather than for readers, and made no effort to see his plays printed. Professor Erne also makes the plausible suggestion that Shakespeare was preparing the plays for a collected edition to be printed in the large folio format, but died before it was completed. So the editorial work passed on to his colleagues, Condell and Hemings.[259]

William Shakespeare was buried in the Stratford Parish Church on April 25, 1616, a month after his last will and testament was signed and witnessed. He wrote his name near the end of each of the three pages. The document seems to have been prepared in haste and experts in handwriting detect signs of a sick man finding it difficult to sign his name. It is hard to tell what his final illness may have been. The bust placed in his monument in the church shows signs of obesity, but that may simply be the sculptor's way of symbolizing wealth and position. A quill pen held in the right hand points to his life as a writer, and his mouth is slightly open, either to suggest an actor or a writer testing a line of verse.

His last verses were carved on the stone covering his grave:

> Good friend for Jesus sake forebear,
> To dig the dust enclosed here!
> Blest be the man that spares these stones,
> And cursed be he that moves my bones.

Whatever his last words were has not come down to us; but there is a piece of gossip recorded near the end of the 17th century by Richard Davies. He made a few additions to some notes about Shakespeare in a manuscript of a fellow clergyman, William Fulman. Davies' last entry is a terse note, "He died a papist." Certainly Davies, a scholar who later became Archdeacon of Coventry, would have no motive to invent a story of Shakespeare secretly making his last confession to a Roman priest. But there were good reasons for Shakespeare to keep things like that under cover and not subject his estate to the fines declared Catholics had to pay.

There are many things we would like to know about Shakespeare. Much is lost in the dusty attic of time and in the mysteries that Shakespeare himself cultivated. Many of his fellow playwrights—Greene, Marlowe, Nashe, and Jonson—achieved a notoriety Shakespeare successfully avoided. And unlike Marlowe, Kidd, Nashe, Jonson, Chapman, and Marston, Shakespeare was careful or cagey enough not to arouse the hostility of authority. On many issues his stand seems more like one of bemused detachment than of open declaration. Certainly his plays and poems reveal a very sharp and playful mind, crammed with observation, opinions, learning, and experience. He expresses things superbly well, but always in the voice of assumed *personae*, making it difficult to know the man behind the masks. He is teasingly apt to imply counter arguments, thus leaving debatable topics open. In fact, it could be said that Shakespeare deconstructs his own works. We can never be sure if his personal thoughts are spoken stage front and center, because when we listen carefully, we can hear opposing statements spoken from the side.

There are no surviving letters to friends or family, and if there were, they would probably turn out to be more concerned with money and investments

2

than with personal reflections on politics, religion, or the art of the theatre. It is a safe bet that he enjoyed his way of crafting dialogue, for without enjoyment he could not have done it so well. Yet in contrast, writing letters may have seemed tedious and easy to postpone.

> Thus far, with rough and all unable pen,
> Our bending author hath pursu'd the story.
> In little room confining mighty men,
> Mangling by starts the full course of their glory.
> Small time; but in that small most greatly lived
> This star of England.
>
> *(Henry V* Epilogue 5.1–6)*

NOTES

CHAPTER 1

1   Jonathan Sumpton, *Pilgrimage: An Image of Medieval Religion*, 1975, pages 198 and 152.

2   The facts about John Shakespeare's life are taken from Mark Eccles, *Shakespeare in Warwickshire*, 1961, and Samuel Schoenbaum, *William Shakespeare: A Compact Documentary Life*, 1977.

3   Peter J. Bowden, *The Wool Trade in Tudor and Stuart England*, 1971, pages 82 and 84.

4   D. L. Thomas and N. E. Evans, "John Shakespeare in the Exchequer," *Shakespeare Quarterly* 35 (1984) 315-318.

5   Samuel Schoenbaum, *William Shakespeare: A Documentary Life*, 1975, page 66, identifies the shepherd as Thomas Whittington.

6   Leslie Hotson, *Shakespeare versus Shallow*, 1931, page 38.

7   E. K. Chambers, *William Shakespeare: A Study of Facts and Problems,* 1930, vol. I, pages 14–15.

8   Thomas and Evans, *op. cit.,* note 4 above.

9   My discussion of marriage customs relies on Ann Jennalie Cook, *Making a Match: Courtship in Shakespeare and his Society*, 1991.

10 That Elizabethan women were active in trades, selling products, finances, and supervising workers, unlike our modern assumption that that was all men's work, see Phyllis Rackin, *Shakespeare and Women*, 2005, chapter 2.

11 Raymond Carter Sutherland, "The Grant of Arms to Shakespeare's Father," *Shakespeare Quarterly* 14 (1963) 379-385.

12 F. V. Emery, "England *circa* 1600," in *A New Historical Geography of England*, ed. H. D. Darby, 1973.

13 All quotations from Shakespeare's text are taken from *The Riverside Shakespeare*, 1974.

14   Quoted in Chambers, *op. cit.,* note 7 above, vol. II, page 247. I have modernized the spelling.

15   Eamon Duffy, *The Stripping of the Altars: Traditional Religion in England, c. 1400 - c. 1580,* 1992.

16   See proclamation in full in E. K. Chambers, *The Elizabethan Stage,* 1923, vol. IV, page 263.

17   These incidents are given in Chambers, *op. cit.,* note 7 above, vol. II, pages 221–223.

18   Records of traveling players were published in Chambers, *op. cit.,* note 7 above, vol. II, pages 77–260.

19   Scott McMillin and Sally-Beth Maclean, *The Queen's Men and Their Plays,* 1998. See also Andrew Gurr, *The Shakespearian Playing Companies,* 1996, chapters 12 and 18.

20   Ronald B. McKerrow, editor, *The Works of Thomas Nashe,* 1966, vol. I, page 188.

21   The Stratford records are summarized in Eccles, *op. cit.* note 2 above, 1963, pages 80–83.

22   R. W. Willis, *Mount Tabor,* 1639, pages 110–113. I have modernized the punctuation and spelling.

23   My summary of the Northern Rebellion is taken from J. B. Black, *The Reign of Elizabeth (1558–1603),* 2nd edition, 1959, and Mary M. Luke, *Gloriana: The Years of Elizabeth I,* 1973.

CHAPTER 2

24   Craig R. Thompson, *Schools in Tudor England,* 1958, pages 41–42.

25   That a schoolmaster be a university graduate, could not always be enforced, Simon Forman was a schoolmaster without having a degree. See Barbara Traister, *The Notorious Astrological Physician of London,* 2001, page 17.

26   Joan Simon, *Education and Society in Tudor England,* 1966, page 331.

27   Gilbert Highet, *The Classical Tradition,* 1950, page 207.

28   Quoted in *The Riverside Shakespeare,* 1974, page 1844. I have modernized the spelling and punctuation here and in all subsequent references to *The Riverside Shakespeare.*

29   Jonathan Bate, *Shakespeare and Ovid,* 1993, page 83 and further in Chapter 3.

30   *Op. cit.,* note 28 above, page 1838.

31   Virgil K. Whitaker, *Shakespeare's Use of Learning,* 1964, pages 33–34.

32   Arthur Quinn, *Figures of Speech: 60 Ways To Turn a Phrase,* 1982, pages 93–95.

33   Quoted in William L. Edgerton, *Nicholas Udall,* 1965, page 35.

34   Quoted in E. K. Chambers, *The Elizabethan Stage,* 1923, vol. II, page 76.

35   Andrew Gurr, editor, *The Knight of the Burning Pestle*, 1968, page 25, and
      commentary, page 102.

36   Richard Mulcaster, *The Training Up of Children*. London, 1581. Reprint, Da
      Capo Press, 1971.

37   Richard Southern, *The Staging of Plays before Shakespeare*, 1973. The probable
      staging of English plays (1461-1589) discussed; for *Jack Juggler* see pages
      423–424.

38   See Antony Hammond, editor, *The Arden Shakesepeare: King Richard III*, 1981,
      page 80.

39   E. F. Watling, translator, *Seneca: Four Tragedies and Octavia*, 1966, page 155 fol.

40   Emrys Jones, *The Origins of Shakespeare,* 1977. Chapter 3. Shakespeare and
      Euripides (I).

41   The allusion to the revenge of the Queen of Troy in the opening scene of *Titus
      Andronicus* was probably made by the co-author, George Peele, rather than by
      Shakespeare. See Brian Vickers, *Shakespeare, Co-Author*, 2002, chapter 3.

42   E. R. C. Brinkworth, *Shakespeare and the Bawdy Court of Stratford*, 1972, pages
      54–55.

43   E. K. Chambers, *William Shakespeare*, 1930, vol. I, page 9.

44   Mark Eccles, *Shakespeare in Warwickshire*, 1963, pages 83 and 45.

Chapter 3

45   Rosemary Wolf, *The English Mystery Plays, 1972.*

46   J. S. Purvis editor, *The York Cycle of Mystery Plays,* 1957, page 7.

47   Mark Rose, *Shakespearean Design*, 1972, page 68, compares with design of the
      panels in the Sistine Ceiling.

48   R.W. Ingram, editor, *Records of Early English Drama: Coventry,* 1986, page xvii.

49   Hardin Craig, editor, *Two Coventry Corpus Christi Plays,* 1957, pages 29–30.

50   The way *Macbeth* is indebted to the Corpus Christi plays on the "Harrowing
      of Hell" and the Herod plays is discussed by Glynne Wickham, *Shakespeare's
      Dramatic Heritage*, 1969, pages 214–224.

51   Quoted in Martial Rose, editor, *The Wakefield Mystery Plays*, 1961, page 16.

52   Samuel Schoenbaum, *William Shakespeare: A Compact Documentary Life*, 1977,
      chapter 4.

53   Alexandra Walsham, *Church Papists*, 1999, page 14.

54   Evelyn Waugh, *Edmund Campion*, 1946.

55   See Schoenbaum, *op. cit.*, note 52 above, chapter 5.

56   The authenticity of John Shakespeare's "Spiritual Testament" has been questioned
      since the original has disappeared and we only know of it by second-hand copy.

202   SHAKESPEARE: A LIFE IN SEVEN CHAPTERS

The story line I use has been developed from speculations by many scholars who find it is consonant with and helps to explain many details of Shakespeare's life. The strongest arguments against the authenticity of the "Testament" are stated by Robert Bearman, in *The Shakespeare Survey* 56 (2003) 184–202.

57   John Henry de Groot, *The Shakespeares and "The Old Faith,"* 1946, pages 27–29.

58   Eamon Duffy, *The Stripping of the Altars*, 1992, chapter 16, and Alexandra Walsham, *Church Papists*, 1999.

59   Two writers survey these matters in great detail. See de Groot, *op. cit.*, note 57 above, and Peter Milward, *Shakespeare's Religious Background*, 1973.

60   David George, editor, *Records of Early English Drama: Lancashire*, 1991, page xxiv.

61   Antonia Fraser, *Faith and Treason: The Story of the Gunpowder Plot*, 1996, page 21.

62   E. K. Chambers, *William Shakespeare: A Study of Facts and Problems*, 1930, vol. II, page 254.

63   Suzanne R. Westfall, *Patrons and Performance: Early Tudor Household Revels*, 1990, page 5.

64   E. A. J. Honigman, *Shakespeare: The "Lost Years,"* 1985.

65   Waugh, *op. cit.*, note 54 above, page 131.

66   Lawrence M. Clopper, editor, *Records of Early English Drama: Chester*, 1979.

67   Quoted in George, *op. cit.*, note 60 above, page 29.

68   Honigmann, *op. cit.*, note 64 above, page 3.

69   The mix-up in Anne Hathaway's name is discussed Samuel Schoenbaum, *William Shakespeare: A Documentary Life*, 1975, pages 65–74.

70   W. R. Streitberger, editor, *Jacobean and Caroline Revels Accounts, 1603–1642: Malone Society Collections*, vol. XIII, 1986, pages 8–9.

71   Leslie Hotson, *Shakespeare Versus Shallow*, 1936, page 38, footnote.

72   Keith Sturgess, editor, *Three Elizabethan Domestic Tragedies*, 1969, page 57.

73   Honigman, *op. cit.*, note 64 above, page 29.

74   E. K. Chambers, *The Elizabethan Stage*, 1923, vol. II, pages 118–127.

75   Schoenbaum, *op. cit.*, note 69 above, page 66.

76   Phyllis Rackin, "Women in Shakespeare's World, "in *Shakespeare and Women*, 2005. See also F.P. Wilson, *The English Drama, 1485-1585*, 1969.

77   Ann Jennalie Cook, *Making a Match: Courtship in Shakespeare and His Society*, 1991, pages 17–18.

78   Mark Eccles, *Shakespeare in Warwickshire*, 1961, page 64.

79   Cook, *op. cit.*, note 77 above, page 75.

80   Cook, *op. cit.*, note 77 above. Chapter 6 explains Elizabethan marriage customs as related to dowries and jointures.

81   Ingram, *op. cit.*, note 48 above, page 587.

82   Craig, *op. cit.*, note 49 above, page xx.

83   A. W. Pollard and G. R. Redgrave, *A Short-Title Catalogue of Books Printed ... 1475–1640*, 1956. See items 14517, 14518, 14519.

84   Hyder E. Rollins, *Index to the Ballad-Entries in the Stationer's Register,* 1967. See items 564, 2877, 2916.

85   Chambers, *op. cit.,* note 74 above, vol. III, page 407.

86   R. A. Foakes and R. T. Richert, editors, *Henslowe's Diary,* 1961, page 17. The entry actually reads, "tittus & vespacia," which I think is simply another misleading spelling.

87   Ingram, *op. cit.,* note 48 above, page 332.

88   F. J. Furnival, *Robert Laneham's Letter ... etc.,* 1907, pages 27–28.

89   Ingram, *op. cit.,* note 48 above, pages 232–233.

CHAPTER 4

90   D. Allen Carroll, editor, *Greene's Groatsworth of Wit,* 1994, pages 84–85. In Appendix G, Carroll includes a thorough review of interpretations of the passage.

91   Tetsumaro Hayashi, *A Textual Study of Robert Greene's "Orlando Furioso" with an Elizabethan Text,* Ball State Monograph Number Twenty-One, 1973, page 1.

92   E.A.J. Honigmann, *Shakespeare's Impact on his Contemporaries,* 1982, pages 1–14.

93   Gerald Eades Bentley, *The Professions of Dramatist and Player in Shakespeare's Time, 1590–1642,* 1986, part II.

94   E. K. Chambers, *The Elizabethan Stage,* 1923, vol. II, page 120.

95   Shakespeare and Kemp were the payees for court performances in the early years of the Lord Chamberlain's Men, organized in 1594. See Andrew Gurr, *The Shakespearian Playing Companies,* 1996, page 284.

96   Bentley, *op. cit.,* note 93 above, page 28.

97   Chambers, *op. cit.,* note 94 above, vol. IV, page 242.

98   Bentley, *op. cit.,* note 93 above, page 213.

99   R. A. Foakes and R. T. Rickert, editors, *Henslowe's Diary,* 1961, pages 16–19.

100   William A. Ringler, Jr., "The Number of Actors in Shakespeare's Early Plays" in *The Seventeenth-Century Stage,* ed. Gerald Eades Bentley, 1968, pages 110–134.

101   Bernard Beckerman, *Shakespeare at The Globe, 1599–1600,* 1962, pages 121–122.

102   Quoted in E. K. Chambers, *William Shakespeare,* 1930, vol. II, page 214.

103   John Downes, *Roscius Anglicanus,* 1708, page 24.

104   William M. Jones, "William Shakespeare as William in *As You Like It,*" *Shakespeare Quarterly* XI (1950) 228–231.

105   Robert Parker Sorlien, editor, *The Diary of John Manningham of the Middle Temple, 1602–1603,* 1976, page 75.

106   Alwin Thaler, "*Faire Em* (and Shakespeare's Company?) in Lancashire,"

Publications of the Modern Language Association XLVI (1931) 647–658. In reviewing the possibility of Shakespeare's being in Lord Strange's Company when the play was first performed, Thaler overlooks the possibility that Shakespeare might have played the Conqueror.

107   C. F. Tucker Brooke, *The Shakespeare Apocrypha*, 1908, pages 285–306.

108   R. A. Foakes and R. T. Rickert, editors, *Henslowe's Diary*, 1961, page 20.

109   Girogio Melchiori, editor, *The New Cambridge Shakespeare: King Edward III*, 1998.

110   Quoted in Chambers, *op. cit.,* note 102 above, page 253.

111   J. R. Mulryne, editor, *The Spanish Tragedy*, 1989, page xxxi. Eleven printings are listed in Lukas Erne, *Shakespeare as Literary Dramatist*, 2003, page 53, footnote 70.

112   My summary of these events is taken from Garrett Mattingly, *The Armada*, 1959.

113   Thomas Nashe, *Pierce Penniless*, 1592. Quoted in *The Riverside Shakespeare*, 1974, page 587.

114   Foakes and Rickert, *op.cit.,* note 108 above, pages16–19.

115   Hereward T. Price, "Construction in Shakespeare", in *The University of Michigan: Contributions in Modern Philology* (May, 1951). Price argues for the skillful dramaturgy of *Henry VI, Part I.*

116   There have been long standing scholarly investigations on how much of *Titus* may have been written by another. A very thorough review by Brian Vickers reaches the conclusion that George Peele wrote at least Act I of *Titus.* See his *Shakespeare, Co-Author*, 2002, chapter 3.

117   From the Induction to *Bartholomew Fair*, quoted in Eugene M. Waith, editor, *The Oxford Shakespeare: Titus Andronicus*, 1984, page 1.

CHAPTER 5

118   F. W. Brownlow, "John Shakespeare's Recusancy: New Light on an Old Document," *Shakespeare Quarterly* 40 (1989) 186–191.

119   Quoted in F. P. Wilson, *The Plague in Shakespeare's London*, 1927, page 52.

120   Scott McMillin, *The Elizabethan Theatre and "The Book of Sir Thomas More,"* 1987.

121   Richard Dutton, *Mastering the Revels: The Regulation and Censorship of English Renaissance Drama*, 1991. Chapter 3 discusses the matter of the More play and Marlowe's case.

122   David Riggs, *The World of Christopher Marlowe*, 2004; Charles Nicholl, *The Reckoning: The Murder of Christopher Marlowe*, 1992.

123   Calvin Hoffman, *The Murder of the Man Who Was Shakespeare*, 1955.

124   From *The Return from Parnassus*, quoted in E. K. Chambers, *William Shakespeare*, 1930, vol. II, pages 200–201.

125   F. T. Prince, editor, *The Arden Shakespeare: The Poems*, 1960, pages xi–xii.

126   Chambers, *op. cit.,* note 124 above, vol. II, page 197.

127   Jonathan Bate, *Shakespeare and Ovid*, 1993, page 100.

128   G. P. V. Akrigg, *Shakespeare and the Earl of Southampton*, 1968, page 193.

129   Martin Green, *Wriothesley's Roses in Shakespeare's Sonnets, Poems, and Plays*, 1993, makes the case.

130   Katherine Duncan Jones, editor, *The Arden Shakespeare: Shakespeare's Sonnets*, 1997.

131   R. A. Foakes and R. T. Rickert, editors, *Henslowe's Diary*, 1961, page 280.

132   Christopher Devlin, *Hamlet's Divinity, and Other Essays*, 1963, pages 74–114.

133   Andrew Gurr, *The Shakespearian Playing Companies*, 1996, chapter 4.

134   Gerald Eades Bentley, *The Profession of Player in Shakespeare's Time, 1590–1642*, 1984, chapter III.

135   Peter W. M. Blayney, "The Publication of Playbooks," in *A New History of Early English Drama*, ed. John D. Cox and David Scott Kastan, 1997, chapter 21.

136   Chambers, *op. cit.,* note 124 above, page 332.

137   Robert Gittings, *Shakespeare's Rival*, 1960, discusses the possibility that the play was rewritten; at first Armado was a take-off on Antonio Perez, but on rewriting, details were added so that Armado became a take-off on Gervase Markham. That some parts of the play were a lampoon on Sir Walter Raleigh is discussed in Walter Oakeshott, *The Queen and the Poet*, 1961, chapter IV.

138   John Russell Brown, editor, *The Arden Shakespeare: The Merchant of Venice*, 1959, page xxiii.

139   Andrew Gurr in "Intertexuality at Windsor," *Shakespeare Quarterly* 38 (1987) 189–200. I was fortunate to participate in Professor Gurr's seminar on the topic at the Folger Library in 1989.

140   Details about the grant of arms are discussed in Chambers, *op. cit.,* note 124 above, vol. II, appendix A, page ii.

141   Samuel Schoenbaum, *William Shakespeare: A Documentary Life*, 1975, pages 173–178.

142   Carol Chillington Rutter, editor, *Documents of The Rose Playhouse*, 1984, page 8. The book includes information about Henslowe, whose work is also reviewed in Bernard Beckerman, "Philip Henslowe" in *The Theatrical Manager in England and America*, ed. Joseph W. Donohue, Jr., 1971, pages 19–62.

143   See Frances A. Yates, *Theatre of the World*, 1969, chapter VI.

144   E. K. Chambers, *The Elizabethan Stage*, 1923, vol. II, pages 391–392.

145   Chambers, *op. cit.,* note 144 above, page 508.

146   Irwin Smith, *Shakespeare's First Playhouse*, ed. by David George, 1981.

147   Rutter, *op. cit.,* note 142 above, pages 103–104.

148   John Orrell, *The Quest for Shakespeare's Globe*, 1983, chapter 6.

149   William Ingram, *A London Life in the Brazen Age: Francis Langley, 1548–1602,* 1978.

150   Leslie Hotson, *Shakespeare Versus Shallow*, 1931.

151   Rosemary Linnell, *The Curtain Playhouse*, 1977.

152   Seymour M. Pitcher, *The Case for Shakespeare's Authorship of "The Famous Victories": With the complete text of the anonymous play*, 1961.

153   Gary Taylor, editor, *The Oxford Shakespeare: Henry V*, 1984. "Introduction," page 4.

154   Kristin Poole, "Saints Alive! Falstaff, Martin Marprelate, and the Staging of Puritanism," *Shakespeare Quarterly* 46 (1995) 47–75.

155   Pitcher, *op. cit.,* note 152 above, page 178 and footnote.

156   It may be significant the Lord Cobham was also a Knight of the Garter.

157   Milicent V. Hay, *The Life of Robert Sidney,* 1984, page 158.

158   Alice-Lyle Scoufos, *Shakespeare's Typological Satire*, 1979, discusses the Falstaff/ Cobham brouhaha.

159   Douglas J. Stewart, " Falstaff the Centaur," *Shakespeare Quarterly* 28 (1977) 5–21.

160   Taylor, *op. cit.,* note 153 above, page 246.

161   Percy Simpson, editor, *The Malone Society Reprints: The Life of Sir John Oldcastle*, 1908.

162   Chambers, *op. cit.,* note 124 above, page 213.

163   Chambers, *op. cit.,* note 124 above, page 266.

164   The circumstances of the composition of the play are reviewed by William Green, *Shakespeare's Merry Wives of Windsor,* 1962.

165   See H. J. Oliver, editor, *The Arden Shakespeare: The Merry Wives of Windsor*, 1971, pages xi–xiii.

166   Duff Cooper, *Sergeant Shakespeare,* 1949.

167   *The Passionate Pilgrim* is reprinted in *The Riverside Shakespeare*, 1974, pages 1787–1794.

168   The relevant sections of Meres' book are quoted in Chambers, *op. cit.,* note 124 above, pages 193-195.

169   Quoted in Chambers, *op. cit.,* note 124 above, page 195.

170   E. A. J. Honigmann, *John Weever: A Biography of a Literary Associate of Shakespeare and Jonson, Together with a Photographic Facsimile of Weever's "Epigrammes" (1599),*1987. The verses are on page E6a of the facsimile and page 33 of the Introduction.

171 Quoted in O. J. Campbell and Edward G. Quinn, editors, *The Reader's Encyclopedia of Shakespeare*, 1966, page 265.

172 Chambers, *op. cit.*, note 144 above, page 400.

173 Chambers, *op. cit.*, note 144 above, page 365.

CHAPTER 6

174 Robert Lacey, *Robert, Earl of Essex*, 1971, chapters 24–30.

175 G. P. V. Akrigg, *Shakespeare and the Earl of Southampton*, 1968, page 96.

176 E. K. Chambers, *William Shakespeare: A Study of Facts and Problems*, 1930, vol. II, page 325.

177 Catherine Drinker Bowen, *The Lion and the Throne: The Life and Times of Sir Edward Coke*, 1956, pages 151–152.

178 Harold Jenkins, editor, *The Arden Shakespeare: Hamlet*, 1982. For the dating of *Hamlet*, see pages 1–13.

179 Michael Hattaway, editor, *The New Cambridge Shakespeare: As You Like It*, 2000.

180 A full discussion of this point will be found in Robert Henke, *Pastoral Transformations: Italian Tragicomedy and Shakespeare's Late Plays*, 1997.

181 Hugh Macdonald, editor, *England's Helicon*, 1949, page xx.

182 *The Downfall of Robert, Earl of Huntington*, and *The Death of Robert, Earl of Huntington* are reprinted in *Old English Plays*, edited by Robert Dodsley, 1744, revised 1876, vol. 4, pages 93–327. Another play based on the history and legends of King John, published in 1591, may have been used. But it too may derive from Shakespeare. See E. A. J. Honigmann, *Shakespeare's Impact on his Contemporaries*, 1982, pages 56–66.

183 Robert Parker Sorlien, editor, *The Diary of John Manningham of the Middle Temple, 1602-1603*, 1976, page 48.

184 Philip J. Finkelpearl, *John Marston of the Middle Temple: An Elizabethan Dramatist in his Social Setting*, 1969.

185 Quoted in Elizabeth Story Donno, editor, *The New Cambridge Shakespeare: Twelfth Night*, 1985, page 4.

186 David Riggs, *Ben Jonson: A Life*, 1989, page 84.

187 James P. Bednarz, *Shakespeare & The Poets' War*, 2001, page 176.

188 Sorlien, *op.cit.*, note 183 above, page 133.

189 M. R. Woodhead, editor, *John Marston: What you Will*, 1980, page 39.

190 Mark Eccles, *Shakespeare in Warwickshire*, 1963, pages 138–139.

191 Leslie Hotson in *Shakespeare's Sonnets Dated, and Other Essays*, 1949, pages 44–45.

192 Alan Brissenden, editor, *The World's Classics: As You Like It*, 1993, page 31.

193 Bernard Harris, editor, *The Malcontent*, 1967, page xvi.

194　Michael Shapiro, *Children of the Revels: The Boy Companies in Shakespeare's Time and Their Plays*, 1977.

195　Kenneth Muir, editor, *The Oxford Shakespeare: Troilus and Cressida,* 1984. Muir cites the critics on page 6.

196　Riggs, *op. cit.,* note 186 above, pages 79–80.

197　Thomas Fuller, *Worthies, Warwickshire*, quoted in Chambers, *op. cit.,* note 176 above, page 245.

198　John Roe, editor, *The New Cambridge Shakespeare: The Poems*, 1992, pages 41–52 and 231–235.

199　See E. A. J. Honigmann, *Shakespeare, the "Lost Years,"* 1998, chapter IX.

200　Andrew Gurr, *The Shakespearian Playing Companies,* 1996, chapters 19 and 20.

201　Keith Sturgess, editor, *The World's Classics: John Marston: The Malcontent and Other Plays*, 1997.

202　Three recent studies draw attention to the influence of Italian theatrical practice on the work of Elizabethan playwrights: Louise George Clubb, *Italian Drama in Shakespeare's Time*, 1989; Robert Henke, *Pastoral Transformations: Italian Tragicomedy and Shakespeare's Late Plays*, 1997; and Michael Wyatt, *The Italian Encounter with Tudor England: The Cultural Politics of Translation*, 2005.

203　Captain Melchior, a Portuguese, on the advantages of the Moroccan trade in 1561, as quoted by T. S. Willan, *Studies in Elizabethan Foreign Trade*, 1959, page 107, in D. W. Davies, *Elizabethans Errant: The Strange Fortunes of Sir Thomas Sherley and His Three Sons,* 1967, page 193.

204　Davies, *op. cit.,* note 203 above, page 193.

205　See E. A. J. Honigmann, editor, *The Arden Shakesepare: Othello*, 1997, page 2.

206　Honigmann, *op. cit.,* note 205 above, appendix 3, "Cinthio and Minor Sources."

207　Jerry Turner, Director of the Oregon Shakespeare Festival in the 1970s, passed that story to me.

208　Leeds Barroll, *Politics, Plague, and Shakespeare's Theater: The Stuart Years,* 1991.

209　Barroll, *op. cit.,* note 208 above, pages 32–49.

210　Chambers, *op. cit.,* note 176 above, pages 328–329.

211　Quoted in Barroll, *op. cit.,* note 208 above, pages 40–41.

212　W. R. Streitberger, *Jacobean and Caroline Revels Accounts, 1603-1642,* 1986, pages 7–9.

213　Maurice Lee, Jr., editor, *Dudley Carlton to John Chamberlain, 1603–1624,* 1972, page 68.

214　Chambers, *op. cit.,* note 176 above, appendix C, page 270, item xxvii.

215　Josephine Waters Bennett, *"Measure for Measure" as Royal Entertainment,* 1966.

216　G. K. Hunter, editor, *The Arden Shakespeare: All's Well That Ends Well*, 1959, page xxiii.

217 A summary of critical opinions is in John Wilders, "The Problem Plays," in *Shakespeare: A Bibliographical Guide*, ed. Stanley Wells, 1990, pages 137–157

218 Francelia Butler, *The Strange Critical Fortunes of Shakespeare's "Timon of Athens,"* 1966.

219 *Eastward Ho* (II.i.130ff.), in *Ben Jonson*, ed. C. H. Herford and Percy Simpson, 1932, vol. IV, pages 487–619.

220 Riggs gives an account of the incident in his biography of Jonson, *op. cit.*, note 186 above, pages 224–226.

221 Antonia Fraser, *Faith and Treason: The Story of the Gunpowder Plot*, 1997.

222 David Scott Kastan explores these questions and other ambiguities in his essay, "*Macbeth* and the 'Name of King,'" in *Shakespeare after Theory,*1999, chapter 9.

223 Henry N. Paul, *The Royal Play of "Macbeth,"* 1950.

CHAPTER 7

224 The matter is meticulously examined by Leeds Barroll in, *Politics, Plague, and Shakespeare's Theatre,* 1991. See especially Figure 1, page 173.

225 See Ann Jennalie Cook, *Making a Match: Courtship in Shakespeare and His Society,* 1991, pages 224–225.

226 My discussion is indebted to Clifford Chalmers Huffman's *"Coriolanus" in Context*, 1971.

227 Frank Marcham, *William Shakespeare and His Daughter Susanna*, 1931. William Hall's will is on pages 20–23.

228 Joan Lane, *John Hall and His Patients: The Medical Practice of Shakespeare's Son-in-Law*, 1996, and Harriet Joseph, *Shakespeare's Son-in-Law, John Hall: Man and Physician,* 1976. Both include annotated facsimiles of Hall's book.

229 Mark Eccles suggests that the Halls never lived in Hall's Croft in *Shakespeare in Warwickshire*, 1961, page 112.

230 Wayne H. Phelps, "Edmund Shakespeare at St. Leonard's, Shoreditch," *Shakespeare Quarterly* (1978) 442–423.

231 Anthony Powell, editor, *Brief Lives, and Other Selected Writings by John Aubrey,* 1949, page 75.

232 E. K. Chambers, *William Shakespeare,* 1930, vol. II, appendix C.

233 Shakespeare and the Huguenots are discussed in Park Honan, *Shakespeare: A Life,* 1996, chapter 16.

234 Eccles, *op. cit.,* note 229 above, page 60.

235 Quoted in Andrew Gurr, *The Shakespearian Playing Companies*, 1996, page 354.

236 Gurr, *op. cit.,* note 235 above, chapters 20 and 21.

237 Frances A. Yates in her study, *Theatre of the World*, 1969, explores the possibility

that Burbage might have been influenced by descriptions of Roman theatres in the work of Vetruvius.

238   Quoted in E. K. Chambers, *The Elizabethan Stage*, 1923, vol. II, page 384.

239   See Brian Vickers, *Shakespeare, Co-Author,* 2002, chapter 5.

240   F. D. Hoeniger, editor, *The Arden Shakespeare: Pericles*, 1963, page lxvi.

241   C. F. Tucker Brooke, editor, "Mucedorus," in *The Shakespeare Apocrypha*, 1908, pages xxiii–xxvi and 103–126.

242   David Cressy, *Bonfires and Bells,* 1989, chapter 4.

243   Alan Young, *Tudor and Jacobean Tournaments,* 1987.

244   Streitberger, *op. cit.,* note 212 above, pages 55–56.

245   Charles Hamilton, *Shakespeare with John Fletcher: Cardenio, or The Second Maiden's Tragedy,* 1994. He argues *Cardenio* is the same as the play called *The Second Maiden's Tragedy* and the manuscript is in Shakespeare's handwriting. This has not won critical acceptance; to me, *The Second Maiden's Tragedy* seems like the work of Middleton.

246   The antimasque in Beaumont's masque is reprinted and discussed in detail in *The Arden Shakespeare: The Two Noble Kinsmen*, ed. Lois Potter, 1997, appendix 3 and 4.

247   Vickers, *op. cit.,* note 239 above. See Chapter 6 on *Henry* VIII and *Two Noble Kinsmen.*

248   Chambers, *op. cit.,* note 238 above, page 419.

249   Chambers, *op. cit.,* note 238 above, page 421.

250   C. Walter Hodges, *Shakespeare's Second Globe: The Missing Monument,* 1973, chapters 6 and 7.

251   Irwin Smith, *Shakespeare's Blackfriars Playhouse: Its History and Design,* 1964, pages 250–252.

EPILOGUE

252   E. R. C. Brinkworth, *Shakespeare and the Bawdy Court of Stratford,* 1972, page 74.

253   Brinkworth, *op. cit.,* note 252 above, pages 132 and 110.

254   My information came by combing the index of Mark Eccles, *Shakespeare in Warwickshire,* 1961.

255   Quoted in Samuel Schoenbaum, *William Shakespeare: Records and Images,* 1981, page 77.

256   Park Honan, *Shakespeare: A Life,* 1998, gives a detailed discussion of the enclosure movement.

257   Brinkworth, *op. cit.,* note 252 above, page 143.

258   E. K. Chambers, *William Shakespeare,* 1930, vol. II, appendix A, "Shakespeare's Will."

259   Lukas Erne, *Shakespeare as Literary Dramatist,* 2003.